D0871985

UNPRINCIPLED VIRTUE

UNPRINCIPLED VIRTUE

AN INQUIRY INTO MORAL AGENCY

Nomy Arpaly

OXFORD

UNIVERSITY PRESS

2003

OXFORD
UNIVERSITY PRESS

Oxford   New York

Auckland   Bangkok   Buenos Aires   Cape Town   Chennai
Dar es Salaam   Delhi   Hong Kong   Istanbul   Karachi   Kolkata
Kuala Lumpur   Madrid   Melbourne   Mexico City   Mumbai   Nairobi
São Paulo   Shanghai   Taipei   Tokyo   Toronto

Copyright © 2003 by Oxford University Press, Inc.

Published by Oxford University Press, Inc.
198 Madison Avenue, New York, New York 10016

www.oup.com

Oxford is a registered trademark of Oxford University Press

Library of Congress Cataloging-in-Publication Data
Arpaly, Nomy.
Unprincipled virtue : an inquiry into moral agency / Nomy Arpaly.
p. cm.
ISBN 0-19-515204-2
1. Ethics. 2. Psychology and philosophy. I. Title.
BJ45 .A76 2002
170—dc21   2002025754

1   3   5   7   9   8   6   4   2

Printed in the United States of America
on acid-free paper

To my friends, who make life worthwhile

ACKNOWLEDGMENTS

I would like to thank a number of people for their help with this work: Kimberlee Kane-Maguire, for igniting the first spark for this project, and for being such a wonderful friend and person. Timothy Schroeder, my one-in-a-million philosophical collaborator, friend, muse, coach, and editor, for endless support, long philosophical discussions, and the rest. George Sher, for philosophy, friendship, support, secretarial help, faith, hope, loyalty, and Pilsner Urquell, all invaluable. Russell Hardin, for increasing overall utility. My Stanford teachers, especially Michael Bratman, Rachel Cohon, Ariela Lazar, Peter Godfrey-Smith, and Julius Moravcsik, and my unofficial mentors, David Copp, Stephen Darwall, Harry Frankfurt, Barbara Herman, Thomas Hill, Rosalind Hursthouse, Peter Railton, Thomas Scanlon, and David Velleman: their help, good will, and wisdom have been simply invaluable to me at various stages of developing these ideas, and I am forever in their debt. Andrew Conway, Maureen Kelly, Simon May, David Mills, Jonathan Schaffer, Erica Stephan, Asya Takken, Todd Takken, and Penny Tucker have all provided invaluable emotional support. I am deeply indebted to my great colleagues at Rice University, one and all; to the people of the philosophy department at the University of Michigan, one and all; and to the faculty and the fellows at Harvard University's Center for Ethics and the Professions. Thanks also to the people who looked at drafts and provided very helpful comments, sometimes enduring the groans with which I greet astute criticism: Elizabeth Anderson, Arthur Applbaum, Sarah Buss, Ruth Chang, John Martin Fischer, Lori Gruen, Gilbert Harman, James Joyce, Angella Keckler, Shua Knobe, Janet Malek, Mary MacLeod, Alfred Mele, Rob Shaver, Heda Sedvic, Andrea Westlund, and various anonymous referees. I must also mention the following students, who kept me honest with fresh intuitions and uninhibited objections: Maud Barriquand, D. J. Braisier, Grace Chu, Andrew Courtwright, Brad Lega, and Philip Mayor. Thanks are due to Louisa and Paulo Orizio of Dolce & Freddo, purveyors of splendid gelato and coffee, for allowing me to pace back and forth on the premises like some madwoman for hours on end while I was writing this book in my mind, and to Ann Pinchak, who can motivate very well. To all the people of whom fictionalized versions appear in my examples: I do hope you forgive me.

I wish to thank Rice University, the University of Michigan, and the Center for Ethics and the Professions at Harvard University for support during the writing of this book. Thanks are also owed to various publishers for permission to reprint previous work. An earlier version of chapter 2 appeared in *Ethics* 110 (2000); some of the ideas presented in chapter 3 are due to appear in a shorter form in the *Journal of Philosophy*; a section of chapter 4 was presented at the Inland Northwest Philosophy Conference in Spring 2001 and is due to appear in a volume edited by Joseph Keim Campbell, Michael O'Rourke, and David Shier for Seven Bridges Press; and some of the cases discussed in chapter 5 appeared in *Philosophical Studies* 93 (1998).

CONTENTS

UNPRINCIPLED VIRTUE

ONE

■ ■ ■

THE COMPLEXITY
OF MORAL PSYCHOLOGY

Agency and the Secret Agent

In John Le Carré's novel *Single and Single* we are introduced to Oliver Single, a young lawyer in a prestigious firm and heir apparent to his illustrious father, Tyger Single, who heads the firm. The firm is heavily involved in organized crime. Oliver has always known that his father makes shady deals, but only gradually does he learn quite how shady. Even when he knows full well that his father acts immorally, he still has no plans to leave his post. He enjoys the money and the prestige and, in addition, he loves his father deeply and wishes to please him. At a critical moment, however, Oliver defects to the side of the law, in whose service he remains to perform some courageous acts for which the reader takes him to be praiseworthy and admirable. Here is how Le Carré describes the moment of Oliver's defection:

> It is midwinter, and Oliver is a little mad. *That much he knows about himself, no more.* The origins of his madness, its causes, duration and degree, are not within his grasp, not now. They are out there, but for another time, another life, another couple of brandies. The neon-lit gloom of a December's night at Heathrow airport reminds him of a boy's changing room in one of his many boarding schools. Garish cardboard reindeer and taped carols compound his mood of unreality. Snowy lettering dangles from a washing line, wishing him peace and

3

joy on earth. Something amazing is about to happen to him and *he is eager to find out what it will be*. He isn't drunk but technically he isn't sober either. A few vodkas on the flight, a half of red with the rubber chicken, a Remy or two afterwards have done no more in Oliver's eyes than bringing him up to speed with the furor already raging inside him. He has only hand luggage and nothing to declare except a reckless ferment of the brain, a firestorm of outrage and exasperation starting so long ago that its origins are impossible to peg, blowing through his head like a hurricane while *other members of his internal congregation stand around in timid twos and threes and ask one another what on earth Oliver is going to do to put it out*. He is approaching signs of different colors and instead of wishing him peace, joy on earth and goodwill among men, they are requiring him to define himself. Is he a stranger in his own country? Answer, yes he is. Has he arrived here from another planet? Answer, yes he has. Is he blue? Red? Green? His eye drifts to a tomato-colored telephone. It is familiar to him. Perhaps he noticed it on his way out three days ago and, *unknown to himself*, recruited it as a secret ally. Is it heavy, hot, alive? A notice beside it reads "If you wish to speak to a Customs officer, use this phone." He uses it. *That is to say, his arm reaches out for it unbidden, his hand grasps it and puts it to his ear*, leaving him with the responsibility of what to say. (Le Carré 1999, 90–91, italics mine)

The quality of this passage is derived as much from its psychological credibility as from its prose style. The reader who at some point has made a drastic career change, left a marriage, a church, or a cult, or otherwise made a hard choice will find something familiar in the description of Oliver on his dark night of the soul. A philosopher reading Le Carré's thriller might also be struck by the difference between Oliver Single and most agents imagined by ethicists and philosophers of action in their discussions of human agency. While I do not wish to imply that all philosophers imagine the same kinds of agents in all their discussions, it is hard to escape a sense that Oliver is unusual, unlike run-of-the-mill exemplars of agency. He is especially different from the person whom we would typically imagine as an autonomous, rational agent, turning his moral life around with a single act. When we imagine such an agent, we usually imagine someone who deliberates and then executes the practical conclusion of her deliberation—perhaps easily, perhaps having to fight *akrasia*. At any rate, she deliberates, and "when you deliberate it is as if there were something over and above all of your desires, something which is you, and which chooses which desire to act on," as Christine

Korsgaard has written (1996, 100). Oliver, at the time of his defection, is not this kind of agent. His picking up of the red phone is not the result of deliberation: he has not planned or decided via deliberation to desert his father. From the moment he steps off the plane, he experiences himself as the passive audience to his own actions, this sense of passivity being stressed by the expressions I have italicized.

In his sense of passivity, Oliver resembles a different type of agent known to the moral psychology literature: the nonagent who performs a nonaction, or who does not participate in his action, or who is "not himself" at the time of his action. This is the person whose autonomy is compromised, or who is irrational, or who is very akratic, or who is not acting for reasons, or who is swayed by an external desire. But Oliver is not a typical victim of his urges any more than he is a typical architect of his fate. He is not, for example, like a person who breaks her low-fat diet or who is addicted to a drug or who is alienated from a fleeting violent urge. Oliver is more complicated. His motivation is not of the type that "mere inclination" conveniently covers: he has gradually become disaffected with his family's immoral dealings, and while his action surprises him, it still has some of the characteristics of an action performed for reasons. It is not an accident that his defection occurs shortly after a series of revelations into the morally bankrupt behavior of his father's firm. It is not an accident that he, "unbeknownst to himself," marked the location of the red phone in the past. It is even, the novelist suggests, not an accident that he drinks before his defection: the drinking, Le Carré hints, is not the cause of Oliver's defection, but, like the marking of the red phone, something that he does to ease himself into the difficult task of defecting, which he unconsciously anticipates.[1] Few of the typically imagined cases of nonaction, unautonomous action, or irrational action are as complicated. How, then, are we to think of Oliver?

Perhaps we can get some guidance from an extremely lifelike case described by David Velleman. Velleman asks us to imagine:

> I have a long-anticipated meeting with an old friend for the purpose of resolving some minor difference; but . . . as we talk, his offhand comments provoke me to raise my voice in progressively sharper replies, until we part in anger. Later reflection leads me to realize that accumulated grievances had crystallized in my mind, during the weeks before our meeting, into a resolution to sever our friendship over the matter at hand, and that this resolution is what gave the hurtful edge to

my remarks. In short, I may conclude that desires of mine caused the decision, which in turn caused the corresponding behavior; and I may acknowledge that these mental states were thereby exerting their normal motivational force, unabetted by any strange perturbation or compulsion. But do I necessarily think that I made the decision or that I executed it? Surely, I can believe that the decision, though genuinely motivated by my desires, was thereby induced in me but not formed by me; and I can believe that it was genuinely executed in my behavior but executed, again, without my help. Indeed, viewing the decision as directly motivated by my desires, and my behavior as directly governed by the decision, is precisely what leads to the thought that as my words became more shrill, it was my resentment speaking, not I. (1992, 464–465)

The process that leads up to the moment of Oliver's defection can be described in Velleman's terms: beliefs and desires cause in him, "unbeknownst to him," a decision to defect, and this decision causes him to pick up the red phone. No sense of "active decision" is involved. If we take seriously the reasons Velleman professes for thinking it is "my resentment speaking, not I," it is hard to avoid the conclusion that in Oliver's case, too, Velleman will say that it is his "firestorm of outrage" moving his arm toward the phone, not he. It is not really his action.

This, however, is not altogether a comfortable conclusion. Oliver, who will later act morally and bravely on many occasions, strikes the reader as a commendable person, and his defection as an important moral step. If Oliver's defection is to be dismissed as an unautonomous action, an action not truly his own, a mere activity (or—choose your theory—nonrational, driven by mere inclination, driven by a desire external to him, etc.), then our intuitive admiration of the hero and appreciation of his momentous step has no basis. He would be a sad case, or perhaps a happy accident (how lucky for the officers of the law that his unconscious sent him their way!), but not a hero. A theory according to which Oliver's action is "not truly his own" or not one in which he participates would make the appeal of Le Carré's story inexplicable, because it would seem that the pivotal action in the middle is not the character's own action. To this extent, treating Oliver as analogous to Velleman's case would clash with common sense.

In a footnote, Velleman attempts to reconcile his view that my yelling at my friend out of unconscious resentment is not my action with the commonsense view that I deserve blame for my rudeness. He does so by suggesting that I have a duty to be vigilant about "unconsidered intentions" and to actively prevent them from running loose, and so I am blameworthy not for yelling but for failing to prevent myself from getting into the state in which I find myself. But if we attempt to make Velleman's case more parallel to Oliver's, and shift from talk of blame to talk of praise, this explanation becomes problematic. Imagine that the "accumulated grievances" that crystallize in a person's mind into a decision to break off her friendship involve her friend's increasingly immoral behavior, which she has been unconsciously ignoring or underestimating. There are occasions on which such a breakup marks a pivotal moral step for a person, or at least an occasion to say "good for you," and hence warrants moral praise. Where does this praise come from? No story about a duty of vigilance can easily explain it, and no story of this sort can easily explain Oliver's praiseworthiness, either, for Oliver and the person ending a friendship have both been led into doing what they do by unconscious motives.

What does the story of Oliver Single show? On its own, nothing much. Our intuitions are not readily accommodated by existing moral-psychological theory, but this hardly shows that there is no way to accommodate them within existing frameworks. And yet the case of Oliver Single is not without interest. For Oliver Single presents us with a sort of agent that moral psychologists have not been trying to understand, and he proves to be an agent who is difficult to understand, in a theoretically adequate manner. He is also far from alone. In the next six sections, I will introduce a collection of cases in which phenomena that appear in real life with substantial frequency appear to be different, in striking ways, from the paradigmatic cases contemporary moral psychologists try to accommodate, and hence puzzling to contemporary moral psychology. My purpose is not to give a counterexample to any particular theory, but to present some complexities in moral life that I think have not been given their due attention and that should be of interest to any moral psychologist.

Wishing to explain these cases motivates the theory of moral worth I present later in the book. Naturally, I think my own theory explains the phenomena I describe, but I would like to make it clear from the outset that my project is a positive one rather than a negative one. My project is to present a theory of moral worth that makes good sense of Oliver

Single and other individuals underrepresented in the literature, to provide a detailed account of how we ought to think about these individuals we have so rarely thought about before. My project is not to show that my theory is the only theory possible, or even to show that my theory is superior to what other theories could say, if only they were to turn their attention to these neglected cases. So in one sense, my project in this book is a rather modest one. But because I will be focusing upon types of individuals whose moral complexities have not been the subject of significant discussion so far, I hope to achieve at least one very significant goal, and that is to expand the domain of moral-psychological inquiry, enriching our philosophical discussion of human beings in all their complexity.

Let us turn to the cases.

Inadvertent Virtue
and Misguided Conscience

Much has been said about people who know what they should do, morally speaking, and do it. Much has been said about people who know what they should do, morally speaking, but somehow fail to do it, perhaps despite trying. Comparatively, there is little on those who appear to be good people with bad principles: those who do not quite *know* what they should do but who often do it anyway. Imagine Peter, who believes, in his own words, that "morality is for wimps." He advocates a quasi-Nietzschean view according to which one should be selfish and strive to increase one's own power. Yet Peter does not perform wrongfully selfish acts, and he performs many unselfish acts, for unselfish motives. When asked about this he offers rationalizations, as if he were rationalizing the breaking of a diet ("But I *was* being selfish, no *really*") or, sometimes, he blushes and says honestly, "Well, I guess I *am* a wimp." But he continues to act well nonetheless.

What is Peter's moral status? If we think of actions as reflecting either an agent's Reason (principles, deliberation) or an agent's Passions (appetite, inclination, "blindly following where his desires take him"), there seems to be little choice but to think of Peter as a bad person—a person committed to false ethical principles—who by a lucky accident of upbringing or temperament happens to act well routinely. To say this is to all but agree with Peter that he is some sort of a "wimp"—a person of weak will—while adding that, given the badness of his principles, it is lucky that he is one. This is certainly how Jonathan Bennett (1974) thinks of analogous cases. In everyday life, however, we are divided in our opinions. We treat some Peter-like people this way, but we also treat many of them as *good* people who happen to be very bad at abstract thinking. In these cases, we do not say, "He's a bad person, but luckily he's weak-willed." We say, "He's a good person. Unfortunately, he has these silly views, but you can safely ignore them." Instead of writing off Peter's good actions as mere lucky accidents of temperament and up-bringing, we are just as likely, in some circumstances, to look at his actions as speaking well of him and write off his principles as an accident: "Well, what can you expect? His parents were fascists. But somehow he turned out to be nice anyway."

Some of the Peters of the world seem to possess inadvertent virtue. That is, they seem to be virtuous just as they think they are at their worst. The most dramatic cases of inadvertent virtue are stark cases of *doing the right thing against one's best judgment*, which I have elsewhere (Arpaly and Schroeder 1999) called *inverse akrasia*. Bennett's (1974) own example of a Peter-like individual, Mark Twain's Huckleberry Finn, beauti-fully exemplifies this special sort of *akrasia*. At a key point in the story, Huckleberry's best judgment tells him that he should not help Jim es-cape slavery but rather turn him in at the first available opportunity. Yet when a golden opportunity comes to turn Jim in, Huckleberry discovers that he just cannot do it and fails to do what he takes to be his duty, de-ciding as a result that, what with morality being so hard, he will just re-main a bad boy (he does not, therefore, reform his views: at the time of his narrative, he still believes that the moral thing to do would have been to turn Jim in). If one only takes actions in accordance with deliberation, or the faculty of Reason or ego-syntonic actions (or any of the other vari-ous entities believed at present to represent the face of the moral agent proper), to be actions for which the agent can be morally praised, Huck-leberry's action is reduced to the status accorded by Kant to acting on "mere inclination" or by Aristotle to acting on "natural virtue." He is no more morally praiseworthy for helping Jim than a good seeing-eye dog is praiseworthy for its helpful deeds. This is not, however, how Twain sees his character. Twain takes Huckleberry to be an ignorant boy whose de-cency and virtue exceed those of many older and more educated men, and his failure to turn Jim in is portrayed not as a mere lucky accident of temperament, a case of fortunate squeamishness, but as something quite different. Huckleberry's long acquaintance with Jim makes him gradually realize that Jim is a full-fledged human being, a realization that expresses itself, for example, in Huckleberry's finding himself, for the first time in his life, apologizing respectfully to a black man. While Huckleberry does not conceptualize his realization, it is this awareness of Jim's humanity that causes him to become emotionally incapable of turning Jim in. To the extent that this is Huckleberry's motive, Twain obviously sees him as praiseworthy in a way that he wouldn't be if he were merely acting out of some atavistic mechanism or if he were reluctant to turn Jim in out of a desire to spite Miss Watson, Jim's owner. Huckleberry Finn is not treated by his creator as if he were acting for a nonmoral motive, but rather as if he were acting for a moral motive—*without knowing* that it is a moral motive.

I think every theory of moral worth needs to account for that thing about Huckleberry Finn which makes him seem more than an accidental good-doer, and better than some people with liberal principles who are still viscerally prejudiced against people of different races. Likewise, it should also account for what makes us admire some Peters.

Inverse *akrasia* is closely related to cases which Thomas Hill discusses under the name *misguided conscience*. These are cases in which a person appears to believe quite honestly that she is doing good but is in fact loyal to a morally irrelevant cause (say, chastity), a morally bad cause (name your least favorite mainstream political party), or a downright evil cause (National Socialism, the Spanish Inquisition). Or perhaps it is not a matter of loyalty to a cause at all, but a case of a person who beats his children severely because he believes that it builds character and that therefore he is in fact acting morally. Think of the village woman who piously helps burn the heretic, convinced that she is doing morality a great service, or of the common Nazi soldier who is convinced he is serving the good and displays what seem to be loyalty, courage, and, as it were, inverse *enkreteia*, doing the wrong thing in accordance with one's best judgment. What do we think about them? Is the Nazi off the moral hook if he honestly believes that the cause he is serving is good? In some such cases, our gut feeling seems to be no. Anyone who is enthusiastically attracted to a cause such as Nazism, we say, must have something morally wrong with him. Who, we ask, but a person with a mind full of hatred would imagine Jews to be ultimate sources of evil? In other cases, our feelings are more torn, and we are tempted to see things more in terms of a "conscience"—something that by itself is good to have—that has been "misguided," put to the wrong use, and perhaps it is better to have a misguided conscience than none at all. This, of course, does not exhaust the range of our responses, but it is a rare person who thinks that "but I believed I was acting morally" always excuses, or that it never does. More often, in the more ambiguous cases, we want to know "what the belief means" to the agent before we judge. Cases of misguided conscience, like cases of inverse *akrasia*, relate to a sense we have that people's relationships with their moral beliefs or principles can at times be quite complex, and that when they act on their moral beliefs their actions do not always lend themselves to a simple "S wants to F because she mistakenly believes it would bring about G" reconstruction.

Cases of inadvertent virtue and misguided conscience have not by and large received the amount of attention they deserve, and they raise complex questions—whether we discuss dramatic cases, like Huckleberry Finn and the devoted Nazi soldier, or more day-to-day cases (my students tend to mention, at this point, fond memories of kind relatives who support hateful politicians, and there is also the case of Peter). I shall attempt to provide complex answers.

Belief Formation "Under the Influence"

There is epistemic irrationality stemming from motivational factors and emotions, known as 'hot irrationality' or irrationality "under the influence" (Lazar 1999; Pears 1984), and irrationality stemming from nonmotivational factors such as lack of intelligence or sleep deprivation, known also as 'cold irrationality'. Most examples of hot epistemic irrationality focus on cases in which one believes something because one wants to believe it. Standard cases of self-deception—the woman who refuses to see that her husband is cheating on her despite the lipstick on his collar, for example—are often believed to be the result of an intention to form a belief. Thus Davidson characterizes self-deception in the following way:

> A has evidence on the basis of which he believes that p is more apt to
> be true than its negation; the thought that p, or the thought that he

ought rationally to believe p, motivates A to act in such a way as to cause himself to believe the negation of p. All that self-deception demands of the action is that the motive originates in a belief that p is true (or recognition that the evidence makes it more likely to be true than not) and that the action be done with the intention of producing a belief in the negation of p. (1985, 88–89)

Self-deception, according to Davidson and many other moral psychologists, is an action, and it requires an intention to effect it, like every action. Much has been written about the riddle of self-deception, and the riddle is often the very question of how such intentional inner action is possible. How, to put it simply, does one cheat oneself without getting caught?

In contrast, others such as Ariela Lazar (1999) and, to some extent, Alfred Mele (2000) maintain that ordinary cases of people believing what they want to believe despite consistent evidence to the effect that they are wrong are not examples of intentional self-deception. Rather, they are cases in which emotions and desires influence belief formation without the intervention of actions or intentions, operating through nonpsychological mechanisms. If we appreciate the sheer force that desires and emotions so routinely have over perception and belief, it is held, we will see that there is no need to assume that a special intention is required in order for people to maintain a false belief in the face of obvious evidence. The wife who does not see her husband's infidelity, the parents who refuse to believe that their missing son is probably dead, or the average American who thinks that he is an exceptional driver[2] are most often best explained not as cases of people who intentionally but unconsciously cheat themselves, but as people whose desires, emotions, wishes, or moods irrationally color their perception, without any intention on their part, just as the anorectic's emotions change what she sees in the mirror.

Lazar and Mele go so far as to suggest that Davidson-style self-deception never occurs,[3] or at any rate that to the extent that it does, it is not "hot irrationality" but cold self-manipulation, akin to auto-suggestion. I find their arguments interesting, but it is not my purpose to evaluate them here. What I would like to do is take a look at the moral significance of the phenomenon. If people genuinely do form irrational beliefs as a causal, but not intentional, result of their other beliefs, wishes, values, and so on—as I am persuaded they do—what are we to think when these irrational beliefs have moral import?

Begin by considering the immense variety of nonintentional hot irrational belief formation. A familiar example is wishful thinking, as exemplified, say, by Sigmund Freud walking down a city street and misreading a storefront sign as "Antiquities." This apparently happened to him often, as he was a great lover of antiquities and was enthusiastic about buying and collecting them. There is also what could be called 'self-hateful thinking': an anorectic, hating herself, may think she is fat when in fact she can see as well as anyone that she is thin. In the same vein, there is also depressed thinking—Peter Kramer, in *Listening to Prozac*, describes a woman who always believed that her cousin was taller than she was, until she recovered from depression, when she learned that in fact the cousin was the shorter one. As we venture further from the traditional territory of the philosopher of self-deception (generally, beliefs about marital fidelity or bodily defects) we run into more spectacular examples of belief formation under the nonintentional influence of motivational factors. I do not know what made the irreverent, intelligent Voltaire believe that Jews are greedy and have long noses, or the Nobel Prize–winning chemist Linus Pauling believe that vitamin C has powerful health benefits, but with people as intelligent as these, one feels one has to posit some "hot" factor. For one last example, consider the opinion, popular among the best and the brightest American doctors in the late nineteenth century, that "neither plague, nor war, nor smallpox, nor a crowd of similar evils, have resulted more disastrously for humanity than the habit of masturbation: it is the destroying element in civilized society."[4]

What such examples have in common, as Lazar and Mele point out, is that there is no use in positing any sort of puzzling, intentional self-deceptive behavior in explaining them. When considering Freud's wishful thinking, for example, no one, I think (probably including Davidson), would assume that Freud ever made an intentional effort to convince himself that there was an antique shop in front of him. Why, after all, would he intentionally set himself up for a disappointment? Likewise, when depression makes a woman think that her cousin is taller than she is, what plausible benefit is she to derive from this which is to explain her intention to deceive herself? When considering the anorectic whom self-hatred motivates to believe that she is fat, one does not assume that she intentionally makes herself believe that she is fat. Whether or not intentional self-deception exists, these are not cases of intentional self-deception. This is exactly what has led many to think that they are not philosophically interesting.

As a result, cases of belief formation "under the influence" have not been discussed much in the moral psychology literature. The person who intentionally induces in herself beliefs that she wants to have is the person most often discussed in this context, followed by the wishful thinker, and this is true to the extent that even Mele calls cases in which people believe negative things out of negative emotions "twisted cases," as if they were unusual in some way, an exception to some norm of useful or wishful delusions. I think, however, that it is a mistake for the moral psychologist not to pay attention to cases of unintentional "belief under the influence"—not because there is something particularly complicated about them, but because their very existence is significant and merits attention. Note how many of the beliefs thus formed are morally relevant beliefs, such as racial prejudices or beliefs in the evil of witchcraft. Chapter 3 argues that attention to such epistemic irrationality helps us to solve some riddles about moral worth—most notably, cases involving misguided conscience. Such attention also makes easier some discussions of rationality and self-control, as I hope will become apparent throughout the rest of this work.

The Ego-Dystonic: External Desires and the Closet Homosexual

There is much discussion in moral psychology of agents who are alienated from elements of their psychology or from their actions. Rarely discussed, however, are agents who are alienated from elements of their psychology or from their actions—but whose alienation, we have reason to believe, is inappropriate.

Once upon a time, the *Diagnostic and Statistical Manual of Mental Disorders* (or *DSM*, American psychiatry's primary diagnostic tool) characterized homosexuality as a mental disorder. In 1973, the American Psychiatric Association decided that homosexuality is not a mental disorder. It did, however, still allow psychiatrists to diagnose patients with 'ego-dystonic homosexuality'. 'Ego-dystonic homosexuality' is a Freudian term for the condition of a person who is homosexual but is disturbed by his homosexuality, feels estranged from it, and deeply wishes he were heterosexual. It is opposed to 'ego-syntonic homosexuality'—the term for the state of the person who is homosexual and proud, or at least accepting, of his homosexuality. As time went by, many American psychiatrists and psychologists began to argue that ego-dystonic homosexuality should not be considered a disorder either, and their view became largely accepted by the psychiatric profession. Their argument was based on the simple idea that, in a society that still by and large disapproves of its gays and lesbians, any person who discovered that she is homosexual would be likely to be surprised and disturbed by her discovery and would have understandable reasons to wish things were different. If homosexuality itself is not unhealthy, and wishing that one were heterosexual is a natural reaction to one's social circumstances, there seems to be no reason to hold ego-dystonic homosexuality to be a disorder.

Since Harry Frankfurt published his seminal "Freedom of the Will and the Concept of a Person" (1971), moral psychologists have been very concerned with the concept of *external desires*—desires that are not truly the agent's own, in a sense that is not quite literal but nonetheless significant. There is no agreement as to what exactly makes a desire external, but there is a wide agreement that externality exists and that it is somehow very significant for questions of free will, moral responsibility, and personhood; there is also a widely shared agreement that whatever external desires are, they are very similar to what an old-fashioned psychologist would call "ego-dystonic" desires.[5] They are desires from which the agent feels estranged ("that's not really me"), desires of which the agent deeply disapproves, whose existence causes the agent distress, or which the agent would never consider a reason for action. A paradigmatic example in the moral psychology literature of the person who has an external desire is the drug addict who very much wants not to be a drug addict. In short, external desires are the desires that do not fit with the agent's "party line"—and much good philosophical discussion has been devoted to determining what exactly that "party line" consists in. I agree that the distinction between ego-dystonic and ego-syntonic mental states is a fascinating topic of inquiry. However, there are cases in which ego-dystonic desires or actions do not lend themselves easily to such dramatic descriptions as "not the agent's own" or "happening without the participation of the agent." Such cases are uncommon in the literature but more common in everyday life, and their moral status is not yet well understood.

Imagine a person, Lynn, who discovers that she is a lesbian and is deeply disturbed by that discovery. Her homosexual desires conflict with her values and her sense of her identity. She does not want her desires to motivate her into action under any circumstances—the very thought scares her more than anything else. If Lynn were to go to her favorite college professor for help, she would likely be told that she should try to accept herself for who she is, refrain from attempts to suppress her true self, and so on. If, on the other hand, she were to read the moral psychology literature and believe its claims, she would probably conclude that she was right and her homosexual desires are not truly her own. For 'Lynn' and 'homosexual desires', we could substitute 'Victorian lady' and 'any sexual desire', 'nice Jewish boy' and 'hostility toward parents', 'severe perfectionist' and 'desire to get some rest', 'the young E. T. A. Hoffman' and 'desire to be a writer', or any of various characters from various novels and their adulterous loves. In all these cases, the agent who dismisses these desires as reasons for action and treats them as "outlaw desires" is likely to feel that they are not really his. In at least some of these cases, the nonphilosopher's intuition tends to follow pop psychology, deeming the agent "in denial" or escaping from himself or having a false self-image. These cases receive considerably less attention in the literature than those in which we tend to think that the agent seems right when she apologizes for "not being herself."

It would be a mistake to endorse the sort of folk-Freudianism that automatically assigns the suppressed desire the status of a "truer self." Sometimes a person who is made weak-willed by drinking reveals her "true colors" in her drunken behavior (*in vino veritas*), while at other times a person under similar circumstances seems to speak the truth when she says, "Sorry, it was not really me talking; I was drunk." When trying to sort out intuitions about the status of ego-dystonic desires and actions, it is a mistake to ignore either sort of case, to ignore either intuition. There is an interesting philosophical challenge in explaining the salient differences between the two sorts of cases and accounting for the fact that they both exist. I shall take on some of this challenge later in the book.

Self-Control and Garden-Variety
Unconscious Motivation

There are forms of unconscious motivation whose existence is not particularly controversial, and they are what I have in mind when talking about "garden-variety" unconscious motivation. The unconscious, in this sense, I take to be less reminiscent of the particular entities postulated by Freud or Jung than of the unconscious as found in such articles as "Knowing More than We Can Tell"[6] and "Telling More Than We Can Know,"[7] on the one hand, and the source of phenomena described in everyday statements with words like "without realizing it, you deeply envy him," on the other hand. Garden-variety unconscious motivation is a form of motivation we recognize everywhere. If George avoids a certain colleague without knowing why, that may well be because he has registered her facial expressions in the past and has concluded, without consciousness of it, that she dislikes him. If Louisa chooses to buy one shampoo over the other and provides you with a list of reasons for why she did so, it may still be the case that the location of the product on the shelf influenced her choice more than any of the factors she describes. Larry may describe to you his lofty moral reasons for supporting a communist regime, but his actual motivation for supporting it may be more along the lines of avoiding cognitive dissonance—having fought for the revolution, Larry concludes that what he did was right.

No contemporary philosopher I know of, moral psychologists included, denies that we have beliefs and desires (plans, memories, etc.) of which we are not aware, that we act on them frequently, or that we make many inferences each day without drawing a syllogism on a mental blackboard. There is, however, some tension between the prevalence of garden-variety unconscious influences and the emphasis in the writing of some philosophers on the importance of the first-person perspective to moral psychology—the very perspective that the discovery of the unconscious showed to be somewhat less trustworthy than it once seemed. Consider the following typical classroom example:[8]

> I see a piece of cake in the fridge and feel a desire to eat it. But I back up and bring that impulse into view and then I have a certain distance. Now the impulse does not dominate me and now I have a problem. Is this desire really a reason to act? I consider the action on its merits and

decide that eating the cake is not worth the fat and the calories. I walk away from the fridge, feeling a sense of dignity.

This could be the inner monologue of a rational, autonomous being, and this is how it is usually presented. It could equally be the inner monologue of an individual with severe anorexia nervosa, weighing eighty-five pounds, or one of the many women who suffer from milder versions of food-related irrationality. Imagine such a case: a woman who appears to herself to be in control of her desires, deciding between them on their merits, but who appears to her friends (or even to her future self, after having recovered from her anorexia or her irrational dieting) to be a person who *is* in fact at the mercy of her desires, or at the mercy of what are commonly called her "emotional issues." It may be that at the root of anorexia there is fear of losing control, but a fear of losing control is still a fear, at the mercy of which the anorectic finds herself, and being at the mercy of a fear is a state that is different from operating under the rule of one's practical reason.

The anorectic is a potential challenge to contemporary moral psychology because she is a person who experiences her psyche in terms of self-control, as if there were something that was *her*, choosing between her desires on the basis of their merits, giving her control over herself, while we have good reasons to believe that unconscious desire or emotion moves her in a manner not characteristic of well-exercised practical reason. To the extent that moral psychology emphasizes the first-person perspective, it risks misunderstanding such cases.

Another example: imagine that you have a friend whose thirst for professional recognition is of the most extreme form. He has received an offer from a prestigious firm, an offer that, while flattering and promising a raise in pay, is in other ways very disadvantageous to him. Your friend is now in the process of considering the offer. Hearing him detail his painstaking deliberation on the phone, you may tell yourself, "There is no way he will be able to resist the allure of this much prestige." What is interesting in such a case is not simply that you can predict what the man will do (presumably, one can predict what an ideally self-controlled person would do under some circumstances), nor is it simply the fact that his decision is likely to make him miserable in the long run (I do not deny that free choices can make one miserable). What is interesting is that you, a keen observer, cannot help but see him, with respect to his choice, as being as much a slave to his desire for prestige as anyone can be: you see him, correctly, as *driven*, as a person who has a false sense of control over his desires, while he is in fact a paradigm of obsession. One can imagine a novelist making good use of the sense of self-control felt by such a man, contrasting it with the way the man's life appears to the reader to be out of control.[9]

These cases seem to suggest several things. First, they suggest that that the mere first-person *experience* of having control over one's mental life is not by itself a surefire indication that one *actually* has control over one's mental life, in any meaningful sense of 'self-control'. Second, the existence of garden-variety unconscious motivation suggests that what occurs so dramatically in the lives of the anorectic and the fame-chaser—namely, the appearance of control paired with all the third-person evidence of lack of control—may also occur in less dramatic form in many of us: every time, for example, that one's choice of shampoo is unconsciously influenced by the emotions invoked by a forgotten advertisement, or every time a businessperson's choice to force herself to work another hour is unduly influenced by her already alarming lack of sleep. In these situations, as in the situation of the anorectic and the fame-chaser, our subjective experience of self-control seems potentially misleading: unconscious motivation seems to move us unawares.

No philosopher, to my knowledge, advocates the view that the first-person appearance of control guarantees control, but some have written without taking sufficiently into account the possibility of a gap between felt self-control and actual self-control. Take Christine Korsgaard as an example. Korsgaard (1996) tells us that while, from the third-person perspective, it may seem as if decisions are forced by desires, "when you deliberate, it is as if there were something over and above all of your desires, something which is you, and which chooses which desire to act on." Now, this focus on the first-person perspective comes just after Korsgaard *agrees* that the mind is not transparent. Korsgaard seems to share the assumption that various garden-variety forms of the unconscious exist. What is especially interesting to me, however, is that Korsgaard moves quickly from the admission that mind is not transparent to a philosophical position that focuses exclusively on the first-person conscious perspective. If the unconscious exists, and if, as Korsgaard writes, we tend to think of other people's actions as compelled by passion and of ours as autonomously chosen, are not *both* perspectives suspect, to some extent?

Some readers would say that Korsgaard simply should not be expected to worry about whether the first-person view of our motivational structure reflects the truth, because she merely says that in order to act for reasons, it is necessary to see things from the first-person perspective. Even if this is true of Korsgaard, there is still much potential for conflict between her theory and the possibility that the first-person perspective is, with respect to our motivational structure, delusional—a possibility suggested, though by no means more than suggested, by cases like the anorectic and her less dramatic cousins. (I will argue in chapter 2 that only *from* the first-person perspective does the first-person perspective appear necessary for acting rationally: from the third-person perspective, there are people who act rationally without conscious deliberation and hence without a first-person experience of distance from their desires.)

For now, however, my point is not that Korsgaard or anyone else holds a false view, but that we as moral psychologists have been consuming an unbalanced diet of examples. Much has been written about agents who experience themselves as choosing between their desires autonomously while being paradigms of self-control, and about agents who feel the pull of temptation and surrender to it. Almost nothing has been written about the agent who steps away from her desires and, as it seems to her, chooses calmly between them, feeling apparent mastery over temptation and emotion, while the very "I" that steps away from the desires is the unconscious dupe of other desires, emotions, or irrationality. I think these agents are common, and I hope to show that paying attention to them has philosophical benefits.

Deliberation, Reflection, and Getting Through the Day

Characters in Hollywood movies encounter a lot of car chases. Characters in novels rarely wash their hands or do their laundry. And in the work of moral psychologists, people deliberate and reflect *a lot*. They deliberate, one sometimes feels, whenever they perform an action, and certainly whenever they act for good reasons. They also form beliefs based on reflection, because that is what rational beings do. This is not to say that most moral psychologists say that we are frequent deliberators, though some of them seem to come quite close. After all, movie producers know very well that car chases are not common. But deliberation is given far more prominence in moral psychology than its position in daily life would suggest, and so the many daily actions, even rational-seeming actions, performed without deliberation rarely make their way into the literature.

This tendency is well illustrated by its most extreme supporters. Michael Smith (1994, 157) seems to hold that when we are rational "our desires and beliefs only generate new desires if we deliberate and only if we do so correctly." Given the standard meaning of 'deliberation' in English, the reader can be forgiven for imagining Smith's rational agent in the following way: whenever a desire (say, your desire to eat some nuts) joins up with a belief (say, your belief that there are nuts in your pocket) to create an instrumental desire (say, the desire to reach into your pocket), this is the result of deliberation on your part. The rational agent has to think, "So I have a desire to eat nuts. What would be the best way to fulfill this desire? Hmmm. Perhaps I should reach into my pocket," and only then does he develop the desire to do so. Consider what this would mean if it were correct. Every trivial act, such as reaching into your pocket for a handful of nuts, would itself require conscious consideration of many beliefs and desires, and many (hundreds? thousands?) of such trivial acts are performed each day, often in circumstances that would make deliberation very difficult (under time pressure, or while the agent is thinking—deliberating—about something else). If every proper derivation of instrumental desires required deliberation, it would be hard for anyone to get through the day.

Smith (as well as others inclined to think deliberation is very common) would remind us that his term 'deliberation' does not always mean conscious, "deliberate" deliberation, but "deliberation or something close enough"[10]—suggesting that it is simply convenient to discuss agents as if they deliberate or reflect, but that what one says about them applies equally to those who perform inferences unconsciously. The problem is that using 'deliberation' to mean "deliberation or something close enough" in this way only works if those other things that are supposed to be "close enough" to deliberation—unconscious processes of inference—are in fact close enough to it that it makes no philosophical difference whether you lump all types of good inference under 'deliberation' or not. But the difference between deliberation and nondeliberation is simply too significant for us to do that. And where deliberation meets moral psychology, there are important consequences of ignoring the difference.

Deliberation is a process that necessarily involves a first-person experience of distancing yourself from your emotions. This has been pointed out most forcefully by Korsgaard, but Humean writers, like Smith and Bernard Williams, often use the term 'deliberation' in that way as well, as this is a natural way to use the term in English ("I have no time to deliberate," etc.). This experience occurs when I sit at my desk and try to decide by deliberation how I should spend the afternoon. This experience does not always occur when I develop a desire to reach into my pocket for some nuts, and it does not occur when George infers, unconsciously and quite correctly, from a woman's facial expression that she wishes to be left alone, and leaves the room, unable to make sense of his motives for leaving. It does not occur when people seem to act rather reasonably while thinking—deliberating—about something else. It does not occur in many cases in which inference seems to happen "at some level" below consciousness. This is the difference between deliberation in the narrow sense and mental processes of inference in general. This difference is often accorded significance—even by the very authors who assume that deliberation is common. Given this difference it will not do for us to say, in effect, "I am talking about cases in which agents deliberate, but *surely* what I say is true for nondeliberative inference cases as well." No one has promised us that the mental process undergone by the nondeliberating actor is so similar to deliberation as to make the distinction negligible.

Let me give one example of the significance of the difference between deliberation and inference in general. Common assumptions about rationality—that *akrasia* is never rational, that rationality requires distancing oneself from one's emotions, that we are always more rational in a cool hour, that only humans act rationally—are plausible to the point of triviality if we think that rationality requires deliberation in the narrow sense, and more debatable if rationality only requires inference in a broader sense. Of any person who acts in a way that seems to be based on an inference but does not involve "deliberate" deliberation, it is possible to ask, Is she rational? To what extent is she acting for reasons? I think there is room for debate here, room for asking, meaningfully, "Are people only rational when they deliberate?" and "Are people ever rational when they act against the conclusions of their deliberation?" This is, in essence, asking how important the first-person perspective is to rationality and to acting for reasons. Those who take acting against one's best judgment or acting out of sheer sympathy as always irrational or a-rational, even if the action is clearly motivated by unconscious practical inference, seem to answer "very important": if you do what you, when experiencing yourself as distanced from your desires, regard as irrational, you *are* irrational. Other views imply that this is not very important: regardless of how irrational you think you are when you perform that distanced thinking, you may still be quite rational. This may be true, for example, if we adopt Scanlon's (1998) view that desire *itself* is reason-responsive or, in a quite different way, if we agree with McIntyre (1993) that *akrasia* can be rational. Either way, one risks equivocation if one tries to answer the question "Are we rational only when we deliberate?" by simply applying the name 'deliberation' to any mental process that shows signs of being responsive to reasons.

Some actions which, like Oliver's defection, are more important than eating nuts, and more morally significant, appear to take place without deliberation in the classical sense. Anyone who has tried to convince someone of a moral truth without success via argumentation, only to watch that person undergo a conversion years later as a result of a significant life event or watching *La Strada*, knows examples of morally important changes that happen without deliberation. This, as well as the very fact that people act as often as they do without explicit deliberation, makes a case for devoting more attention in our discussions to actions not deliberated upon. It may be that theories developed to accommodate explicitly deliberating agents can also explain cases involving non-deliberating agents, but whatever one's theory, there may be profit in not ignoring them.

It may also be noted that if one is concerned with psychological accuracy, there are some risks associated with taking less common phenomena as paradigmatic of the way humans act and think. Consider this example:

> I perceive, and I find myself with an impulse to believe. But I back up and bring that impulse into view and then I have a certain distance. Now the impulse doesn't dominate me and now I have a problem. Shall I believe? Is this perception really a reason to believe? (Korsgaard 1996, 93)

The reader steeped in the relevant literature may need to read this passage more than once in order to notice that Korsgaard describes a scenario that *almost never happens*. True, there are rare contexts in which it does happen. If I were to—apparently—clearly perceive a Malayan tapir in my room, my nature as a reflective animal would make me wonder if sense experience is a good enough reason to believe that there is a Malayan tapir in my room, as opposed to a reason to believe that I have gone too long without adequate sleep. However, this kind of postponement of belief, involving as it does the doubting of a clear perception, would be an unusual, profoundly distressing experience in the life of anyone who does not use hallucinogens regularly. In daily life, in most circumstances, seeing *is* believing—or at least it is true that if you see a black cat in front of you, you do not stop to back up and examine the merits of your "impulse" to believe that there is a black cat in front of you as a reason to believe that there is a black cat in front of you. In many circumstances one does not even bother to make a mental note to oneself that there is a cat present. One simply pets it, or removes it from the keyboard, or keeps going about one's business. Even when called upon to think consciously about the presence of the cat—perhaps someone asks you, "Where is the cat?"—you do not deliberate about its existence before you shout back, "Right here!"

To these facts about everyday experience, one is tempted to add the fact, documented in many experiments, of what is called "belief perseverance"—the fact that even intelligent, reflective humans seem to cling, consciously or otherwise, to false beliefs long after being given obvious reasons to dismiss those beliefs. If one used to believe that one has a slippery character because one is a Scorpio and later came to the conclusion that astrology has no basis in reality, one will often find it curiously hard to give up the belief that one has a slippery character. If one is introduced as "the man who did not rob the bank," even rather conscientiously reflective people will have trouble ridding themselves, by reflection, of the belief that one is somehow associated with bank robbery. Examples like these seem to show striking limitations to our capacity to do what Korsgaard describes and choose what to believe, even when we are perfectly aware of good reasons for changing our beliefs. Another striking fact is that even when one *does* exercise reflection—for example, one wonders how to judge the quality of a student's work or whether to believe what a politician says—one does not experience anything like the direct conflict between belief and sense-perception that Korsgaard describes. Perceptual beliefs ("there is a cat here") and unconscious beliefs (a prejudice against people who wear straw hats) do not, prima facie, seem to behave in the same way that reflective beliefs do.

It is worth emphasizing that Korsgaard herself does not argue that the sort of scenario she describes happens often. If her goal is simply to show that human beings are reflective in a way that other animals are not, she is successful: I, but not the Malayan tapir, have the ability to tell myself, "Look, there can't really be a Malayan tapir here. Let's call a neurologist." Korsgaard's example, then, works well for this purpose. My point is not so much to criticize Korsgaard as to point out that a moral psychology that feeds on an unbalanced diet of examples in which people form beliefs by reflection and practical judgments by practical deliberation risks missing out on important parts of moral life.

Rationality and Garden-Variety Unconsciousness

The rich varieties of unconscious motivation introduce puzzles about practical rationality that are as little addressed as puzzles they pose for theoretical rationality or self-control. Even when self-consciously reflecting from within the first-person perspective, one sometimes does not know rationality from irrationality (in the sense of not knowing if one is rational or not, not simply in the sense of not knowing what course of action one should take).[11] Imagine Tamara: she is trying to decide whether or not to marry Todd. Though she loves him, Tamara is very concerned about the differences in background between her and Todd (she is a religious Jew, he is a West Virginian goy; she is bookish, he likes country music, etc.). On the other hand, she notes to herself that she has been happy with him, that he has moral merits, and that they have dealt well with difficult relationship issues in the past. Facing a marriage ultimatum, Tamara is extremely perturbed; like Oliver Single's, her experience cannot be easily described in terms of a rational side of the self standing in opposition to the irrational (or nonrational) appetites. At times, she sees herself as consisting of her Reason, which sees the good reasons not to marry Todd ("After all, we are from such different backgrounds. It's simply madness."), and her Unreason (a.k.a. "my foolish heart"), which wants to marry him. At these times, she experiences the "part" of her that wishes to marry Todd as a dark, automatic, almost atavistic inclination: an appetite tempting her to violate her good sense. Then suddenly, as if observing a duck-rabbit picture, a shift occurs in her consciousness, and she experiences herself as consisting of Reason, which sees the desirability of marrying Todd ("After all, we have gotten along happily for many years, we have many compatible interests, and we love each other. These are the things that matter—every rational person should see that."), and Unreason (a.k.a. "fear of commitment" or "the tribal xenophobia I inherited from my parents"), which recoils at the thought of marrying Todd. Now it is the part of her wishing to marry Todd that plays the role of Reason in her inner drama, and the part of her rejecting the thought of marrying Todd that seems to her an opaque and nearly atavistic Appetite (or, in this case, Aversion). A little bit later, the roles of Reason and Unreason may switch again, and after a while she may feel confused and honestly wonder which is the advice of her Reason and which the blandishment of Appetite.

It seems to me that, while there is a fact of the matter as to which of her attitudes toward Todd is rational and which is not, this fact has little to do with whether these attitudes have the characteristics generally associated with the Faculty of Reason. It *could* be that her pro-marriage attitudes are rational and her anti-marriage attitudes are irrational, or the reverse could be true, or both could be equally irrational.[12] Her resistance to marrying Todd may be her response to a plethora of evidence—that is, it could follow from her many true beliefs about the situation which indicate that marrying Todd would be bad for her—or it could be the result of irrelevant factors, such as a childhood-ingrained visceral belief that non-Jews are bad people, or that she is not worthy of a nice husband. If her reluctance to marry Todd is based on the latter, it is irrational, *even if Tamara developed it while deliberating calmly*, and if her reluctance to marry Todd is based on the former, it is rational, *even if Tamara developed it in while in tears and dismisses it as a mere inclination that must be ignored.* This makes possible the following scenarios: Tamara, deciding in a calm, cool hour to banish all thought of Todd from her heart, correctly strikes all of her informed friends as being perfectly crazy even as she takes pride in her reason; Tamara, eloping with Todd while mumbling, "Why on Earth am I doing this, I'm crazy," makes her informed friends say, rightly, "Thank God, I knew her common sense would finally prevail"; and lastly, Tamara, still unsure what to do, saying to her friends, "I have these reservations about Todd. Do you think I am irrational?" The claims made here will be defended and elaborated in chapter 2.

It is important to note that Tamara is confused not simply about whether marrying Todd would be the rational thing to do (i.e., the thing that the rational person would do in her place) but also about whether she is being rational in wishing to do it—whether her *motives* are properly reason-responsive or crazy. Her friends, too, judge her as rational or irrational in a way that is based not simply on whether they believe she does "the rational thing to do" but also on their perception of whether she seems to be responding to good reasons. "Her common sense prevailed" is a different judgment from "Well, she's crazy, but this time her craziness led her to do the same thing that a rational person would have done." "She is crazy" is a hypothesis about the rationality of a person's internal mental state, not just about the desirability of the action she finally commits. When Tamara fears that she is irrational, she fears not only that she is making the wrong decision but that her motives for action are unreasonable ones (wishful thinking, xenophobia, etc.).

Now imagine that Tamara decides that her desire to marry Todd is, all in all, irrational—only wishful thinking, she concludes, could have led her to the belief that she and Todd could get along well together in the long run. Imagine that you, an older, wiser, more acute observer of human nature, knowing both Tamara and Todd very well, find it obvious that she is mistaken; on the contrary, you think, only a very insecure and pessimistic person (such as Tamara herself) would fail to see that Tamara and Todd have as good a chance for a successful marriage as anyone has. Her urge to marry Todd appears to be there for all the right reasons—motivated not by wishful thinking but by all the good things she knows about him—while her fretting and doubting seem to be attributable to factors that have nothing to do with the case but rather with whatever it is that Tamara's parents, say, did to make her insecure and pessimistic regardless of her circumstances. Suddenly, what sounded, from a first-person perspective, like the voice of Reason appears instead to be the voice of Tamara's neurosis or insecurity; if she does marry Todd, however reluctantly, it will look not like *akrasia* but like her having enough common sense to do the right thing in spite of her silly notions.

"Rational deliberation" is a common phrase in philosophical works. "Irrational deliberation" is not. Yet we all suspect that deliberation is at times a source of irrationality. Many people have told themselves, in a calm, cool, inner voice, things such as "Stop panicking: just because he hit you twice doesn't mean the relationship is doomed" or "Sure you want a new television set, but on a professor's salary you can't afford it yet." Since much of moral psychology was and is written in a culture concerned with the "sin" of lust, and the (these days, more widely reviled) "sin" of gluttony, it is not surprising that most discussion of irrationality is focused on irrational *temptation* fighting rational *resolution*. But irrationality comes in many forms, not all of them resembling temptation (an obvious example would be fear or worry). Rationality also comes in many forms, not all of which involve resolution—or deliberation. The nontemptation types of irrationality and nonresolution forms of practical rationality are, I hope to show, quite interesting in their own right.

Beyond the neo-Kantian use of "Practical Reason" as a noun, it is hard to find contemporary moral psychologists committing themselves explicitly to the colloquial distinction between the Rational Part and the Emotional Part of the soul, although there are exceptions. Gary Watson, for example, in his influential "Free Agency" (1975) explains quite clearly that his distinction between desires and values is derived from the Platonic idea of Reason and Appetite, Eleonore Stump (1988) identifies Reason with the higher faculties, and Kantian ethicists never completely drop talk of conflicts between Reason and Inclination. When Barry Stroud (2000) and Tim Scanlon (forthcoming) argue that the idea of Reason and Passion as capacities is ill-conceived, they are not so much attacking a specific theory but a certain resonance that the Platonic division of the soul, or its more sophisticated Aristotelian counterpart, still has in some moral psychologists' discussions. (In Aristotle's metaphorical language, Reason is the master and the emotions are dogs that can bring the master information and respond intelligently to his orders, but they still are not such that they can lead to rational behavior; no rational agency is possible unless the master rules.)

The resonance is found in the fact that when we are given examples to stir our intuitions, we are rarely given cases such as Tamara's and are almost always given cases that the Aristotelian or Platonic picture, or the folk-psychological model of "the rational part and the irrational part," "the head and the heart," can explain. Agents are often described as acting for reasons that they endorse or as blindly following their desires, as if these were jointly exhaustive categories. If an agent in a moral psychologist's example feels the pull of emotion against the push of reason, the pull that the agent attributes to reason is always a pull toward an action that seems rational to the reader. Rational agents in examples often deliberate in a "cool hour": they hardly ever wake up with a painful, warranted realization in the middle of the night.[13] Irrational agents always "act against their best judgment" because they are tempted, or fail to deliberate in the heat of passion: they never conclude disastrously irrational business deals while feeling calmer than ever, only to wonder "What was I thinking?" a year later. This does not, by itself, mean that contemporary action theorists cannot explain people like Tamara. It raises, however, the suspicion that cases like Tamara's—not altogether that rare—may not have been given due consideration.

The Plan

I have brought up a number of puzzling cases: people who appear to act for rational reasons, even for moral reasons, without knowing that they are acting from them or even denying that they are; people whose irrational beliefs are caused by their emotions or desires without the intervention of their own agency; people whose explicitly declared moral beliefs are at odds with the way they act and feel; people who wonder if they are very rational or very foolish; and people who seem to be alienated from parts of themselves that seem to us to be an important part of them.

These cases have received too little attention from moral psychologists. Cases in which the mind of the agent seems quite transparent to her, cases in which she either acts for reasons that she understands and endorses or is carried to action by some atavistic force, cases in which what she regards as important to her is important to her, and cases in which, even when she is irrational, she knows she is—these are all cases familiar from the literature. And yet the unconscious does not usually get its due.

It has been suggested to me more than once that the reason moral psychologists rarely write about cases involving unconscious factors of the sort I sketched in this chapter is that these cases are very complicated (or even, according to some, strange or "deviant") and that, as even the simplest cases in moral psychology are hard to deal with, a theory has no better option than to start with the simple cases and maybe, given some good luck, go from there. I disagree. Yes, it is true that life is complicated, and the part of life of most interest to moral psychology—human behavior and cognition in morally significant contexts—is a particularly complicated part of it. This, however, is not necessarily a reason to base our investigations into human nature on simple or simplified cases. On the contrary, this is a reason to wonder how far we can possibly get by studying simple or simplified cases. It can be admitted that strange cases can lead to bad theory, but the cases that I have mentioned are not really strange. Cases involving people growing out of seeds or aliens coming to Earth may be strange, and some (e.g., Hardin 1988; Wilkes 1994) argue that this is a reason to be judicious in their use. In a different sense, cases involving bizarre, ill-understood individuals, artificial situations of the kind created by the television show *Survivor*, or horrible moral dilemmas that verge on the grotesque may be strange enough to make bad theory— even if the bizarre individual existed in real life or the grotesque moral dilemma was imposed by a sadistic, bored Nazi on his prisoners. My cases, by contrast, only display the sort of murkiness and complexity which is *the rule*, not the exception, in life, and especially in the part of life interesting to us as moral philosophers. I take the goal of the moral psychologist to include understanding the interesting cases—Kant's sorrowing philanthropist, Aristotle's brave man, the amoralist, the kleptomaniac, coworkers who claim that they are under stress and therefore not blameworthy for their actions, and so on. All of these cases are quite complex, and yet no one suggests that we quit discussing them or pretend that they are simpler than they are.

In this book, I will offer a theory of moral worth or moral praiseworthiness and blameworthiness (though not a theory of right or wrong, or of the good). In developing this theory, I shall take cases of inadvertent virtue and misguided conscience as important cases I need to make sense of. I will take it as a working assumption that actions not deliberated upon, unconscious motivation, and the other phenomena described in this chapter are salient and important features of moral life, too important to be left to the "extra credit" stage of developing a theory. But I shall also attempt to make sense of the more usual suspects (Kant's sorrowing philanthropists, Aristotle's brave man, etc.). Chapter 2 prepares the ground by arguing against one common assumption in moral psychology, the assumption that *akrasia* is always irrational, or at least, always, other things being equal, less rational than the corresponding self-controlled action. Chapter 3, the heart of the book, presents my positive theory of moral worth and argues for it. Chapters 4 and 5 are concerned with the concept of *agent-autonomy*. My theory of moral worth makes no central use of any such concept, and the goal of these final two chapters is to defend the positive theory from potential objections to the effect that there is something wrong with its failure to invoke autonomy, while clarifying along the way what the theory implies about some issues in moral responsibility that are often discussed in connection with autonomy (including the responsibility of kleptomaniacs, drug addicts, makers of Freudian slips, and people driven to murder by mad hypnotists). My views in these chapters owe a lot to the view, advocated by some compatibilists, that we are blameworthy, roughly, for acts of ill will and praiseworthy for acts of good will,[14] but this will not, for all that, be a work on free will.

It should be stressed that the puzzling phenomena I will push to the forefront are not claimed to refute any existing research program in moral worth. At most, it will sometimes be argued that *particular* theoretical positions do not accommodate them, and that richer visions may be needed if the problems are to be rectified. This is not, except in passing, a work of criticism of others. I will keep largely to the task of understanding the place of the mind in moral merit in a way that is as responsive as possible to the complexities of the cases I have raised, without presupposing, attacking, or defending any particular larger theoretical framework. I will simply aim for the truth about the particular issues I discuss and see where it takes me, with the hope of enriching existing discussions along the way.

■ ■ ■

TWO

ON ACTING RATIONALLY
AGAINST ONE'S BEST JUDGMENT

There are at least two ways to think of theories of rationality. One way is to see the ideal theory of rationality as providing us with a manual of sorts: follow these instructions, and you will always make rational decisions or you will, at least, know whether or not you are acting rationally at the moment.[1] Another way is to see theorizing about rationality as aiming, not at providing us with a manual, but at providing us with a third-person theory—a theory that tells us when people act rationally and when they do not, so that given full information about a person's circumstances, beliefs, and motives, one would be able to tell how rational or irrational said person would be in performing a certain action. These two tasks—to which I will refer as the creation of a *rational agent's manual* and the creation of an *account of rationality*—are more different than they may look, and conceptual blunders may ensue if one does not always know which of them one pursues.

 Consider, for example, a person facing a complex situation. One attempts to decide whether to take up a certain risky career, whether or not to leave a marriage in favor of a new love, or (to borrow from Bernard Williams) whether to leave one's family and move to Tahiti to become a great painter. Desperate, one wonders, Am I crazy for wanting to take the job? Would it be irrational of me to leave my husband? Should I decide to go to Tahiti and just see what happens? Now let us assume that a certain theory of rationality does not help us very much in answering these questions, thus being of little use in making our complex decision. If we see the task of the theory as the writing of a rational agent's manual, such a failure to help is necessarily a failure on the theory's part. On the other hand, if the task of the theory is to provide an account of rationality, it may be no failing on the theory's part if it entails that in certain situations it is extremely hard or impossible for an agent to know when she is rational and when she is not, and hence what the rational choice for her is. It might even be possible that just as the right account of delusion must imply that one cannot tell if one is deluded or not, the right account of rationality must imply that, at least in some situations, one is a very bad judge of one's own rationality.[2]

Another difference between the manual perspective and the account perspective is that a manual, by nature, contains advice, and so everything in a rational agent's manual should consist of good, coherent advice. However, not everything that is good advice translates into a good descriptive account of the rationality of an action, or vice versa. Moore's paradox—the fact that the utterance "It's raining but I do not believe it" is absurd while the truth of the claim is harmless—has its parallels in matters of rationality: "Never pay attention to anything I say" is incoherent advice, but it may still be true that a rational agent would never listen to anything I say. "Go to the party, but do not do it just because I told you so" may be, under some circumstances, impossible to follow, but it may well be what the rational person would do. "Never act out of a conviction that is the result of self-deception" (or, as Williams says, "Do not leave your family in order to go to Tahiti and paint unless you are reasonably convinced that you are a great painter")[3] is not very useful as advice; neither is "Never act out of an unconscious wish that has nothing to do with the task at hand." Still, it may be true of the rational agent that she would never act out of such motives—that she would not simply try to avoid doing so, but in fact would never act out of them. Perhaps, just as Williams has it, no theory could have provided Gauguin with an algorithm for figuring out whether going to Tahiti was a crazy idea, but that does not exclude the possibility that with a true account of rationality and full information about Gauguin's psyche we might have been able to figure out, before knowing the results of his action, whether Gauguin's idea was crazy or not.

"Act against your best judgment" is also an absurd piece of advice. I use the term 'best judgment' in the manner of contemporary philosophers of action—to refer to the judgment that one reaches, having taken into account all the reasons one judges to be relevant, as to what would be best for one to do in a given situation. I use 'acting against one's best judgment' and '*akrasia*' interchangeably. Thus, if Tamara deliberates and reaches the conclusion that, all things considered, she should marry Todd, it is her best judgment that she should marry Todd. If Tamara, being a human being, deliberates imperfectly and forgets to consider a thing or two before concluding "All things considered, I should marry Todd," it is still true that *her best judgment* tells her that she should marry Todd. If, without changing her judgment that she should marry Todd, she fails to marry Todd, she is thus acting against her best judgment, or acting akratically, or displaying weakness of will.

Let us now see why "Act against your best judgment" is an absurd piece of advice. Faced with the question "Should I marry Todd, as I think I should, or should I act against my best judgment and not marry him?" I cannot quite answer "Act against your best judgment and don't marry him," for if my interlocutor is convinced by my advice, her best judgment will no longer be that she should marry Todd. A rational agent's manual cannot instruct the agent to act against her best judgment. It can instruct the agent not to marry Todd, it may instruct the agent not to make certain types of decisions pertaining to her emotional life, such as marrying Todd, in the face of strong emotional resistance, or it may instruct her, if she has strong feelings against such a decision, to consider whether her instincts have something to them and perhaps revise her best judgment if there are reasons to do so. A sophisticated agent's manual may even instruct an agent to do something such as drink alcohol with the purpose of making her more "weak willed"—more likely to act against her best judgment—but this will be similar in all ways to the manual instructing the agent to take a pill that makes her irrational: while taking the drug may be recommended by the manual, neither "act irrationally" nor "act against your best judgment" can be recommended itself. A rational agent's manual is a deliberator's manual, and acting against one's best judgment is not the sort of thing one settles on doing as a result of good deliberation. Similarly, "I, the agent, should act against my best judgment"—itself a best judgment rather than advice—is flagrantly absurd. Acting against one's best judgment is not something that one can, as a result of deliberation, resolve to do; one just changes one's best judgment as to what to do.

As acting against one's best judgment is something that no rational agent's manual can advise, it is little surprise that it is almost a universal assumption in contemporary philosophy—at least among those philosophers who believe that acting against one's best judgment is genuinely *possible*—that acting against one's best judgment is never an instance of rational action. In a paper originally published in 1970, Donald Davidson (1980, 31) describes a man who decides, after deliberation, that he should not get out of bed to brush his teeth, as it is not worth the trouble. The man gets up, against his best judgment, and brushes his teeth anyway. "What is wrong," says Davidson, "is that the incontinent man acts, and judges, irrationally, for this is surely what we must say of a man who acts against his own best judgement" (41). Since Davidson,[4] one rarely hears challenges to the claim that acting against one's best judgment is never rational. Most often, it is simply assumed to be true.[5] If asked to name kinds of irrationality, the student of action or agency will usually name, in no particular order, self-deception and *akrasia*. In this chapter I will argue that if we aim purely at providing an account of rationality, without any view to creating a rational agent's manual, we have to accept the conclusion that acting against one's best judgment can sometimes be rational. Or rather, to be more precise, I would like to argue that *sometimes an agent is more rational for acting against her best judgment than she would be if she acted in accordance with her best judgment*. I still agree that every agent who acts against her best judgment is, as an agent, *less than perfectly* rational, as the schism between best judgment and desire[6] indicates a failure of coherence in her mind. However, I will argue that it is not always the case that an agent is less rational (and less coherent) in following the desire than she is in following her best judgment. In fact, I will show that there are cases where following her best judgment would make the agent *significantly* irrational, while acting akratically would make her only trivially so—and as rational as most of us ever are. Do I offer the advice, then, that we should sometimes act against our best judgments? I do not. As it is not my intention here to contribute to the writing of a rational agent's manual, my subject matter is not to suggest what should or should not be done. What I would like to argue is that sometimes, when we do act against our best judgments, we are, in doing so, rational (or rather, more rational than we would have been in acting in accordance with our best judgments), though we may fail to realize it at the time of acting. The significance of this result for specifically moral issues will become clear in chapters 3 and 4.

As I said before, the assumption that acting against one's best judgment is never rational is uncontested within action theory and moral psychology, with very few exceptions, notably those expressed by Harry Frankfurt (1988),[7] Robert Audi (1990), and Alison McIntyre (1993).[8] Some doubts about the universality of the assumption may also be implicit in Thomas Hill (1986).[9] Unlike other possible arguments against this assumption, the argument I intend to offer does not depend on any commitment to the existence of external reasons for action. On the contrary, I will assume, for purposes of argument, that one only has a reason to act in a certain way to the extent that the relevant course of action is likely, given one's beliefs, to satisfy one's desires, and that acting rationally, whatever it turns out to be, involves doing what one has overwhelming reasons to do, for these reasons.[10] I would like to start my discussion from a context in which, however implicitly and unexpectedly, the assumption of the universal irrationally of acting against one's best judgment has been challenged: the debate over Michael Smith's *The Moral Problem*. As we shall see, Smith, in answering his critics, comes as close as anyone to actively attempting to defend, rather than assume, the claim that acting against one's best judgment is always more irrational than not doing so. By treating this claim as worth defending rather than assuming it to be obviously true, Smith provides a good starting point for our discussion.

Smith on Failures to Desire What We Think We Should

In *The Moral Problem* (1994), Smith defends the claim that if one believes that one should φ, one rationally should desire to φ. In defending this claim, he relies on an attempt to explicate the meaning of "I should φ." According to Smith, a judgment such as "I should φ" means "If I were fully rational, I would want to φ."[11] If this is so, he argues, it is clear that:

> C2. Agents who believe that they have a normative reason to φ in certain circumstances C rationally should desire to φ in C. (Smith 1994, 148)

It is not hard to see a connection between Smith's C2 and the claim that it is always irrational to act against one's best judgment. According to him, it is irrational not to desire to do what one believes would be rational for one to do. If Smith is right, a person who believes she should give money to the Tapir Preservation Fund (TPF) in circumstances C and fails to do so because she has no desire whatsoever to give to the TPF in C is acting irrationally. Presumably, then, if she believes that, *all things considered*, the most rational thing for her to do at this moment is to give to the TPF, and, despite having some desire to do so, her desire to keep the money motivates her more forcefully, her failure to be *effectively* motivated to give to the TPF is a sign of irrationality on her part. My point here, however, is not to insist that Michael Smith believes that acting against one's best judgment is always irrational (though it would surprise me if he believed otherwise).[12] My point is that a certain type of criticism of Michael Smith's C2 has implications for the common assumption that acting against one's best judgment is never rational.

There is something appealing about Smith's view that it is rational to want to do what one believes it to be rational to do — or rather, to want to do what one believes that one would want to do if one were rational. The person who has beliefs such as "If I were rational, I would want to concentrate on my studies right now" or "If I were a reasonable human being, I would want to stop smoking more badly than I want not to gain weight" often thinks of herself as more irrational for the fact that these beliefs, by themselves, do not in the least motivate her to concentrate on her studies or stop smoking. But as James Dreier (1996) and Geoffrey Sayre-McCord (1997, 63) point out, there is also something genuinely puzzling about Smith's claim that it is always rational to want to do what one believes one would want to do if one were rational. Does the mere fact that I *believe* a certain desire would be rational for me to have make it rational for me to have it? What if my belief is false?

Smith tries to convince us by suggesting an analogy between desire and belief: he postulates that if we believe that we have good reasons to believe that P—that it is rational for us to believe that P—then it is indeed rational for us to believe that P. But this analogy between desire and belief lends more support instead to the objectors, for we often do not hold the fact that an agent takes her belief to be rational to be any evidence of the rationality of her beliefs, *contra* Smith. Many people think of themselves as rational and appear to be wrong. In fact, practically everyone who has conscious irrational beliefs also believes that she is epistemically rational in having these beliefs: if we were to deem rational every person who *believes* herself to have good reasons to hold her beliefs, there would hardly be an epistemically irrational person left in the land. Imagine, for example, that Kathleen believes that aliens habitually invade the Earth and that the U.S. government makes an effort to hide this fact. Kathleen also believes that it is rational for her to believe in her conspiracy theory, and that this is the theory she would believe in if she were fully rational. If asked, she gladly offers a plethora of considerations which she takes to be excellent reasons to believe in the existence of alien visitors and a government cover-up. If we suspect Kathleen's belief in aliens to be irrational, the fact that she believes it to be rational does not seem to count against our suspicion in any significant way. It is irrational for Kathleen to believe in aliens and even more irrational for her to believe that she is rational in believing in aliens.

If the fact that Kathleen thinks of her belief as rational does not make it rational for her to have her belief, why should the fact that an agent takes her desire to be rational (or to be a desire she would have if she were rational) make it rational for her to have that desire? Imagine the outlines of the kind of case Dreier alludes to—a case in which it seems an agent has a *false* belief as to what he would do if he were fully rational. Let us imagine that Sam believes that he should become a hermit of sorts—that he should restrict his social life to a bare minimum and devote himself to nothing but academic study. He believes that if he were rational, he would be motivated to become such a hermit. Let us also imagine that, given Sam's overall set of desires and the evidence available to him, it would be clear to him, if he were fully rational, that becoming a hermit would make him miserable, which is exactly the predicament Sam would most like to avoid. If he were fully rational, he would not be motivated in the least to become a hermit but would seek a more balanced existence. In this case, it seems that it is irrational for Sam to desire to become a hermit. Sam, in being mistaken as to what he would do if he were fully rational, seems also to be simply mistaken as to what is rational for him to desire right now. In invoking, at least by implication, cases such as Sam's, Dreier and Sayre-McCord, perhaps without noticing, do a lot more than attack Michael Smith: by suggesting that a person with a false view as to what it would be rational for her to do may not be irrational if she is not motivated by her view (and hence, presumably, not moved to act on it), they cast doubt on the assumption that it is always irrational to act against one's best judgment. Let us see how Smith addresses this doubt.

In his scattered replies to Dreier (see Smith 1996, 162; Smith 1997, 100), Smith addresses the possibility of people like Sam—people who have a false belief as to what it would be rational for them to want to do—in the following way: he admits that they cannot be fully rational, even if their desires match their beliefs, but he maintains that given their false beliefs that φ-ing would be rational for them, it would be more rational for them to φ than not to φ. In the case of Sam, this would mean that should Sam desire to become a hermit, he would not be fully rational, because he would, after all, desire something that he would not desire if he were fully rational. However, given the fact that Sam believes that it would be rational for him to desire to become a hermit, it would be more rational of him to desire to become a hermit than not to desire to do so. Why would it be more rational for Sam to desire to do what he believes it to be rational for him to do? Because, says Smith, other things being equal, Sam's overall set of beliefs and desires, his overall psyche, would be more coherent if his desire matched his belief. To have a belief that it would be rational for you to become a hermit and a desire to become a hermit is to have a more coherent psychology than someone who has the belief that it would be rational for her to become a hermit and no desire to match her belief, or a desire not to become a hermit.

In arguing this way, Smith appeals to coherence of the agent's mental states as the core of rationality. If it seems strange to us that a person such as Sam should be thought of as more rational for being motivated to follow an ill-conceived plan to become a hermit than not to do so, Smith can argue that it only seems strange to us because we tend to think of rationality as always leading to the optimal outcome, while Sam is making a mistake; but rationality, Smith points out, is not about always finding the optimal outcome, but about having a coherent and consistent set of beliefs and desires, and Sam, believing that he would be rational to try to become a hermit, is more coherent and consistent if he also desires to become one (and, one could extrapolate from Smith, if he believes that all things considered he should become a hermit, he is more coherent if his desire to become a hermit triumphs over competing desires). If it seems even stranger to us that Kathleen should be thought of as more rational for having an unfounded belief in alien visitors, Smith could analogously say that we only feel odd about this state of affairs because we think of the rational person as always discovering the truth: but rationality, he could say, is not about always discovering the truth (rational people err all the time) but about being coherent, and *given* the fact that Kathleen believes that she has clear evidence for the existence of alien visitors, she would be more rational if she believed in the existence of alien visitors than if she did not.

I would like to argue that the concept of rationality as consisting in having a more coherent belief/desire set does not support Smith's position. In fact, the idea that rationality consists in having a more coherent belief/desire set supports the view that, *contra* Smith, there are cases in which one is more rational in failing to desire to do what one believes it would be rational to do, or even in developing a desire not to do it, than one would be in desiring to do what one deems rational. For these reasons, this conception of rationality also supports rather than undermines the view that there are some cases in which one is more rational in acting against one's best judgment than one would be in acting in accordance with it.

Let us imagine Sam's case in more detail. Sam, a college student, looks at his wall calendar and discovers that his final exams are only three weeks ahead of him—he had had a vague impression that more time was available to him. He becomes somewhat anxious about his chances of success in his exams, and somewhat angry at himself for having left a little more academic work for the last moment than he is comfortable with. Alas, he thinks, too much time has been spent interacting with interesting people rather than studying. "What I really should do," Sam thinks, "is restrict my social life to an absolute minimum until I finish my degree and find a job. My education is very important to me, and it is too easy for me to procrastinate when there are friends around me. There will be a lot of time for social interaction later in life, when the structure provided by a job will reduce the need for self-discipline on my part. I really should become a hermit." Sam, however, fails to become a hermit, as he cannot muster the motivation. He does not manage, even though he tries, to develop an actual desire to live like a hermit. "This is very irrational of me," we can imagine him saying, as if reading from Smith. "If I were rational, I know I would embrace the opportunity that being in this expensive, first-rate college presents to me and want nothing more than to become a hermit, doing nothing but studying for the duration of my student years."

While Sam is thus deliberating, let us further imagine, he fails to consider the following facts: whenever he is alone for too long his productivity does not increase but rather decreases, because in the absence of friendly social interaction he becomes depressed and tends to soothe his depression by watching television. Sam has gone through such a process more than once, and his memory of his typical reaction to loneliness is not buried deep in his unconscious—it is just not at the front of his mind while he is deliberating in front of his wall calendar. Perhaps it would be recalled if he were a little less worried, in which case he would be likely to conclude that his desires to be a good student, get a good education, and avoid last-minute panic would not be served by becoming a hermit. Sam also has a strong desire to be happy, which is deeper and more important to him than the desire to be a good student. He has a plethora of beliefs and desires which collectively entail that he cannot be happy as a hermit. It is also true, let us say, that if a fellow student were to tell Sam that she wished to become a hermit for similar reasons, Sam would call her crazy or say she is "overreacting." As a whole, Sam has a large number of desires that would be badly frustrated by acting on a desire to become a hermit, given his beliefs.

According to Smith, given Sam's belief that he should become a hermit, it is obvious that his psychology, and especially his desire set, would be more coherent were he also motivated—had he also the desire—to become a hermit. But given the whole story of Sam's beliefs and desires, a desire to become a hermit would make Sam's overall desire set *less* coherent. Sam has many desires that, given his beliefs, are incompatible with a desire to radically reduce social contact. Some of these desires are central to his belief/desire set: giving them up would be incoherent with the great majority of his beliefs and desires. He has, on the other hand, only a few desires that would be served by becoming a hermit, and they are fairly isolated. Sam's overall set of beliefs and desires is not optimally coherent, but the reason for that is not that he has a belief that he should become a hermit without a desire to become one, but rather the existence of the belief itself. If he were optimally consistent, he would have neither a belief that he should become a hermit nor a desire to become a hermit, but given that he already has the belief, having the desire only makes things worse. Developing a desire to become a hermit, a desire incompatible with most of his desires, to accommodate a marginal, isolated normative belief would not increase coherence in

Sam's mind but decrease it.[13] In fact, if rationality is simply psychic coherence, and rational desires and actions are those that best cohere with the agent's beliefs and desires, then surely it is more rational for Sam not to desire to become a hermit (and thus fail to become one), or, in fact, to develop and act on a desire not to become a hermit, than it is for him to desire to become a hermit.[14]

Had Sam been our friend or son, we would probably treat his belief that he should become a hermit as a forgivable, perhaps endearing, irrationality. Had Sam suddenly developed a desire for social isolation, a desire strong enough for him to take appropriate action, we would most likely see it as a sign of loss of mental balance.[15] We would think that while irrationally believing that one should adopt a hermit's existence is a common irrationality in college students facing final exams, Sam is showing more than average irrationality by actually reaching the point of *following through* with his mad plan.

Smith (personal communication) has suggested that he could take the following step in response to my objection, amending his view to some extent. To his original claim that it is always rational to desire what one believes one would desire if one were rational, Smith could add "provided that the belief itself was formed in response to evidential considerations, rather than irrationally, as the result of the intervention of self-deception, delusion, depression, and so on." On this revised view, Smith can accept the conclusion that Sam would not be more rational for desiring to become a hermit. After all, when Sam concludes that he should become a hermit, he is not responding merely to evidential considerations: his deliberation seems to be distorted by the sheer psychological force of his anxiety at the prospect of his final exams. His deliberation is influenced by undue fear, and perhaps also by excessive guilt, inspired by a Protestant work ethic. While he experiences himself as engaging in clear, cool deliberation, his deliberation is in fact distorted by fear.

By giving in to the idea that Sam is more rational in not becoming a hermit, Smith's revised position would present a great break from the way we look at cases in which one is motivated to act against one's best judgment. The literature pertaining to weakness of will routinely assumes that if a person believes that she should not eat a piece of cake but proceeds to eat it, she is acting more irrationally than if she sticks to her resolution; it does not, as a rule, add "unless, of course, the decision not to eat is the result of anorexia." Smith would have to agree that there are some cases in which an agent is, if not more rational, at least not less rational for acting against her best judgment. However, taking this revised position would still represent an attempt on Smith's part to salvage the idea that, in general, there is something special about one's best judgment—one's belief about what would be rational for one to do—that makes acting against it irrational. In the agent's web of beliefs and desires, her best judgment is not just another belief, but a belief that has a special normative force—unless there exists depression, delusion, and so on. If one contemplates, however, what it takes for a belief about what one would desire if one were rational to be a belief that "responds to evidence," one realizes that with the proposed modification, Smith would be giving up a lot more than he seems to at first glance—in fact, he would effectively be accepting the minimal significance of one's own beliefs about one's own rationality.

It might seem to one, in the spirit of *The Moral Problem*, that ruling out irrational best judgments, irrational beliefs about what one would want if one were rational, is as easy as ruling out a few obvious cases—cases in which depression, fatigue, stress, or other such factors intervened in the agent's belief formation. To the factors that Smith mentions as irrational it seems easy to add just a few more: fear, as in Sam's case, low self-esteem, and the other usual suspects. Making an exception for irrational best judgments this way—listing easily recognized "excluded conditions"—makes it seem as though Smith resists the full force of the objection while making a small concession to it. But this is not the right way to picture things. Consider Sam's case again. We take Sam's belief that he should become a hermit to be irrational, not to be formed in response to evidential considerations. What makes us take it to be so? It is not simply the fact that Sam experiences intense anxiety while he deliberates. It is impossible to determine a belief's rationality simply by whether or not it is formed in a proverbial "cool hour." At four in the morning, in a state of emotional turmoil, a person might realize that she needs to leave her husband, and her belief might be perfectly rational. At noon, in an air-conditioned room, calmly and confidently, a sleek presidential aide might reach certain conclusions regarding changes in economic policy, and her conclusions might be tragically irrational. A belief formed in some sort of an emotional state—even a belief generated by an emotional state—is not necessarily a belief that does not respond to evidential considerations. Imagine, for example, that Sam has a fellow student, Paul, who also experiences anxiety when he discovers, looking at the calendar, that final exams are near. Unlike Sam, Paul has a rather extreme tendency to procrastinate, and unlike Sam, after spending a little while flooded with anxiety, Paul does not conclude that he should become a hermit, but rather that from that day onward, he should devote three hours daily to his studies. While Paul's decision is formed while he is anxious, and is as likely as Sam's decision to seem a result of his anxiety, it does not appear irrational to us, and appears to respond to evidential considerations—at least, given banal assumptions about Paul's beliefs and desires. If Smith wishes to incorporate into his thesis an exception for judgments that have been skewed by emotions, he needs to tell us what the difference is between cases in which emotions are merely present and cases in which emotions indeed skew our judgment. In the case of Sam and Paul, one of them seems more rational than the other, not because of anything pertaining to the origin of their decisions, but simply because of the relation between decision and evidence—Paul's decision makes sense as a practical conclusion from the rest of his beliefs and desires, while Sam's does not. Whatever it is that caused Sam to be irrational, to reach a conclusion so much at odds with his own beliefs is not of the essence; whatever made him irrational—be it anxiety, guilt, fatigue, a nefarious neurosurgeon, or his purely intellectual limitations—did so not simply by its existence but rather by the fact that it disrupted the path from Sam's evidence to a warranted conclusion.[16] A situation in which one is irrational in concluding that one should φ is simply a situation in which a conclusion that one should φ is not warranted by one's other beliefs and desires. Thus, Smith's claim that it is rational for one to desire to do what one believes one would do if one were rational unless that belief is itself irrational is not a strong, sweeping generalization with a few excluded conditions, but instead is the rather uninteresting claim that it is rational to desire to φ unless a conclusion to φ is not warranted by one's other beliefs and desires—that is, unless it would be irrational to φ.

Thus, if we take seriously Smith's own idea that rationality is a matter of coherence, then it is impossible for him to show that there is something especially malignant in the fact that an agent fails to have a desire to comply with her best judgment, or even in the existence in an agent of a desire contrary to her best judgment. In other words, he cannot show that such an occurrence in an agent is anything worse than ordinary incoherence—incoherence that is in some cases rather small compared to the larger-scale incoherence that would be produced by the agent desiring in accordance with his best judgment. Sometimes an agent who acts against his best judgment is acting on a desire that does not cohere with the rest of his beliefs and desires; other times, he is acting on a desire that wonderfully coheres with all his desires and beliefs—except one. Coherence considerations do not make acting against one's best judgment necessarily less rational than not doing so.

Beyond Coherence: Acting against One's Best Judgment as Ill-Motivated

At this point, proponents of the view that acting against one's best judgment is always less rational than following it are likely to suggest that even when an action performed against one's best judgment is the action that best coheres with the rest of one's beliefs and desires, this action is still irrational, because all akratic actions, whatever their logical relation to the agent's beliefs and desires, are brought about by some sort of an irrational process.

Let us agree, for the sake of the argument, that Sam's original decision to become a hermit is an irrational decision. Let us also agree that if Sam were rational, he would not desire to become a hermit, and in fact would desire not to become one, and that, in not becoming a hermit, Sam is doing what in fact is the rational thing for him to do—his course of action best coheres with his overall desires and beliefs. Is the process by which Sam fails to become a hermit a rational process? This is where many will say no. There are all kinds of ways for an action to be caused by the agent's beliefs and desires, they might say, and only some of them can produce rational action: any instance of acting against one's best judgment is an instance of an action produced in an irrational or nonrational way. This has been nearly universally agreed upon among writers on weakness of will. There are countless views about the nature of the irrational or nonrational process that supposedly lurks behind every case of *akrasia* (division of the mind, failure of a self-control mechanism, lapse of reason . . .),[17] but there is general agreement on the view that there must be some such process.[18] By and large, these authors see something like the following as a paradigmatic case of acting against one's best judgment.

Nicole believes that she should become a singer. Her belief, let us suppose, is irrational: Nicole believes that she should become a singer despite rather obvious evidence, which she has come across, suggesting that she has no particular talent as a singer and would make a fool of herself if she were to become one, and, generally, that becoming a singer would bring more desire frustration than satisfaction. Despite her firm belief that she should become a singer, Nicole does not become one, imagine, because she suffers from a strong inhibition against assertive and ambitious behavior. This inhibition is also, in this paradigmatic case, irrational: in her childhood, Nicole's sexist family severely chastised her whenever she dared to put her own wishes before those of others, which produced in her a strong visceral sense that she somehow deserves less than others and that she would always somehow be punished for any assertive behavior. As trying to break into the entertainment business requires plenty of assertive behavior and involves working hard in order to realize one's own ambition, Nicole finds it impossible to bring herself to act out her resolution, as the psychological force of her childhood shame overcomes her when she thinks of the necessary steps she needs to take in order to do so. *Ex hypothesi*, Nicole's course of action—not becoming a singer—is exactly the course of action that best coheres with the rest of her beliefs and desires: it is the course of action she has overwhelming reasons to take. However, Nicole does not take this course of action for these reasons, but rather is moved to action by the sheer psychological force of her childhood shame. This shame itself is not an overwhelming reason for action; Nicole is moved by it, to use Davidsonian terms, by its causal force far out of proportion to its force as a reason. Thus, the fact that Nicole does not become a singer is no credit to her rationality. However well her action fits as a practical conclusion from her beliefs and desires, it is still a result of some kind of fortunate mechanical glitch, some sort of mental "faulty wiring" (however it was brought about). To her original irrationality in the process of forming her best judgment Nicole adds the additional irrationality of her inhibition against following through on it, and only by accident is the resulting action the same action she would take if she suffered from neither of these two irrationalities. Though her original best judgment is irrational, she is more irrational for violating it than she would be for following it, because by now she has fallen victim to two glitches instead of one.

Why, action theorists might ask, would Sam's case be any different from Nicole's? Continuing his social life may be the course of action he has overwhelming reasons to take, but surely, in not pursuing his decision to become a hermit, he is not acting for these reasons. He is rather simply too weak-willed to pursue his decision, and this is lucky for him but nothing more. While a desire to continue his social life may fit much better into the web of his beliefs and desires than a desire to become a hermit, and thus he has better reasons to continue his social life than to become a hermit, he continues his social life not because he has good reasons to do it, but rather as a result of a mechanism that is not reason-responsive—perhaps simply because the psychological force of the temptation to be with his friends somehow gets the better of him, perhaps because of his laziness, or depressive tendency, or lack of self-control. Failing to become a hermit in this fashion, Sam adds a second irrationality to the irrationality of his original decision to become one.

But why assume that this is the case with Sam? Granted, this is one scenario that would explain why he fails to become a hermit, and in this scenario Sam would be analogous to Nicole. But it is not the only scenario that can be imagined, and I shall now offer another one. Sam might be neither lazy nor depressive nor lacking in self-control, nor suffer from anything of the kind. He might be exactly the kind of person who is inclined to quickly accept reasonable conclusions, and he might be failing to muster the motivation to abide by his decision to become a hermit exactly because it is an unreasonable decision. When Sam deliberated and reached the conclusion that he should become a hermit, he overlooked many reasons not to do so—reasons that were, given Sam's overall beliefs and desires, overwhelming reasons not to become a hermit. All these reasons were given by the nature of Sam's overt psychology—they were not hidden from him in some black box of the unconscious, but rather were simply overlooked in his deliberations at the time, his vision of himself being clouded due to his fear of exams and such. In failing to become a hermit, Sam might, unbeknownst to him, be acting for the same reasons he overlooked in his deliberation.[19] His visceral reluctance to abide by his decision, which he perceives as weakness or laziness, was (let us imagine) in fact the result or the embodiment of an awareness, inaccessible at the moment of his deliberation, of all the things that are, given his beliefs and desires, overwhelmingly wrong with becoming a hermit. Far from being the result of fatigue, major depression, or some general lack of self-control—conditions equally likely to prevent him from following through with a good decision as with a bad one—Sam's lack of motivation was a response to the badness of his decision, or rather to the same factors that make his decision bad. This is a way of understanding the case in which we may think of Sam not as a weak-willed man, but as a man who has some "crazy notions" sometimes but whose common sense prevails "in real life." And this is the way in which I would like to argue that Sam would be considerably less rational (or more irrational) if he were to follow his best judgment that he should become a hermit, utterly oblivious to the glaring evidence of its falsity, than if he were to act against this judgment, acting, though unbeknownst to him, in response to this very evidence. He is irrational for keeping his conviction despite his evidence,[20] but not for continuing his social life, for he had overwhelming reasons to do so and was responsive to them.

To better illustrate the features of what I take to be cases in which an agent is more rational for acting against her best judgment than she would have been otherwise, here is another example. Emily's best judgment has always told her that she should pursue a Ph.D. in chemistry. But as she proceeds through a graduate program, she starts feeling restless, sad, and ill-motivated to stick to her studies. These feelings are triggered by a variety of factors which, let us suppose, are good reasons for her, given her beliefs and desires, not to be in the program. The kind of research that she is expected to do, for example, does not allow her to fully exercise her talents, she does not possess some of the talents that the program requires, and the people who seem most happy in the program are very different from her in their general preferences and character. All of these factors she notices and registers, but they are also something that she ignores when she deliberates about the rightness of her choice of vocation: like most of us, she tends to find it hard, even threatening, to take leave of a long-held conviction and to admit to herself the evidence against it. But every day she encounters the evidence again, her restlessness grows, her sense of dissatisfaction grows, and she finds it harder to motivate herself to study. Still, when she deliberates, she concludes that her feelings are senseless and groundless. One day, on an impulse, propelled exclusively by her feelings, she quits the program, calling herself lazy and irrational but also experiencing a (to her) inexplicable sense of relief. Years later, happily working elsewhere, she suddenly sees the reasons for her bad feelings of old, cites them as the reasons for her quitting, and regards as irrationality, not her quitting, but rather the fact that she held on to her conviction that the program was right for her for as long as she did.[21]

Emily, I would like to argue, acts far more rationally in leaving the program than she would in staying in the program, not simply because she has good reasons to leave the program, but also because she acts for these good reasons. To illustrate this, compare Emily to Alice, who has the same good reasons to leave the program that Emily has but ends up leaving the program for *bad* reasons. She, too, feels restless and ill-motivated in the program, but unlike Emily her bad feelings are a result of a deep lack of self-esteem, which would have caused her to feel similarly even if the program fit her interests and aptitudes perfectly. Emily's bad feelings grow in response to encountering real incompatibilities between her interests and the program; Alice's bad feelings grow in response to the fact that her classmates seem to chuckle and giggle a lot when she speaks in class or the fact that Professor Lorimer sounds grim when he speaks to her, despite the fact that her classmates chuckle and giggle audibly most of the time and that Professor Lorimer sounds grim even when he gives someone the time of day. The real incompatibilities between her interests and the program, though they should be obvious to her, have no bearing on her feelings. In leaving the program, Alice is twice irrational—first, like Emily, for holding a false conviction in the face of evidence, and second for leaving the program due to psychologically powerful bad reasons. Emily, on the other hand, leaves the program for good reasons, and her only irrationality is in her failure to give up her errant conviction.

My accounts of Sam and Emily as rational in taking their courses of action assume that one can act for good reasons (where good reasons are thought of in terms of desire satisfaction given one's beliefs) without *knowing* that one is acting for good reasons: Sam thinks that he is acting out of sheer laziness, Emily thinks her behavior makes no sense, and still I maintain that they act for good reasons. This assumption is not any more bizarre than the common view in epistemology that one can *know* that P without *knowing that one knows* that P. The reader well versed in moral psychology and action theory, however, may find herself reluctant to accept it, because we routinely assume that acting for reasons necessarily involves deliberation. Sam and Emily, one may concede, are motivated by facts that are in fact overwhelming reasons for them to take their course of action, but, one may insist, they are acting merely because of these reasons, not *for* them. But why think so? As opposed to the case of Nicole, the objector cannot answer simply that Sam and Emily's motives are effective in a way that is disproportional to their force as reasons, as we assume that in both cases there is no disparity between the power of their motives as causes and as reasons. The root of the feeling that Sam and Emily cannot be acting for reasons seems to lie in the fact that they do not *deliberate* upon these reasons, and their ultimate actions are not the result of deliberation. It is not enough, one may say, that one's action be caused by factors that are in fact good reasons; it has to be caused by them "in the right way" — and the right way is, presumably, via deliberation.

But, I would like to argue, "the right way" is not always via deliberation. If we were only to call people rational when their actions were caused by deliberation, we would have to call people rational considerably less often than we do, and if we were to deny that people act for reasons whenever their actions are not the result of deliberation, then we would find that it is uncomfortably rare for people to act for reasons.

In order to show that deliberation is not necessary for rationality, it will help to look at a few kinds of cases in which a person who is not deliberating or reflecting is intuitively judged by us to be rational, or criticized for not being rational, where the criticism does not imply that she should have deliberated but rather that, as the nondeliberator that she is, she can be acting for good reasons and be rational, or acting for bad reasons and be irrational. The cases I will be looking at are fast action, including fast conversation; cases of belief formation; and, most surprising of all, the case of deliberation itself.

Cases of Rationality
without Deliberation

Consider cases of *fast action*. Here I am talking not about cases of acting against one's best judgment, but cases in which there is no "best judgment" regarding the relevant action — the agent simply does not deliberate about it. It is not a provocative view that an accomplished tennis player, for example, does not have time to deliberate on all her moves during a fast-paced game. Not only that, but given the complex factors to which she responds, she is unlikely to be able to reconstruct all her reasons for action after the game. However, even after the ball is served, we can legitimately judge her moves as rational ("That was brilliant!") or criticize her for irrationality ("What on earth were you thinking there?"). If actions not deliberated upon are irrational by definition, it is hard to see how we can praise the player for the brilliance (rationality) of her action, and it is also hard to see how we can criticize her for a "crazy" (irrational) action, for we do not expect a person to be able to deliberate in the middle of a fast-paced game. (I am assuming here that the tennis player is accomplished, and both our praise and our criticism of her do *not* concern simple internalization of the rules of the game, a task she has completed long ago.)

It could be objected that what makes an action committed by the tennis player during a game rational is a decision, made by the player prior to the game, to count on her good instincts. I do not think this argument works. First, not all situations where a nondeliberative action strikes us as rational are situations in which such a decision can be said to have been made. Think, for example, of a case in which James enters a room and walks quickly out of it. Except for a feeling of discomfort in the room, he does not know why he leaves, and only retrospectively does he come to the conclusion that he left because, in a manner not deliberated upon, he registered that the people in the room were hostile to him. Such an action may seem to us to be wise (if it seems to be based on good evidence), but it would be artificial to insist that before James entered the room, or earlier in life, he decided to follow his instincts in such cases. As far as we know, this could be the first time he encounters such a situation. Second, a further piece of evidence for the fact that the tennis player's action could be rational in itself, without recourse to prior deliberation, is that an action committed under similar circumstances by the player can also be criticized as irrational. If all that made the player's action rational was a prior rational decision to count on her instincts, then as long as the decision to follow the instincts could be shown to be rational, any instinctive action committed during the game could be rationalized by the decision. If the coach yelled at the tennis player for making an uncharacteristically crazy move, she could reply to him, "But I made a rational decision to follow my instincts and that's exactly what I did. It's ridiculous to say I am irrational." In practice, however, such a retort would be nonsensical—which suggests, I submit, that it is not a previously deliberated-upon decision that makes an un-deliberated-upon action rational, but something about the "instinct" itself which the agent follows—whether it is the right reasons (acting with the appropriate force) that trigger the action. A major part of what it is to be a competent tennis player is to have the ability to play tennis rationally—to act for good reasons rather than bad reasons in all of your game-related actions. Similarly, in the case of James, if what led him to leave the room was not the perception of hostility but rather perception of the fact that one of the people in the room had the same build as his bad-tempered uncle, we would regard his action as irrational ("neurotic," we might say, or "prejudiced" or the result of a "hang-up"). If James perchance *did* make a decision in the past to trust his instincts in such matters, and if that decision was rational, given his overall level of social competence, James still cannot escape the charge of acting neurotically, and thus irrationally, on this particular occasion.

Another example of fast action that does not involve the usual trappings of athletic action is that of fast-paced *conversation*. A witty conversationalist, one who finds an entertaining and clever answer to every question, does not have time to deliberate upon her actions any more than the athlete does. Yet she acts for good reasons in her choice of answers even if she never makes a decision to trust her instincts—in fact, even if her view of herself as a conversationalist is very low. In the rare cases in which the conversationalist says something embarrassing or foolish despite the fact that she should know better—perhaps she is tired or briefly forgets her interlocutor's well-known hatred of all things rural—she acts irrationally, even if she did make a decision to trust her instincts regarding wit.

A second type of case in which we judge people to be rational or potentially rational despite the fact that they do not deliberate are certain cases of belief formation. It is possible for a person to be epistemically rational in reaching a certain conclusion even if she does not reach her conclusion via deliberation, and we routinely regard certain cases of belief formation as rational despite the fact that no deliberation was involved. Why, then, should we regard it as impossible or odd for a person to be rational in being motivated to action simply because she did not deliberate? The simplest cases of belief formation without deliberation are those involving perception. I see a black cat in front of me, and as a result

I believe that there is a black cat in front of me. No deliberation is involved in the formation of this belief. Nor does deliberation bring about my belief, in response to certain sounds, that a car is passing by my window. Yet there is no reason, in ordinary circumstances, to doubt the rationality of either belief. And it is possible to rationally form, without deliberation, beliefs of considerably more complex character. In showing that we sometimes regard a person as epistemically rational for forming a belief despite the absence of deliberation, I will focus on what I will call, for lack of a better term, cases of *dawning*—cases in which people change their minds, sans deliberation, as a result of a long period of exposure to new evidence.

Candide, a young man who lives in an idyllic setting, accepts the authoritative Dr. Pangloss's view that this is the best of all possible worlds, in which everything is for the good, humankind is nice, and so on (one need not assume here that these are precisely Voltaire's or Leonard Bernstein's characters, but these are familiar names for the sort of people I am imagining). Then, after gaining some experience with the wider world, Candide still swears that this is the best of all possible worlds, as his initial emotional investment in the view has been immense, but there is less conviction in his voice, or perhaps there is an excess of conviction in his voice (as he protests too much) but his face is no longer that of the wholehearted optimist. Then one day, when asked if he believes that this is the best of all possible worlds, he discovers that he does not think so and has not for some time. Here we have a process, starting with firmly believing that this is the best of all possible worlds and ending with disbelieving the same proposition. At no point in the process, let us suppose, did deliberation occur: never, upon encountering a piece of counterevidence to the Panglossian view, did Candide think something along the lines of "Hmm, this does seem to be in conflict with my teacher's idea," or "How can this be the best of all possible worlds if it has war in it?" Or, if such deliberation ever did occur, it always ended with Candide finding what to him seemed irrefutable evidence that this was, despite appearances, the best of all possible worlds. The truth that this world is not all sweetness and light was not something that Candide reached after deliberation, but rather it *dawned* on him. But we do not regard Candide's change of mind as irrational. In fact, we regard it as rational. Finally, the young man came to his senses.

Or consider an alternative ending to Emily's case. In my original story, Emily leaves the chemistry program while still holding the best judgment that she should not do so. In the alternative ending, Emily "comes to her senses" during her first year in the program and one day realizes, to her surprise, that her conviction regarding her vocation has disappeared, as if it had evaporated, and she no longer thinks a Ph.D. in chemistry is right for her. Thus she is able to leave the program wholeheartedly. Here, again, Emily undergoes a process that begins with her being convinced that she should study chemistry and ends with her being convinced otherwise. The first step in the process is her *akrasia*: Emily feels a sense of restlessness and disaffection in response to facts that she registers—just as Candide registers facts about the badness of the world—but does not acknowledge when she deliberates. She is deeply convinced that chemistry is her vocation, and due to assumptions she makes about herself and the world, she never doubts it for a moment: whenever she surveys her beliefs and desires, she does not see any reason to do so. When the odd feeling moves her, she writes it off as a sign of laziness or irrationality on her part and tries to get over it. People, after all, do not give up their convictions so easily. Gradually she encounters more and more data that are inconsistent with her conviction, though it still fails to affect her deliberation, and at a certain point, not easy to define, she realizes that she does not find the program right for her anymore. Alternately, she realizes suddenly that for a while she has been very unsure about what used to be obvious—the chemistry program being the right place for her. At this stage, Emily can articulate very good reasons for leaving. The facts she recites as reasons had to "dawn on her" gradually (rather than, say, be found out by laborious research), but since they are indeed good reasons, no one doubts the rationality of her decision. There is no intuitive reason to say that Emily's conclusion is rational only if she had deliberated about it.

Dawning processes are perhaps the main way in which people change their minds, especially concerning subjects they regard as important—the very subjects regarding which an attempt to argue with them and talk them out of the error of their ways is likely to encounter the sternest irrational resistance. Very few people who give up racist prejudices, for example, give them up via a process of deliberation. More often, the irrationality of their prejudice dawns on them after spending long enough with people of the relevant race and realizing, bit by bit, that they are very similar to themselves. Memoirs by intelligent people who dogmatically adored Stalin's Soviet Union as Heaven on Earth and then changed their minds rarely include the protagonist thinking something along the lines of "The people I saw in Russia looked uncannily skinny and hungry. Therefore, the Soviet Union cannot be perfect." They rather describe a painful process, often lasting years from the initial availability of obvious counterevidence, in which this evidence, so to speak, continually eroded the writer's dogmatic conviction, in the face of strong incentives to self-deception. And many times we regard such a change of mind, when completed, as rational nevertheless. Here again, we have a type of case in which we regard people as rational despite the fact that their rationality is not the product of deliberation.

Of course, I do not argue that all "dawnings" are rational, nor do I need to do so. Just as a person can be rational or irrational in her deliberation, and a person can be rational or irrational in her response to a situation on the tennis court, a person can be rational or irrational in a way in which some conclusion dawns on her. Here is a case of irrational dawning: A guest on a talk show tells us a story of how it dawned on her that Jesus exists, saying, "I was all alone in a foreign country. I was sad because my father had recently died. I tried several times to get a job as an actress and failed. Then I discovered that one of my last boyfriends had AIDS. That was the worst moment of these dreadful two weeks. I was due for another audition the next day, and I didn't know how I could concentrate. I felt completely alone, and it scared me. Suddenly, when I was in bed, trying to sleep, it dawned on me that I can't really be so alone. It is simply impossible for life to be so unbearable; someone must be watching me. Jesus must be watching me. I felt an immense relief and found myself calm enough the next day to audition successfully." The dawning of a belief in the existence of Jesus in this case is an irrational process, while Emily's dawning process is a rational process. Why does Emily's change of mind look rational while the guest's conversion does not? The conversion seems irrational because the relationship between the accumulating evidence (the death of the agent's father, her failure to find a job, her discovery concerning her past lover, her apparent aloneness) and the conclusion (that Jesus must be watching) is not compelling. As in traditional descriptions of self-deception, the agent's belief formation (that is, her dawning process) seems to be unduly affected by a wish—the wish to have a life she can bear. Even if we assume, for the sake of the argument, that Jesus is watching us, it would still not be rational to infer his presence from the fact that one lived through two horrible weeks. In addition to irrational dawning processes, it should be noted that there are also rational dawning processes leading to false conclusions (imagine, for example, the John Le Carré character on whom it dawns that her husband must be hiding an affair, while in fact he is hiding his unlikely assignment as a spy).

Candide and Emily change their minds (develop new beliefs) without deliberation, and yet they do so rationally, do so for good reasons, as a legitimate response to good evidence of which they are aware. Why should it be any stranger to claim that Sam and our original Emily are moved to action rationally, for good reasons, as a legitimate response to good evidence of which they are aware, even though they do not deliberate their way into their actions?

In addition to fast action and processes of belief change, I would like to mention one more psychological process that is not the result of deliberation and that is often rational: deliberation itself. Deliberation is itself an action, and this action is rarely the result of deliberation. Imagine that I deliberate about which book to assign my introductory class. As likely as not, my deliberation did not spring from deliberation: one moment I was thinking about something else, and the next moment I was wondering what book I should assign to my class. If we were to assume that actions are only rational if they are the result of deliberation, my act of deliberating about my textbooks would not have been a rational act. It is, though: it is a sign of my (relative) rationality that I begin to deliberate about next semester's textbooks just about now. Furthermore, the thought that deliberating, in order to be a rational action, would have to be the result of deliberation seems to threaten an infinite regress: before deliberating about my textbooks, I would have had to deliberate about deliberating about my textbooks, and before that deliberate about deliberating about deliberating, and so forth, in order for all these intellectual acts to prove to be rational.

In a similar vein, it can be pointed out that the course of my deliberation about my textbooks depends on nondeliberative inferences. When I ask myself, "Which books should I assign?" it is not an accident that the initial list of books that occur to me as candidates does not include *What Does It All Mean?* or *Being and Time* but does include *Philosophical*

Ethics and *Knowledge and the Flow of Information*. From prior knowledge of students in my institution, I have concluded without deliberation that *What Does It All Mean?* would appear deceptively easy to my challenge-hungry engineering majors, who would as a result not study it hard enough, and that *Being and Time* would appear, and actually be, too difficult for all my students. Thus, neither book appears on my list, though either could have appeared on it if I were teaching different students. When I turn to trying to decide between the books on my list, I quickly turn to wondering whether *Knowledge and the Flow of Information* is too difficult: I do not waste much time wondering if *Philosophical Ethics* is too difficult. If you were to interrupt my reflection by asking why I do not worry about the accessibility of *Philosophical Ethics*, I might tell you in reply that *Philosophical Ethics* is obviously accessible to my university's students, but if you were not to ask me this question, the thought would never consciously occur to me. Thus, every step I take in deliberation is informed in a nondeliberative way by beliefs and desires that do not participate in it.

That every step in deliberation, including the first step, is thus informed by our prior knowledge in a nondeliberative way is also the conclusion of empirical study. In his book *Descartes' Error* (1994), Antonio Damasio describes the predicament of patients who have lost the ability to have emotional feelings as a result of brain injury, while their intellects have remained intact. If one believes in the traditional dichotomy between Reason and Appetite, one will expect these "cold-blooded" people to be hyper-rational. However, these people seem to be utter failures exactly in the realm of practical reasoning—or, as the author puts it, in choosing the best means to reach their aims. In attempting to keep a job, make a good business deal, or win a card game, the people studied by Damasio consistently make very bad decisions. Why are the nonfeelers bad at practical rationality? Consider again my deliberation involving textbooks. My deliberation focuses on *Knowledge and the Flow of Information* because the thought of assigning it invokes a feeling of uneasiness or worry. It does not focus on *Philosophical Ethics* because assigning the latter "feels right." I never considered *Being and Time* because the idea would make me laugh. Thus, even my calm, academic deliberation seems to be guided by subtle emotional cues—cues that I hardly notice. We should not pretend that for the deliberation to proceed, I have to tell myself, "Okay, I feel uneasy about this book; maybe that's a reason to reconsider it," the way a master may wonder why his dog is barking. This scenario is possible, but another scenario is at least as likely, in which I take no such reflecting step: I simply proceed from coming up with a list of possible books to thinking further about one book, as opposed to the others, without taking any time to reflect on my feelings. My uneasiness about *Knowledge and the Flow of Information* simply is part of my process of reasoning—the part in which my previous experience with students, books, and so on, weighs in to guide my decision. Brain-damaged nonfeelers, despite an unharmed ability to deliberate and reflect, make bad decisions because they are denied such feeling-based access to their own background knowledge in making those decisions. Thus, despite being able to deliberate, they end up doing things that no rational person would have done—the same way that no rational person would have assigned *Being and Time* to my students in Introduction to Philosophy. The rational person, and not the brain-damaged person, would *feel amused* at the thought and give it no further attention.[22]

Two things, then, appear to be true. First, if we were to assume that only actions that are the result of deliberation are rational, we would discover that it is never rational for an agent to deliberate, as the act of deliberation must at some point spring from something other than deliberation. Second, no action and no belief is purely the result of deliberation. Assigning *Philosophical Ethics* to my students is the result of deliberation, but it is also the result of many beliefs and inferences that formed no part of my deliberation.

To recapitulate: there are cases in which people do not deliberate but act rationally, and there are rational mental processes that do not involve deliberation. Thus, if Sam fails to live a hermit's life or Emily leaves the Ph.D. program, against their respective best judgments, the fact that their actions are not the result of deliberation is not in itself an argument against the claim that they are more rational in acting against their best judgments than they would be acting in accordance with their best judgments. In fact, if we admit that (1) there are cases in which people do not deliberate but still act rationally, and (2) there are cases in which people act as a result of deliberation but are acting irrationally, it is hard to avoid the conclusion that sometimes an agent who acts against her best judgment is acting more rationally than she would have acted had she followed her best judgment. Sam's deliberation, which led him to his best judgment, was irrational; on the other hand, his reluctance to become a hermit is rational. If he is to become a hermit, he is to become a hermit for bad reasons, acting out of little more than his excessive fear of examinations. If he is not to become a hermit, he is not to become a hermit for excellent, legitimately overriding reasons. If our interest is not in writing the rational agent's manual (which, as I said earlier, cannot command anyone directly to act against her best judgment) but in an account of rationality, it is hard to see how a person who acts for excellent reasons can be less rational than he would be if he acted for bad reasons, whatever else is true of him.

Whither Rationality?

One lingering worry one may have after reading the foregoing arguments is the possibility that both the conclusion (some people who act against their best judgments are more rational for doing so than they would be for following their best judgments) and some of the claims I use to support it (that fast actors act for reasons and that people on whom something dawns change their mind for reasons) imply a dangerous blurring of the boundary between rationality and irrationality. One may wonder, furthermore, what kind of theory of rationality would make sense if all I said so far were right.[23]

In response to the worry, I would like to admit that my findings imply that it is sometimes very hard to distinguish rationality from irrationality *in practice,* and that, in particular, it is sometimes very hard to distinguish rationality from irrationality *in ourselves* in practice, but this does not necessitate any conceptual or theoretical blurring of the boundaries of rationality. Standard action theory makes it appear that if I deliberate in the best way that I can and come to the conclusion that the paper I am writing is finished and I should go out and have some ice cream, and yet I am struck by, and surrender to, a strong urge to come back to the computer and revise the paper yet again, it should be very easy for me, and for anyone who is standing next to me, to see that I am irrational in surrendering to the urge. If one takes my conclusions seriously, however, it is not so easy at all. If I want to know whether I am irrational or not, I need to ask myself questions such as, Is the urge to look at the paper the result of some defect in the paper that I perceived, a belief that is for some reason inaccessible to my attempts at deliberation, or is the urge simply the result of deep-seated "Protestant work guilt"—a tendency to feel always as if I should be working regardless of the evidence at hand? My rationality depends on the answers to these questions, and it may be the case that I simply do not know them. I take it to be an advantage of my view that it correctly predicts a world in which people often have reason to ask others to judge their own rationality. "Am I crazy?" they ask. "Do you think these qualms I have about my paper—my husband, my career—are reasonable, or am I just being neurotic again?"

Through the last two paragraphs I have been suggesting that though the present line of argument implies that rationality and irrationality may be hard to distinguish in practice— all too often they may look the same—we should not conclude that they are thereby rendered any more similar in theory. This leads us to the second question I raised at the beginning of this section: what sort of theory of rationality would be compatible with the theses in this chapter? The answer is this: any number of them, with a few provisions. (1) A theory of rationality should not assume that there is something special about an agent's best judgment. An agent's best judgment is just another belief, and for something to conflict with one's best judgment is nothing more dramatic than ordinary inconsistency in belief, or between beliefs and desires. (2) When discussing beliefs, one should count all of the beliefs the agent actually has, not only the beliefs that she knows she has at times of deliberation. For example, when Emily the would-be chemist deliberates, she ignores many of the beliefs that she has formed about her stay in the chemistry department— which is another way to say that she "ignores available evidence." She might not even know that she has some of these beliefs, but they are there. (3) It may well be that, for an agent to have a reason to φ, φ-ing should be a good practical conclusion from his beliefs and desires; but it is not necessary that he be able to actually *reach* this conclusion by deliberation, not even "in a cool hour." In other words, for one to have a reason, one does not need to believe, or be disposed to believe, that one has a reason. Finally, (4) for an agent to be acting for a (good) reason R, she does not need to know that she is acting for (good) reason R. Given these four requirements, one can still talk of rationality in the good old way in other respects, to a surprisingly unchanged extent.

Consider some well-known theses about rationality: other things being equal, a more rational person has a more coherent set of beliefs and desires; a rational person changes her beliefs and desires in response to evidence; a rational agent is motivated by reasons proportionally to their force as reasons. I have not argued against any of these widely held views, and as far as I am concerned, they are all true. Let us begin with the last one. Consider again Nicole, the irrationally inhibited would-be songstress. Davidson seems to suggest that Nicole is irrational because she is acting against her best judgment. I argued that he cannot sustain this position, as acting against one's best judgment is not always irrational. But this should not matter that much to Davidson, because he does not *need* to use this explanation at all. Davidson's theory provides a different explanation for Nicole's irrationality: she is acting from causes that are bad reasons. This explains her irrationality well enough, and any reference to her best judgment is redundant. Similar things are true for Michael Smith's depressed, sick, and fatigued individuals: if their actions really are the result of nothing but the causal force of their ennui or disease, that makes the case for their irrationality. Even if they were not acting against any sort of best judgment, they would be irrational in their actions. If the tennis player, for example, acted because of causes that are bad reasons on the court (for example, she played too aggressively because the person in front of her looked too much like her abusive father), she would be irrational for the same reasons as Nicole, even if she had no deliberated-upon best judgment while playing. Sam, the student who cannot make himself live a hermit's existence and do nothing but study, on the other hand, is acting in response to causes that are excellent reasons, and thus his case is different.

Similarly for coherence. If a person's set of beliefs and desires is grossly incoherent, that makes her irrational, and it should not matter whether any best judgments are involved. If a person's action seems likely, given her beliefs, to frustrate her most important desires, we can safely conclude that she is irrational in performing that action, without inquiring if she acts against her best judgment or if she has one at all. Smith and others seem to assume that people who act against their best judgments are always less coherent than people who do not; I argued that this is false, but that does not rule out coherence as an important ingredient in rationality. Rather, it implies that we should look for evidence of true overall coherence or incoherence rather than take a shortcut and look for evidence of *akrasia* or its absence.

Coherence, evidential warrant, goodness and badness of reasons, relevance and irrelevance of factors—all of these can still legitimately be considered even if one does not believe best judgments have any privileged role. This is not the place to argue about these concepts, refine them, or find their right places in a theory of rationality, and I do not know what an ultimate account of them would look like. I have argued, however, that such an account should not ignore the ways in which we can act irrationally just when we think we are at our most rational, and act rationally just when we cannot make any sense of our actions.

Appendix:
What Is Deliberation For, Then?

Since first presenting my views on rationality, I have been asked many times what I think deliberation is "good for." I take it that those who ask this question are not particularly concerned with the technical details of the evolution or biological function of deliberation. The idea behind the question, I take it, is that if it is possible to be rational without deliberating, then it is unclear what deliberation adds to our lives. More specifically, what does the ability to reflect and deliberate give to us that other animals do not have?

I do not think the answer is "the ability to act for reasons." My account allows that some (higher) nonhuman animals may be able to act for (simple) reasons, as I am told dog trainers maintain. But there are plenty of other things that deliberation and reflection alone make possible. Philosophy, for example. Science. Engineering. Law. And yes, morality as well.[24] Let me elaborate. What exactly is done by deliberation and reflection is a complex question for philosophers of mind, but outlines of likely answers are easy to see. I have argued that we do not deliberate as often as moral psychologists would have us believe, but it is interesting to look for a moment at those instances in which we *do* deliberate, in everyday life, and contrast them with instances in which we do not deliberate. You probably do not deliberate as you walk to a previously visited coffee shop in a familiar city; you do start deliberating when you discover that you are lost. Medical students have to deliberate a lot when they encounter their first patients; accomplished doctors make many nondeliberative decisions based on unconscious inference each day. Most people do not need to reflect and deliberate when it comes to whether other people like or dislike them—studies show that most of us pick up subtle facial cues extremely well. However, if you are very insecure, if your "guts" have been proven wrong too often, or if you are adjusting to the company of people from a different culture, you may use your reflective faculty to make decisions and form beliefs in this matter. You deliberate when you plan your budget or your flight itinerary. You deliberate when someone tells you that your behavior has been upsetting people. And, of course, you deliberate aloud when you discuss your dilemmas with others.

Our higher faculties, it seems, are a wonderful asset when it comes to dealing with *new information* and *unfamiliar data*. Visceral knowledge takes a long time to accumulate; while it serves you extremely well in your interactions with familiar people, places, and things, it will not take you very far when you start interacting with people in a foreign culture, or when you have become lost, or when complex data overwhelms you. It serves you in finding your way around your town, but not a new town. Deliberation and reflection help you find your way around the new town or avoid insulting the unfamiliar people. Deliberation and reflection help you acquire certain kinds of complex knowledge—scientific, technological, and legal knowledge are examples—but they also help you *apply* practical knowledge that is not yet internalized: if you are a medical student, deliberation helps you apply your new medical knowledge to your first patient,[25] and if you have just learned in therapy that you tend to be too aggressive, the ability to deliberate before you act helps you apply this insight before it really "sinks in"—in fact, it helps to make it sink in. Another central property of deliberation and reflection is that they *focus your concentration*, allowing you to pull together mental resources from many different corners of your psyche in order to solve whichever problem you have decided to reflect on. The very fact that you ask yourself, consciously, "What am I going to do about Uncle Arthur?" and write down various options on your mental blackboard makes it likely that more and more of your relevant beliefs will become salient to you, increasing the chances of a satisfactory solution and of an all-things-considered, or at least most-things-considered, judgment. Last but not least, it stands to reason that the ability to deliberate—which for many of us is like talking to ourselves or presenting illustrated slides to ourselves—is closely related to the ability to use language, consult others, read books and maps, and so forth. Because of all these things, the ability to deliberate and reflect helps make us, as humans, be rational much more often, about many more things, in many more contexts.

Some of the items on my list may make one wonder if I am not taking back some of what I said before. I have mentioned the usefulness of deliberation in second-guessing our well-ingrained gut feelings in the name of a new insight, and its usefulness in arriving at all-things-considered judgments. How do these work if deliberation does not have the kind of authority that some action theorists invest in it—that is, if acting on a gut feeling may turn out to be more rational than the insight born of deliberation, and if all-things-considered judgments sometimes do not consider all things? But this is like saying that it makes no sense to install Norton Utilities on my computer's hard drive simply because Norton Utilities is a fallible computer program that occasionally erases a good file. All in all, deliberation increases our chances of being rational. Occasionally, however, it only stands in the way of reasonableness.

■ ■ ■

THREE

MORAL WORTH

The previous chapter demonstrated that reasons for action need not enter into consciousness to be excellent reasons or to justify actions, and similarly that those reasons entering consciousness may be the worst of one's reasons for acting, failing to give substantial justification to any action at all. Thus, awareness of one's reasons need play no role in an evaluation others might correctly give of those reasons. These conclusions will serve us well as we turn from rationality to morality and ask about the moral significance of those reasons, conscious and unconscious, for which agents act.

Moral Worth

Sometimes a person does the right thing, but we are not particularly impressed. The reader of Gustave Flaubert's *Madame Bovary* is told of the protagonist's good works:

> She sewed clothes for the poor, she sent wood to women in childbirth; and on coming home one day, Charles found three tramps eating soup in the kitchen. Her little girl, whom her husband had sent back to the nurse during her illness, returned home. She wanted to teach her to read; even Berthe's crying no longer irritated her. She was resigned,

universally tolerant. Her speech was full of elevated expressions. She would say: "Is your stomach-ache any better, my angel?" (Flaubert 1965, 155)

The average reader does not admire Madame Bovary for her charitable actions. Neither does Flaubert, who refers to her as "indulging" in "excessive charity." But why, really? Madame Bovary's charitable actions are clearly not "excessive" in any sense that implies that it is somehow morally wrong of her to perform so many of them. Another character in another novel who sewed clothes for the poor and sent wood for women in childbirth might simply be deemed charitable, her feeding of the tramps humane, and her use of sentimental platitudes unimportant. But Madame Bovary's good works, we are told, are something she takes up after a long illness brought about by the traumatic end of her first extramarital affair and are part of a conversion that, for all its remarkable intensity ("She saw a state of purity floating above the earth, mingling with heaven. She wanted to become a saint" [154]), is relatively short. Madame Bovary loses her interest in orphans as soon as her next lover comes along.

Perhaps Madame Bovary's charitable acts are excessive in the sense that it is excessive for a teenager to spend all of her savings on a hobby she is to abandon next week or to spend every waking moment with a certain boy due to a passing infatuation. Madame Bovary's actions appear to be motivated by a mere infatuation with morality, as opposed to a serious love. Perhaps her actions are indulgent in that even though she desires to be moral, and performs her good works because they are moral, one suspects that she has an ulterior motive of sorts. Like the romantic who is in love, not with her lover but with love itself, Madame Bovary seems to be in love not so much with morality but with the romance of morality—with an image of herself as one of the grand ladies who retired into solitude to shed at the feet of Christ the tears of hearts that life has wounded. The desire to become the kind of person who cares about morality may be a worthy motive, but something about Madame Bovary's dwelling upon the long-trimmed trains of these ladies' long gowns, something about the quasi-sexual passion with which she kisses the image of Christ, seems suspicious—as if there were more than one way in which one might aspire to be devoted to morality, and this is not the right one. Why the same actions prompt us to morally praise (or condemn) some agents more or less than others is what I call the question of moral worth.

A Few Clarifications

The moral worth of an action is the extent to which the agent deserves moral praise or blame for performing the action, the extent to which the action speaks well of the agent. I will speak interchangeably of "a morally praiseworthy action" and "an action with positive moral worth." Deviating from the Kantian use of the term 'moral worth', I will also speak interchangeably of an action with negative moral worth as an action for which the agent is blameworthy and as a "morally blameworthy action." Obviously, the extent to which an agent deserves praise or blame for her action depends in part on the action's *moral desirability*. We talk about an action's moral desirability when we ask whether it is right or wrong, or how grave a wrong it is, or whether it is the best possible action. To send money to Oxfam is morally desirable; to speed, while intoxicated, through a residential neighborhood is not, and so on.

Two actions that are equal in moral desirability may be of different moral worth. To give a simple example, two people may donate equal amounts of money to Oxfam, but one of them may do so out of concern for improving the state of the world, while the other does so purely at the urging of her accountant. Even if the two agents' charitable actions are equally morally desirable — both of them have done the right thing — it is not true that both agents deserve the same degree of praise. Similarly, a person who is rude to her colleagues due to the stress caused by grave news may merit less blame than a person who is rude to her colleagues due to her belief that her status as a mathematical genius allows her to dismiss the feelings of mere mortals.

While this distinction between moral desirability and moral worth appears to be trivial, it is often ignored in casual (and sometimes serious) philosophical discussion. For example, one often hears that "Kant is concerned with the motives for our actions, while utilitarians only care about the results." If one pays attention to the distinction between moral desirability and moral worth, one finds this classroom cliché to be quite false. When it comes to moral desirability, Kantians are not interested in motives for actions but in whether the action, under a certain description, is permitted by universal law. Recall Kant's Prudent Grocer, who prices his merchandise fairly because a reputation for honesty tends to increase his profits. Despite the Prudent Grocer's unimpressive motive, Kant never denies that the grocer does *the right thing* or that he performs the action required of him by duty. In this sense, Kantians clearly care about results. On the other hand, when it comes to moral worth, a number of utilitarians are just as concerned about motives as the Kantians. In fact, just as Mill (1979,17–18) repeats the claim that the rightness or wrongfulness of actions has nothing to do with the agent's motives, he also repeats the claim that motives are relevant to our moral evaluation of the agent:

> The motive has nothing to do with the morality of the action, though much with the worth of the agent. . . . The motive, that is, the feeling which makes him will so to do, if it makes no difference in the act, makes none in the morality [of the act]; though *it makes a great differ-ence in our moral estimation of the agent.* (Italics added)

As the moral worth of an action involves that kind of "estimation" mer-ited by the agent for performing the action, it is not implausible to think of Mill as allowing motives to be relevant to the moral worth of actions, even if they have nothing to do with the rightness or wrongness of the ac-tion. And quite apart from the right interpretation of Mill's text, it is per-fectly consistent to view the moral desirability of actions as depending entirely on their expected consequences, and the moral worth of indi-vidual actions as depending to some degree on the agent's motives. One can believe that giving to charity is desirable because it promotes happi-ness, but that an agent giving to charity out of a desire to promote happi-ness deserves more praise for her action than does her counterpart who is merely concerned with her tax situation or with the impression she makes on her peers; and one can believe so even while holding that we are morally required, for the sake of utility, to lavish indiscriminate praise on all who help the poor.

The last point made—that the moral worth of an act need not cor-respond to the moral desirability of treating an agent as if she were praise-worthy or blameworthy—is worth further elaboration. When I say that an agent is praiseworthy (or blameworthy) for an action, I do not mean to imply that the agent should necessarily be praised (or blamed) for this action: what people deserve is not always what they should be given. If, for example, an armed criminal enters a crowded room and shouts, "Give me some moral praise, or I shall kill everyone," it may be morally imperative to praise her, but that alone does not make her praise*worthy* for her action. The praise that we may be required to give her is *unwarranted*, or undeserved. The moral worth of an action is the extent to which the agent deserves praise or blame for the action, not the extent to which the agent should be morally praised or blamed for it. The purpose of this chapter is to capture the conditions under which such praise or blame is *warranted*, not those under which it is *required*.[1]

Responsiveness to Moral Reasons

Consider again the case of the prudent grocer. One does not need to know the details of Kant's discussion to agree that there is a sense in which the grocer, who is motivated only by a desire for profit, is not particularly praiseworthy for his policy of fair pricing. One is happy, of course, that the grocer does the right thing. But one cannot shake off a sense that this is a mere accident. The grocer aims at increasing his profits. By a lucky accident, it so happens that the action that would most increase his profits is also a morally right action. While this is all well and good, one is not inclined to give the grocer moral credit for this accident. But what, exactly, is this "accidental" quality that we perceive in the grocer's doing of the right thing? It is *not* simply the fact — if it is a fact — that the profit motive does not reliably produce moral actions. We can, with some difficulty, imagine a world in which some invisible hand or other makes it true that the profit motive reliably produces morally right actions, and we can place Kant's grocer in that world, and still we shall not free ourselves from the sense that there is something accidental in the fact that he does the right thing. It is accidental in the same way as it is accidental that a person who reads *Lolita* for the love of scandal reads an aesthetically superior book, or the fact that a person who buys cheap beer because he likes it accidentally makes a money-saving choice. The former is attracted to the novel for reasons that are of no interest to the aesthetician who pronounces it beautiful, the latter is attracted to cheap beer for reasons that are of no interest to the thrifty, and Kant's grocer is attracted to fair pricing for reasons that are of no interest to the ethicist.

The salient feature of Kant's case, I would like to suggest, is that the grocer's morally right action does not stem from any responsiveness on his part to moral reasons. In pricing fairly, the grocer acts for a reason that has nothing to do with morality or with the features of his action that make it morally right. The reasons for which he acts have to do only with his own welfare; and whatever it is that makes his action morally right, the fact that his action increases his welfare is certainly not what makes it morally right. His *reasons for action* do not correspond to the action's *right-making features*. An important truth about moral worth seems to be the following:

> *Praiseworthiness as Responsiveness to Moral Reasons (PRMR)*: For an agent to be morally praiseworthy for doing the right thing is for her to have done the right thing for the relevant moral reasons—that is, the reasons for which she acts are identical to the reasons for which the action is right.

To put the point another way, what we praise in the morally praiseworthy agent is her responsiveness to moral reasons. Which reasons exactly are moral reasons is not a question I can deal with here, as the moral reasons to perform an action are the same reasons that make the action right, and what exactly makes an action right is a question that Kantians, utilitarians, Aristotelians, and others are still debating. Here I will make do with intuitive assumptions: what makes the grocer's action right is surely not the fact that it increases his profits and surely has to do with fairness. There are also action-theoretic concerns that will need to be left for another occasion, such as those having to do with hierarchies of motives and intentions. But I trust that the notion of the reasons for an action's rightness being the same as the reasons for which an agent acts (i.e., an action is right because it alleviates the suffering of a person, and an agent performs it in order to alleviate the suffering of a person) makes sense. PRMR is the intuition that Kant invokes when he argues that only the good will is necessarily good, and Aristotle appeals to it when he makes clear his view that defending one's city would not be virtuous if motivated by the desire for fame or a fee. Thus, it may look tempting, or even trivial, to move from PRMR to the more elegant Kantian claim that all and only morally praiseworthy actions are right actions performed *from duty*, or the venerable Aristotelian view that to act virtuously one needs to perform fine actions *for the sake of the fine*. But as these claims are often understood in contemporary discussion, such a move would be an error. Usually, "acting from duty" and "acting for the sake of the fine" are taken to indicate not simply acting for moral reasons, but rather acting for reasons *believed* or *known* to be moral reasons—acting out of a desire to do that which is right. But moral worth is fundamentally about acting for moral reasons, not about acting for reasons believed or known to be such, and distinguishing the two is important in evaluating moral agents.

Moral Responsiveness *De Re*

Consider the Kantian claim that all and only morally praiseworthy right actions—or, in his language, all and only dutiful actions that "have moral worth"—are performed from duty. This claim is often understood as stating that an agent who does the right thing deserves moral praise for her action if and only if she does the right thing out of concern for morality: an agent is morally praiseworthy for her action if and only if she did the right thing because she was concerned with doing the right thing. In "On the Value of Acting from the Motive of Duty" (1993), Barbara Herman phrases the doctrine of the motive of duty in the following way:

> For a motive to be a moral motive, it must provide the agent with an interest in the general rightness of his actions. And when we say that an action has moral worth, we mean to indicate (at the very least) that the agent acted dutifully from an interest in the rightness of his action: an interest that therefore makes its being a right action the non-accidental effect of the agent's concern. (1993, 6)

Herman is mistaken if "an interest in the rightness of his action" is interpreted in the most obvious way—that is, as an interest in doing the right thing or the moral thing *under this description*, in a *de dicto* sense: a concern for doing what one feels or believes, even as a background belief, that one morally ought to do. For a right action to have (positive) moral worth, it is neither sufficient nor necessary that it stem from the agent's interest in the rightness of his action.

To see that it is not *sufficient*, one can look at cases in which an agent does the right thing out of concern for doing the right thing, and still the fact that he did the right thing appears to be an accident. This is often the case when the agent has a mistaken view of moral rightness, and thus no matter how earnestly he tries to do the right thing, he still does not act for moral reasons. Here is such a case:

> *The Extremist*: After the assassination of Yitzhak Rabin, some Jewish extremists expressed the opinion that the murder was a horrible thing simply because it involved a Jew killing a Jew. Imagine for a moment that Ron is such an extremist, believing deeply that killing a person is not generally immoral but that killing a fellow Jew is a grave sin. Ron would very much like to kill Tamara, but he refrains from doing so because he wants to do the right thing and he believes the right thing to do is to refrain from killing Jews like Tamara.

Here is a case of a person doing the right thing—refraining from killing Tamara—because he very much wants to do the right thing and he believes, rightly, that refraining from the murder would be the right thing to do. He does not, however, do the right thing for the relevant moral reasons. The morally right reasons not to kill Tamara have to do with her being a person; they have nothing to do with her ethnicity. Ron's reasons for (in)action have nothing to do with the right-making feature of his (in)action. Hence the impression that it is merely *accidental* that Ron did the right thing in this case. After all, he might just as well have done the wrong thing had Tamara been Latino instead of Jewish. Just as, in the case of the prudent grocer, it is fortunate that the prudent action also happens to be the moral one, in Ron's case it is fortunate that favoring Jews in a certain way (not killing them when one would otherwise like to) is moral. Ron is not morally praiseworthy for his action, for he does not act for the morally relevant reasons, but rather for reasons that he mistakenly believes to be morally relevant. (There will be more on the likes of Ron in the sections on misguided conscience.)

Thus, for an agent to be morally praiseworthy for her right action it is not sufficient that her action be motivated by a desire to do what is right. One might be tempted to suggest instead that one is morally praiseworthy for one's right action if and only if one acts out of a desire to do what is right and has a decent conception of the right—moral knowledge, or knowledge of the virtues. An agent has to act out of a sense of duty, but the sense of duty ought to be combined with knowledge of what one's duty is.

But even if acting on a desire to do what is right assisted by knowledge of the right is sufficient for granting one's right action moral worth, it is not *necessary* for it. In the case of the extremist, a person acts out of concern for morality (a desire to do the right thing) and still does not act for moral reasons. Let us now look at cases where a person does the right thing for moral reasons but does not in any way act out of a desire to do the right thing. It is exactly ignorance of the virtues, or lack of moral knowledge, that can lead a person to this state. The same ignorance that led the extremist to mistake racist reasons for moral reasons can sometimes cause a person to mistake moral reasons—for which he acts—for something else. Sometimes we are smarter or act more reasonably than we think, sometimes what we take to be our lesser work is our best, and sometimes we act for moral reasons just when we think we do not.

Let us look first at a case of what I have elsewhere called 'inverse *akrasia*' (Arpaly and Schroeder 1998). I use the term 'inverse *akrasia*' to refer to cases in which an agent does the right thing but does so against her best judgment. Perhaps the most famous case of inverse *akrasia* in world literature, already briefly mentioned in chapter 1, is the case of Huckleberry Finn. Huckleberry Finn befriends Jim, a slave, and helps him escape from slavery. While Huckleberry and Jim are together on a raft used in the escape, Huckleberry is plagued by what he calls "conscience." He believes, as everyone in his society "knows," that helping a slave escape amounts to stealing, and stealing is wrong. He also believes that one should be helpful and loyal to one's friends, but loyalty to friends is outweighed by some things, such as property rights, and does Miss Watson, Jim's owner, not have property rights? Hoping against hope to find some excuse not to turn Jim in, Huckleberry deliberates. Like many children (and adults), Huckleberry is not very good at abstract deliberation, and it never occurs to him to doubt what his society considers common sense. Thus, he fails to find a loophole. "What has poor Miss Watson done to me," he berates himself, "that I can see her nigger go away and say nothing at all?" Having thus deliberated, Huckleberry resolves to turn Jim in, because it is "the right thing." But along comes a perfect opportunity for him to turn Jim in, and he finds himself psychologically unable to do it. He accuses himself of being a weak-willed boy, who has not "the spunk of a rabbit" and cannot bring himself to do the right thing, and eventually shrugs and decides to remain a bad boy.

Obviously, Huckleberry Finn does the right thing. His action is morally desirable. It is fortunate that he takes the course of action that he does. Does his action have positive moral worth? The answer to this question depends on our reconstruction of Huckleberry's motives, and, on the reconstruction I find most plausible, Huckleberry is morally praiseworthy for his action. Now there are many stories one can tell about Huckleberry's motives. In some of these stories, it would be rather clear that Huckleberry's helping Jim instead of turning him in would be a morally desirable action with *no* moral worth. For example, if Huckleberry's action were motivated by an unconscious desire to do things that would make the adults around him angry, then it would not have much moral worth. There would simply be no connection between the reasons for which he acts and the right-making features of his action. Similarly, if Huckleberry were to help Jim because of the operation, within himself, of some purely atavistic mechanism—akin, perhaps, to the tendency some animals have not to harm creatures with infantile features— we would also not regard his action as morally praiseworthy, because he would not be acting for reasons at all (this is, perhaps, what Kant imagines when he talks of acting out of *mere inclination*, and it may also remind us of Aristotle's idea of "natural virtue"). This is the interpretation favored by Bennett (1974), who sees Huckleberry Finn as merely squeamish, soft-hearted, unable to see a man in chains. In these two scenarios, Huckleberry is a racist boy who accidentally does something good. There is, however, a scenario in which Huckleberry is morally praiseworthy for his action, and I would guess this is the scenario Mark Twain had in mind, though whether he did is of no consequence for my argument.[2] On this interpretation, Huckleberry Finn is acting from neither squeamishness nor a desire to upset the adults. Rather, during the time he spends with Jim, Huckleberry undergoes a perceptual shift. Even before meeting Jim, the way Huckleberry viscerally experienced black people was inconsistent with his "official" racist views. There are people who sport liberal views but cross the road when a person of a different race appears or feel profound disbelief when that person says something intelligent. Huckleberry, from the beginning, appears to be the mirror image of this sort of person: he is a deliberative racist and viscerally more of an egalitarian. But this discrepancy between Huckle-

berry's conscious views and his unconscious, unconsidered views and actions widens during the time he spends with Jim. Talking to Jim about
his hopes and fears and interacting with him extensively, Huckleberry
constantly perceives data (never deliberated upon) that amount to the
message that Jim is a person, just like him. Twain makes it very easy for
Huckleberry to perceive the similarity between himself and Jim: the two
are equally ignorant, share the same language and superstitions, and all
in all it does not take the genius of John Stuart Mill to see that there is no
particular reason to think of one of them as inferior to the other. While
Huckleberry never reflects on these facts,[3] they do prompt him to act toward Jim, more and more, in the same way he would have acted toward
any other friend. That Huckleberry begins to perceive Jim as a fellow
human being becomes clear when Huckleberry finds himself, to his surprise, *apologizing* to Jim—an action unthinkable in a society that treats
black men as something less than human. As mentioned above, Huckleberry is not capable of bringing to consciousness his nonconscious
awareness and making an inference along the lines of "Jim acts in all
ways like a human being, therefore there is no reason to treat him as inferior, and thus what all the adults in my life think about blacks is
wrong." He is not a very clear abstract thinker, and there but for the grace
of God go all of us. But when the opportunity comes to turn Jim in and
Huckleberry experiences a strong reluctance to do so, his reluctance is
to a large extent the result of the fact that he has come to see Jim as a person, even if his conscious mind has not yet come to reflective awareness
of this perceptual shift. To the extent that Huckleberry is reluctant to
turn Jim in because of Jim's personhood, he *is* acting for morally significant reasons. This is so even though he does not *know or believe* that
these are the right reasons. The belief that what he does is moral need
not even appear in Huckleberry's unconscious. (*Contra* Hursthouse
1999,[4] my point is not simply that Huckleberry Finn does not have the
belief that his action is moral on his mind while he acts, but that he does
not have the belief that what he does is right *anywhere* in his head—this
moral insight is exactly what eludes him.) He is also unaware, or only
dimly aware, of the fact that he is acting for these reasons in the first
place. But he is acting for moral reasons all the same, in the *de re* sense
of the expression "moral reasons." Huckleberry Finn, then, is not a bad
boy who has accidentally done something good, but a good boy. No
doubt he is imperfect, and one who would be better if some of his moral

convictions were changed, but as he is, he is better than many, including his counterpart who is liberal in conviction but not in deed.

Huckleberry Finn is not an isolated case. While inverse *akrasia* may be a dramatic phenomenon, it is not dissimilar to a considerably more common type of behavioral inconsistency—the person whose explicit views with regard to morality and politics are terribly wrong but who in everyday life "cannot hurt a fly." We all have friends, family members, or acquaintances of this sort. We can all recall the likes of a student who, waving his copy of *Atlas Shrugged* in one's face, preaches that one should be selfish and then proceeds to lose sleep generously helping his peers. If philosophers were right in believing that only those actions subjected to prior deliberation are done for reasons, or that only actions derived by deliberation from one's moral principles are done for moral reasons, we would have to view these people as bad people who happen to have some fortunate inclinations in their makeup. More commonly, however, we treat these people as fundamentally good people who happen to be incompetent abstract thinkers. While the existence of such people may sometimes be baffling—note the fascination with the character of Oskar Schindler—such people are as commonplace their opposites: people with wonderful convictions who are immoral in their actions and emotions. The idea that we can sometimes act for moral reasons without knowing that we act for moral reasons is not strange when posed against the background of epistemology and psychology, fields in which many have maintained that we can know without knowing that we know, believe without knowing that we believe, or act for a reason without knowing that we act for a reason. It only seems strange if we are used to imagining people as divided, more or less, into the Faculty of Reason—the seat of deliberation from which all meaningful action springs—and that shady realm of emotion, inclination, and instinct, more or less atavistic forces that mechanically push and pull the agent. On this picture, an agent who is pulled into action by the Appetite can only be blamed indirectly (for failing to restrain his appetites or emotions properly) and can only be praised indirectly (for managing to train his appetites or emotions so that they appear in the right place at the right time). One may attempt, with difficulty, to force the plethora of different cases in which one condemns the viscerally racist liberal, the honesty-preaching Polonius, or the child-beating Christian into a picture in which it is only a lack of self-control that one condemns. But Huckleberry Finn, Oskar Schindler, and our *Atlas Shrugged*–toting friend are obviously not praiseworthy for any kind of self-training or character-building on their parts. They are praiseworthy because, despite any character-building imposed on them by their misguided selves or others, some of their moral common sense, much of their moral goodness—that is, their responsiveness to moral reasons—remains intact.[5] (Issues surrounding the development of self-control will be dealt with in fuller detail in chapter 4.)

Blame and Moral Unresponsiveness

To recapitulate: some people do the right thing by some sort of lucky accident, while others do the right thing in response to moral reasons. Those who do the right thing in response to moral reasons are those who are morally praiseworthy for their actions. It makes sense, then, that something similar is true for people who do the wrong thing. Sometimes the fact that one did the wrong thing appears to be accidental, while at other times it seems to stem from what can be called *ill will* or from a deficiency of good will. I take good will to be the same as moral concern (to be discussed in the next section) and as responsiveness to moral reasons. I take a person to be *responsive to moral reasons* to the extent that she wants noninstrumentally to take courses of action that have those features that are (whether or not she describes them this way) right-making and not to take courses of action that have those features that are (whether or not she describes them this way) wrong-making features. If good will—the motive(s) from which praiseworthy actions stem—is responsiveness to moral reasons, deficiency in good will is insufficient responsiveness to moral reasons, obliviousness or indifference to morally relevant factors, and ill will is responsiveness to sinister reasons—reasons for which it is never moral to act, reasons that, in their essence, conflict with morality. In other words, the person who is deficient in good will acts without regard for the wrong-making features of his action, while the person who has ill will performs his action exactly because of its wrong-making features.

Imagine, for example, that Jeanne is very rude to Joseph and, unsurprisingly, hurts his feelings. Many scenarios can be imagined that fill in her motives. Perhaps she comes from an aggressive culture in which "shut up" is a commonly used phrase and has not yet met people who find it grossly offensive when used by a peer. In this case, the fact that she did something wrong is, in a clear sense, accidental. Perhaps, on the other hand, she has no such excuse, and she acts the way she does because she desires to vent the tensions of a long day by saying exactly what comes to her mind, which happens to be offensive to Joseph in an obvious way. In this case, she is blameworthy, because her action indicates a failure to respond to morally relevant considerations; she should be motivated by the fact that Joseph is likely to be hurt by what she says, but she is unmoved by this and so acts in an inconsiderate manner. A third possibility is that she is rude to Joseph because she enjoys inflicting suffering on others and wishes to hurt Joseph. In this scenario, she is even more blameworthy than in the previous one, as her action not only expresses a deficiency of good will but also expresses ill will. There is nothing about the desire to vent one's feelings that essentially conflicts with morality. Like the more celebrated motives of love and money, it can sometimes accidentally conflict with morality while at other times it leads to morally good or neutral actions. On the other hand, whether one thinks of morality in Kantian, utilitarian, Aristotelian, or simple, commonsensical terms, a desire to inflict suffering for its own sake is essentially in conflict with morality. To do something purely because it would inflict suffering on a fellow human being is to act for sinister or "anti-moral" reasons: it is to perform a wrong action for reasons that are, to a substantial degree, *the reasons for which it is wrong*. While in the "venting" case the features of Jeanne's action that make it wrong seem to be ignored by her, in the sadism case she performs the action exactly because of the features that make it wrong. Other things being equal, a person is more blameworthy for a given wrong action if she acts out of ill will (for sinister reasons) than she would be if she were to act out of a lack of good will (for neutral reasons, while ignoring moral reasons to the contrary). This does not, however, imply that a sadist or a proponent of a sinister ideology is always an all-around worse person than an opportunist. A chilling, profound indifference to moral reasons, the kind compatible with, say, killing for profit, is much worse than a mild predilection for the mildly immoral, such as a taste for unnerving one's underlings.

I said that to act specifically in order to hurt a person is to act for a reason that essentially conflicts with morality. I should emphasize that I assume here that it is possible to act in order to hurt a person and have this be one's reason for action *simplicter*, without a further motive of obtaining pleasure and also without something like Kantian self-love in the background—that is, it is possible to decide to indulge one's sadistic desire. Very few of us believe that everything we do is done for pleasure or for self-interest, and the view is one against which Tim Scanlon (1998) and Stephen Darwall (1997) have argued convincingly. It is also false that all we act for is self-interest *unless we act for moral reasons*. I said that cruelty for its own sake should be seen as an anti-moral reason no matter whether one has a Kantian, utilitarian, or commonsense view of morality. Here, when referring to a Kantian view of morality, I am referring to a view of moral desirability or rightness that is based on the idea of respect for persons or on something resembling Kant's universal law formula. Some proponents of Kantian *moral psychology* could argue that 'anti-moral reasons' is an oxymoron of sorts, and that both in the case of the sadistic agent and the case of the selfish agent, the proper way to formulate the agent's reasons for action would be to say that an agent has chosen the satisfaction of an inclination over morality. In this sense, both agents act out of self-love or self-interest, even though different inclinations served as "incentives" for their decisions. I think, however, that such a view risks underestimating the moral difference between the sadist and the egoist. Intuitively, other things being equal, we are more morally outraged by a person who performs an action out of cruelty for its own sake, or out of an Iago-like desire to defile all that appears good, than we are by the person who performs the same action because he is tempted by money or fame, or even because he clearly cares about money or fame above all other things. The latter makes us feel that we are in the presence of ruthlessness and selfishness, or of weakness; the former makes us feel that we are in the presence of pure evil. Even on a small scale, a Jeanne who is rude to her colleagues because she is inconsiderate is less bad than a Jeanne who is rude to her colleagues out of sadism or out of racial prejudice. Being *overly* susceptible to love or money is bad; being susceptible *at all* to sadistic pleasure is bad—even if one never acts on one's sadistic motives, attempts to suppress them as much as possible, and never makes a decision to indulge them. It is these day-to-day intuitions that my account explains and that other views need to explain as well.

I shall assume, then, that there are sinister or anti-moral reasons for action: it is possible, in other words, to perform actions for reasons that are, morally speaking, reasons to avoid them. (I take the burden of proof to be on anyone who wants to show that it is not possible.) Now consider again the person who acts not for sinister reasons, but who fails to respond to relevant moral factors. What is it to lack responsiveness to moral reasons? There seems to be more than one form this lack of responsiveness can take. Sometimes, one is deficient in some sort of moral perception—blind, as it were, to some kinds of moral factors. One is almost tempted to accuse such a person of *localized amorality*. Some people, for example, do not seem to be able to grasp the idea of personal autonomy. Imagine the sort of parent who not only fails to see that something could be wrong with her extremely paternalistic treatment of her adult son, but who also does not understand the concept of paternalism even after it has been explained over and over. ("But if no one tells you what to do, how would you know?" she asks in bewilderment.) More often, however, one perceives all of the morally relevant features of a situation but is not sufficiently moved by them. One need not be an amoralist or sociopath of any kind for this to happen. It is enough that one be a more common though much less discussed figure: the all-too-human person who cares about morality, but *not so very much*.[6] One might call such a person "the half-moralist." Here is one story about a half-moralist:

> Mary realizes perfectly well that if she does not promptly mail her former roommate, now in Russia, the book he lent to her, she will break a promise, in addition to causing unnecessary pain. Even so, she does not send it, because it is ten degrees below zero outside and because it would be nice if she finished writing her novel before her birthday, and so she cannot really spare the time to make a special trip to the post office. She is not akratic but is acting on a decision. Not being an amoralist, it is not the case that she is indifferent to the institution of promising, the interests of her fellow human beings, or other relevant moral factors. She cares about these things enough to have avoided more serious breaches of trust, but not enough to go to the post office.

The first kind of morally unresponsive person is analogous to the person who does not notice when his clothes do not match. The second kind is analogous to the person who notices very well when his clothes are unmatched but does not care about his appearance enough to make sure that he is never stuck with nothing to wear but his orange shirt and purple pants.

Deficiency of perception and deficiency of motivation are, admittedly, hard to tell apart. Many people have wondered if their spouses don't *see* the dust on the floor or don't *care* that it is there, and the diagnosis is hard because there is often a combination: a person who does not care about cleanliness tends to be less trained at spotting dust, and a person who is not good at spotting dust may find it hard to be motivated to learn to see it and add a new worry to his life. Similar things apply to the person of mediocre moral sensibilities. A person who does not care much about morality may not give much thought to some things to which a more morally concerned person would pay more attention, and she may thus be less competent in perceiving other people's feelings, putting herself in their shoes, and so on. In fact, this is almost always the case, a fact on which I will draw later in this chapter when I discuss the marks of moral concern. Still, it seems useful to distinguish, in comparing people's moral responsiveness, the motivational from the perceptual—much in the same way that, when comparing two people's health-consciousness, it may be useful to point out that one of them seems to be more aware of health factors but the other one seems to be more motivated by factors of which he is aware. By distinguishing the motivational from the perceptual side of responsiveness, I do not preclude the possibility that failing to care about morality is irrational (after all, failing to care about one's health or bank account may be irrational as well), nor even the view that moral factors when noticed are always *somewhat* motivating. All that I assume here is that two agents can be motivated by the same moral reasons exactly, but one may be motivated by them much more than the other. This does imply that moral motivation is not proportional to understanding of morality and/or noticing morally relevant factors, and thus it does not imply anything incompatible with the most Platonic views of moral *akrasia*. It is simply to say that people can be aware of moral factors and yet not be maximally motivated by them. Again, I take the burden of proof to be on anyone who wishes to argue that Mary the half-moralist must have a problem *understanding* or seeing the moral reasons she has to return the book to her former roommate.

Degrees of Moral Concern

This discussion of moral unresponsiveness has brought to the fore-ground the idea that, given that a person is motivated by moral (or anti-moral) reasons, she can be motivated by them more powerfully or less powerfully. Let us go back to the realm of praise. Kant's prudent grocer and his ilk demonstrate to us that moral praise is warranted for the agent who acts for moral reasons, as opposed to other reasons. But suppose we know that an agent acts for moral reasons. What bearing should the strength of his moral motivation, the amount of concern that he has for moral considerations, have on our assessment of his action's moral worth? I would like to offer the following answer:

> *Praiseworthiness as Responsiveness to Moral Reasons (revised version)*: For an agent to be morally praiseworthy for doing the right thing is for her to have done the right thing for the relevant moral reasons—that is, for the reasons for which the action is right (the *right reasons* clause); and an agent is more praiseworthy, other things being equal, the deeper the moral concern that has led to her action (the *concern* clause). Moral concern is to be understood as concern for what is in fact morally relevant and not as concern for what the agent takes to be morally relevant.[7]

What does being *deeply* or *strongly* concerned for something, or being *more concerned* for something than someone else, amount to?[8] I take concern to be a form of desire. To say that a person acts out of moral concern is to say that a person acts out of an intrinsic (noninstrumental) desire to follow (that which in fact is) morality, or a noninstrumental desire to take the course of action that has those features that make actions morally right. To say in general that a person has moral concern would be to say that she has an intrinsic desire (*de re*) that morality be followed or that the courses of actions that have those features that make actions right be taken (which would imply, for example, a desire that other people act morally as well). Much work has been devoted to the study of desire, and very different views have been defended by philosophers of mind.[9] Giving a full account of concern in general or moral concern in particular would require choosing a theory of desire, which I do not wish to do here. What I would like to do is, first, sharpen our intuitive idea of concern by making a few points about what depth of concern does *not* amount to and, second, point out what I take to be important markers of depth of concern in everyday life.

It is important to note what depth or strength of concern does not amount to. It does not amount simply to *intensity of feeling*. I may care about the well-being of my friends more than I care about drinking Coca-Cola, even though now, thirsty as I am, I experience my desire for Coca-Cola considerably more intensely than I experience my concern for my friends. You care for your loved ones even while you are so angry at them that you do not "feel" any love toward them, or you are so panicked about missing a flight that nothing is further from your mind than your loved ones. Nor does being deeply concerned with something amount to a type of reflective endorsement. Two people can reflectively endorse identical things but be very different in their level of concern for these things. Erica and I may reflectively endorse the same kind of political action, but she may be more concerned with it than I am, which may explain why she is at a demonstration while I am writing. It is also natural to say that I am less *committed* to political action than Erica is, and this may tempt some readers to think of caring in terms of *commitment* — reflective endorsement with some sort of emotional backing, perhaps. This would also be misleading, as we may deeply care about things that we do not reflectively endorse at all. Tamara may care deeply about Todd and her relationship with him even though she believes she should not do so, or even though she is utterly unaware of her deep concern, ignoring it in practical deliberation. A frustrated but perceptive Todd may say, "She does not know how much she cares about me, and that is why she is not committed to the relationship." Ultimately, Tamara may say that she had not known how much she cared about Todd until, for example, Todd was in danger. Similarly, one may care about beauty, religion, money, or the opinions of other people even though one does not reflectively believe that any of these is important.

Let me now discuss three features *associated*, other things being equal, with strength of concern. I shall talk generally about moral concern or concern for morality (where "morality" is used in the *de re* sense). But what I say about such concern also holds true for more particular moral concerns — for example, concern for the happiness of others, concern for justice, and even more specific moral concerns. The first feature of concern I wish to mention is a *motivational* one—what can be called the "diehard" quality of stronger concerns as motivators. It appears to be the case that the more you care about something, the more it would take to stop you from acting on your concern. Other things being equal, the person who cares more about the football team will show up for a game on a stormy day while the person who cares less will stay at home. Both go to games for the same reasons, but one of them does so from a deeper love of the team. Thus, other things being equal, the person who cares very much about morality (again, in the *de re* sense of morality), or about any specific moral consideration, would tend to be motivated to action by it in situations in which the rest of us would not. I will say more about this feature in the subsequent discussion of benevolence.

A second feature has to do with the concerned person's *emotional makeup*. Other things being equal, caring about a team makes wins pleasant and losses painful. More than this, the person who cares about a team is likely to experience shame at its bad performance, pride at its good performance, anxiety when an important game approaches, a sense of utter despair if it turns out that a key player has been involved in a serious drug fraud, and other such emotions that utterly baffle the person who does not possess such a concern. More of these phenomena exist, and the more one is concerned with the team, the more their intensity increases. The morally concerned person, other things being equal, will find the thought of doing something wrong quite painful. As a result, she will not simply think, "I have done something wrong," but will also feel pain at the thought—that is, she will feel *guilty*. She will also feel anger when reading about atrocities in the paper, sadness when wondering, as Kant did, if "anything straight can be fashioned from the crooked timber of humanity," as well as admiration for moral heroes and disgust at the thought of being in the company of some immoral individuals. We imagine the amoralist as someone who never experiences these emotional reactions in any form (even if, for some reason or other, he does not happen to live a life of crime). The more one cares about morality, the more it colors one's emotional world (though again, this is true other things being equal, and other things are hardly ever equal when it comes to people's emotional lives). A third and related feature of moral concern is a *cognitive* feature. A person concerned with morality is, other things being equal, "morality conscious"—he notices morally salient things that a person indifferent to morality would not notice. It is a feature of the human mind that we learn more about things in which we are emotionally invested: other things being equal, a child who cares about playing the piano learns better how to play the piano than a child who is forced to do so. A person who cares about birds will notice a bird on the roof, while in the same situation a person who does not care about birds may not notice it at all. If one cares about morality, moral facts matter to one emotionally, and they are salient to one. As a result, other things being equal, a person of more moral concern will be more sensitive to moral features of situations—more apt to notice, for example, that a fellow human being is showing signs of distress or that a joke has the potential to offend certain people. I will say more about the emotional and cognitive markers of concern later in this chapter, in my discussion of blameworthy moral beliefs. The emotional and cognitive features of concern will also be relevant in the section on character, as the virtuous person is at times described as a person who has a collection of concerns that produce both an uncanny ability to recognize morally salient situations and a tendency to have the right emotional reactions at the right time.

In this section, I will focus on the first feature—"diehard" motivation. Imagine a person who cares so much for her fellow human beings, or for what she takes rightly to be her moral duty to them, that she would act benevolently even if severe depression came upon her and made it hard for her to pay attention to others. Now imagine benevolence's fair-weather friend, who acts benevolently as long as no serious problems cloud her mind but whose benevolent deeds would cease, the way some people drop their exercise programs, if there were a serious crisis in her marriage or her job. Last, imagine the person who acts benevolently on a whim. It is Sunday morning and she is awakened by a call from a charity asking for a donation. Our agent thinks, "Why not do something right?" and is moved to do something right so long as her credit card happens to be close enough to the bed.

The first agent is more praiseworthy for her actions than the second agent, because to act benevolently for moral reasons while one is depressed takes more concern for those moral reasons than to do so in happy times. Kant would have offered a different explanation. He would say that the first agent is more praiseworthy than the second agent because she acts out of one motive, duty, while the second one acts out of a motive called 'inclination', a basically hedonistic motive that is as different from duty as water is from oil. This, however, need not be the case. It is quite unlikely that my first agent changes her motive from inclination to duty the moment her life becomes harder. My second agent, unlike Kant's own happy philanthropist, is not someone who "gets her kicks" out of doing good deeds (like Jane Austen's Emma), and her disposition need not be particularly sunny. She is just an ordinary person who does good for moral reasons but whose moral concern is not deep enough to override some other concerns when they appear. Certainly, she sometimes feels a sense of satisfaction with herself, but one needs to be quite a psychological hedonist to think that any action which results in pleasure is motivated solely by it. There is no reason to say that her motives are different from the motives of the first agent, any more than there is a reason to say that the person who is truly devoted to her exercise program goes to the gym for different reasons than the person whose devotion is somewhat weaker. Both may go to the gym for health reasons, but one cares *more* about her health. Similarly, my first and second philanthropists both act benevolently for moral reasons, but one of them cares more. The contrast is *not* that happy philanthropists are less praiseworthy for their actions than sad philanthropists, but rather that *fair-weather*, frivolous philanthropists deserve less praise than those whose concern for morality or for the well-being of others is more *serious* or *deep*. The third agent—the person whose moral concern is skin deep—may be called the *capricious* philanthropist and would be very presumptuous to expect much praise for an action that almost seems accidental, attributable to the charity's call and the location of the credit card more than to her depth of concern for her fellow human beings. Still, there is no reason to doubt that she has acted for moral reasons. When a person whimsically asks for milk instead of cream in the coffee she has with her chocolate cake, one does not doubt that she does it for health reasons but doubts merely the seriousness of her concern.

My account is un-Kantian in two ways: I accept the view that it is possible for people who understand morality equally well to care about morality to different degrees, and I also reject the view that the fair-weather philanthropist acts on inclination—that is, on a hedonistic motive (which qualifies her as a "happy" philanthropist)—and grant that it is possible for her to act on moral motives. If we were to believe that only foul-weather, die-hard philanthropists act for moral motives, we would have to believe that only *very* morally virtuous people ever act for moral motives and ordinary people never do.

A natural question concerns Kant's cold-hearted philanthropist—the one who, at ordinary times rather than in sorrow, has to force himself to help people despite having no inclination to do so. Neither the cold-hearted philanthropist nor the sorrowing philanthropist just discussed enjoys his actions very much, which makes it deceptively easy to look at them as rather similar instances of "acting out of duty." However, each of them has a different story behind the fact that he drags his feet on his way to charity. The sorrowing philanthropist drags himself to action because he cares about the welfare of others so much that his concern lasts even when sorrow tempts him to stay home. The cold-hearted philanthropist has to drag himself to his good work because his philanthropy, even at the happiest times, is *half-hearted.* This could mean that he cares about the good of others just enough to wish he cared more, or it could mean that his concern for the good of humans is offset by essentially conflicting attitudes,[10] such as disdain for his fellow humans. The fact that one's concern, whether for humanity or for one's wife or one's art, is enough to motivate one—albeit barely—even though one is grief-stricken is a testimony to the strength of one's concern. The fact that one's concern, in the best of times, is only enough to motivate one barely, shows a deficiency of concern or a half-heartedness. Thus, under many descriptions, the cold-hearted philanthropist is less praiseworthy than he would be if it were not for his cold-heartedness. The picture becomes complicated, however, when one remembers how underdescribed Kant's case is. I have followed Hursthouse (1997) in taking the coldness of this philanthropist's heart to be a sign of half-heartedness, but truly, many different things can cause a person to appear cold or to experience himself as indifferent, and these things differ in morally significant ways (recall that what one cares about most is not always that about which one feels most strongly and warmly). Thus, a cold-looking or even cold-feeling philanthropist may in fact care about morality much more deeply than a philanthropist known for a "Mediterranean temper" or a "sweet temper." As the concept of hysteria teaches us, concerns that produce songs and tears are not always more serious than those that do not. Also, even if my act of philanthropy is itself half-hearted, it may be a part of a *serious* effort (as opposed to a whimsical one) to habituate myself into being a better person, and such an effort is a praiseworthy action all by itself.[11]

Having mentioned "half-heartedness," I should say a few more words about it. One way to be half-hearted is simply not to have enough motivation; so much is straightforward. Another way to be effectively, or functionally, half-hearted—half-hearted in a sense opposite to that of Frankfurt's wholeheartedness—is to have concern for something that essentially conflicts with the concern in question. A person may have attitudes that conflict with each other accidentally, such as a desire to be a great philosopher and a desire to excel at basketball. These desires conflict accidentally because there are simply not enough hours in each day or days in each week to pull off both projects in the same life. On the other hand, a person who values puritan Christianity but who also loves sex may have two *essentially* conflicting attitudes, and thus we may say that her love of Christianity, as well as her lust, are effectively rendered half-hearted. If her love of Christianity is much greater than her lust, or if her lust stands alone while her love of Christianity is intrinsically supported by her other attitudes, her lustful acts may even be, so to speak, quarter-hearted or less—in other words, the deeper her essentially antilustful attitudes, the less it would be true, other things being equal, that acts performed out of such lust reflect who she is. Thus, a person who lives a life of crime, sensual pleasure, and extravagance, and who goes to church and prays for forgiveness every so often, will usually be considered a person whose Christianity is effectively superficial (and not very praiseworthy, if Christianity is praiseworthy generally), even if her guilt is resilient enough to move her to go to church her entire life.

The difference between essential and accidental conflict of attitudes is implicit in my discussion of the philanthropist. There is no essential conflict between sadness and philanthropic concern, so the fact that the philanthropist helps in spite of depression only serves to underscore the depth of her philanthropy. On the other hand, if the philanthropist helps despite a contempt for her fellow human beings or an indifference to their suffering (I am ignoring here the possibility that this help is part of a self-improvement project, as above), the presence of this contempt or indifference reduces the wholeheartedness of her philanthropic acts to a level that would be expressed by someone who was not conflicted but less concerned. Naturally, it is not always so easy to tell an essential conflict from an accidental conflict. If I love the person Albert Einstein and hate physics, does my hatred of physics merely test my love of Einstein, or does it diminish my wholeheartedness in loving Einstein? It is hard to tell. Note, however, that those who take the second attitude would probably say something along the lines of "Physics is part of *who Einstein is*"—thus conceptualizing the conflict as essential rather than accidental. Very few people would say that loving them requires liking the job they hold at a fast food restaurant.

What, then, of blameworthy actions? There are two types of blameworthy actions: those done for sinister reasons and those done for morally neutral reasons, as a result of some indifference to moral considerations. It makes sense that a person who acts for sinister reasons is more blameworthy the stronger the ill will indicated by his action. Consider, however, the wrong action motivated by moral indifference—perhaps the more common sort of misdeed. If my various philanthropists are judged differently by the depth of concern for moral considerations their actions express, various wrongdoers can be judged by the depth of indifference to moral reasons that their actions reveal. The more moral concern it requires to take the right course of action in a certain situation, the more praiseworthy an agent is for taking it and the less blameworthy an agent is for not doing so. Imagine that in a certain situation it is right to act charitably and wrong to act uncharitably. Imagine also that in this situation it is hard, and therefore requires deep moral concern, to be charitable if one is in great sorrow, but it is easy to be charitable if one is happy (perhaps the situation involves being energetic and making phone calls on behalf of a charity for a few hours). Thus, the person who is charitable in sorrow shows herself to be more praiseworthy for her action than the person who is charitable generally, but not in sorrow. Accordingly, it does not take a great deal of moral indifference to be uncharitable while sorrowing, but it does take a lot of such indifference to be uncharitable while happy. Thus, if the sorrowing philanthropist is more praiseworthy than the happy philanthropist, the sorrowing failed philanthropist is less blameworthy than the happy failed philanthropist. Hence, for example, the use of "She was under stress" to excuse minor wrongdoing. In a more dramatic vein, if one wonders if actions such as hiding Jews from the Nazis are required by morality or are supererogatory, one compromise suggestion can be that such actions *are* required, but performing them requires a degree of moral concern so rare that the person who fails to perform them shows hardly any moral indifference and thus is not particularly blameworthy.

If the depth of one's concern for the right-making features of one's action changes an action's moral worth, how does Huckleberry Finn measure up? Huckleberry, we said, cannot be denied praise for helping Jim, because he is acting for the right reasons—he performs his action because of its right-making features. But can he be said to be acting out of deep concern for the right-making features of his action? Yes—at least on the interpretation described above—because concern does not amount to reflective endorsement and does not have to be conscious. Let us compare Huckleberry to another inverse akratic, whose action I do not take to be morally praiseworthy. Joseph Göbbels, as is evident from his diaries and some of his public speeches, suffered from surprisingly frequent attacks of what he called weakness of will, attacks that he attributed to fatigue and stress. These attacks consisted in feeling compassion for the victims of the Nazi regime, and Göbbels repressed and overcame them with relative ease, the way a civil person may overcome a desire to be rude at a family dinner. Let us suppose that on a certain occasion, Göbbels, tired at the end of a long day, perhaps having had a drink, finds himself momentarily unable to resist his compassion. Against his best judgment, he does something which he will regret the next day and for which he will compensate with a new hardening of his policy. Perhaps he signs an order that will enable a Jewish acquaintance to leave Germany—an action that is easy and not particularly costly for a man of his position. Let us assume for a moment that Göbbels acts for the same reasons as Huckleberry. Of all the things that go by the name of compassion, we shall assume that Göbbels experiences the kind that involves being moved to action by the humanity of the person. Still, Göbbels's action does not impress us in the same way that Huckleberry's does. The reasons seem to be the following. Göbbels's inverse akratic compassion strikes us as shallow or capricious—not so much because of the short time his attacks last but because of the ease with which they are overcome. His compassion is also offset by the strength of his essentially conflicting attitudes—his hatred of Jews, which normally causes him to overlook their personhood, and his deep concern for the Nazi cause, for which he appears to be willing to die. Thus, his action seems to be the product of alcohol, fatigue, and stress more than anything else. We can almost imagine his friends regarding this as a condition that excuses him from blame. For us it "excuses" him from praise.

Things appear to be different with Huckleberry Finn. Huckleberry does not need fatigue or alcohol to help Jim. As he is described in the novel, one gets the impression that he helps Jim because his concern for his fellow human beings in general, and for Jim as a human being in particular, is strong enough to make him act despite any reservations he may have. The strength of his concern for Jim as a person is a testimony to the shallow nature of his racist attitudes, not the other way around. To call Huckleberry's compassion capricious simply because it conflicts with these attitudes is like calling a Mafia boss's actions capricious because he sometimes goes to church. Thus, even though both Huckleberry and Göbbels act—let us assume—for the right reasons, and even though both of them act against their best judgments, we view them differently. One of them appears to be a good (though imperfect) boy who performs a morally praiseworthy action, while the other appears to be a bad man who, thanks to fatigue, alcohol, and a changeable mood, performed a morally desirable but negligibly praiseworthy action.

Character

It is tempting to rephrase what I have said about Huckleberry Finn in terms of character. Huckleberry Finn's concern with all that is human seems to be a deep feature of his character, while his racist convictions do not seem to be so. He is basically a good person; Göbbels is basically a bad person. It is not an accident that talk of character comes naturally here. Just as the idea of doing the right things for the right reasons, or out of concern for the right-making features of one's action, accounts for the appeal of the doctrine of the motive of duty, the idea that deep concern for these features is worth more than shallow concern for these features accounts for the appeal of the Aristotelian idea that right (or fine) actions are only praiseworthy (or virtuous) if they follow from the agent's *character*.

Consider Aristotle's treatment of bravery. For an instance of defending one's city in war to be praiseworthy, it is not enough for Aristotle that it is performed for the right reasons ("for the sake of the fine"). However pure the defender's motive is, if he is only capable of defending his city because he is pathologically fearless, or because he is such a skilled soldier that war does not frighten him, or because he has used drink to calm his nerves, his action is not morally praiseworthy. If, like the half-hearted philanthropist, he needs only the aid of soldierly self-control to drag himself to action, he is only partially virtuous. The only agent who is fully morally praiseworthy for defending his city is the agent whose ability to overcome the fear of death is the result not of wine or even of mechanical self-control, but of the fact that he genuinely *fears moral disgrace more than he fears death*—in other words, his concern for the right-making features of his action is so strong that it defeats the fear of death. Such deep concern for the right-making features of defending one's city is to be found in the *brave* person—the person in whom risking his life for the sake of doing the right thing expresses a virtue of character. The virtuous person is different from the rest of us in his possession of the markers of moral concern. He has a die-hard disposition to do what is fine (in the case of the brave person, fight for his city); he has a different emotional life from that of the nonvirtuous person (in the case of the brave person, the thought of disgrace frightens him; in general, Aristotle makes clear that virtuous people are pleased and pained by things that would not please or pain the rest of us), and he has an ability to recognize the right occasions for certain kinds of action that a mere theoretical knowledge of ethics does not give us. That the mental life of the virtuous person is to a large extent colored by her concerns has been pointed out by John McDowell (1979).

For the Aristotelian, the moral worth of every fine action depends to a large extent on the character of the agent performing it. This claim should not be confused with the common saying that for the Aristotelian, the reason an action is right is that the virtuous person would perform it. There are some reasons to doubt the latter claim: Aristotle never says that defending one's city in war is a fine action *because* that is what the virtuous person would do. However, he does take pains to explain that of all of the many people who would perform the fine action of defending their cities in war, only those of virtuous character deserve genuine praise for their actions.

Why should Aristotle, or anyone else, believe that the praiseworthiness of an individual action depends on the character from which it stems? If one thinks of character as a stable disposition of some sort, the idea may seem fairly strange. Why should the moral worth of the right action that Steve performs on November 13, 1999, be any different if we know that Steve has performed similar actions for twenty-six years and will most likely continue to do so for the rest of his life?

The answer is that the mere frequency or predictability of an action should not matter at all to its moral worth—unless frequency or predictability are taken to be signs of *deep moral concern* in the agent. After all, the pathologically fearless man or the merely well trained soldier may have just as stable a disposition as the brave person to defend the city in war, and they, too, may act for the right reason among other reasons—but their actions do not express virtue.[12] Or consider Steve. Steve, a professor, has not missed class in twenty-six years. When I mention this fact about Steve, I am complimenting him: it says something good about Steve that he has never missed a class in twenty-six years. But why? Because, I would like to claim, we normally take the fact that a professor never misses class as a sign of his devotion—a sign that he cares about his students and his role as a teacher very much. Steve's stable disposition in matters of teaching is *evidence* that his teaching and his students matter to him very much. Such evidence, however, can be overridden, in which case Steve's stable disposition to come to class would not be perceived as virtuous at all. Imagine, for example, that Steve's incredibly stable disposition to come to class is due to the fact that he, unlike other teachers, experiences pain or discomfort in very few circumstances, so that coming to class while injured or sick is not onerous for him. Or imagine that Steve, having only an average amount of concern for teaching, still cannot imagine avoiding a class, because he deeply desires to be perceived as a perfect worker, is deeply afraid of getting fired, or is blindly devoted to a work ethic regardless of whether he works at the university or at a chemical weapons factory. If any of these were the case, we would no longer be inclined to think that Steve's clockwork predictability in coming to class says anything particularly good about him. Steve's devotion to his students is his virtue: his actions over the last twenty-six years are mere evidence—as we have seen, incomplete evidence that can be overridden—of this virtue. If we wish to be neo-Aristotelian, we might want to say that Steve's coming to class on a particular day despite having a severe migraine, say, is especially praiseworthy because it stems from a virtue of character. This would not be tenable if "stems from a virtue of character" meant "stems from a stable disposition," but it makes perfect sense if it means "stems from a markedly deep morally relevant concern"—in this case, deep devotion to one's students. Note that "deep concern" does not mean "long-lived concern." It happens to be empirically true that deep concerns usually do not change overnight, and so, if Steve's behavior toward his students changed from day to day, we would be inclined to assume that his benevolent actions toward them are at least somewhat *capricious*—that is, they do not reflect a particularly deep concern for them. Such an assumption would seem more plausible than thinking that Steve is a sort of Dr. Jekyll, whose genuinely deep concerns change—whose character fluctuates—with alarming frequency. But on the rare occasions when our assumption that deep concerns do not change frequently or rapidly proves mistaken, we do not tend to think of the changed person as capricious. For example, if it were known to us that a teacher, previously indifferent to his students, having read *Up the Down Staircase*, underwent a conversion of sorts and developed a genuinely deep concern for his students, we would have no reason to regard his devotion to his students as any shallower than Steve's—even if the conversion happened only a year ago and thus did not have a chance to manifest itself for twenty-six years. We might say naturally that the person's character changed. Of course, in real life, nobody knows for sure if such a person's new concern is deep or not, and so we tend to postpone our judgment until we see if it lasts, but the "test of time" is only that—a mere *test* for the depth of a concern, and an imperfect one at that. Brevity does not make a concern shallow any more than longevity makes a concern deep—in a comfortable climate, one may be a fair-weather friend for many years.

Thus, the idea that character matters for the moral worth of individual actions makes sense if one takes character to be about depth of concern and not about predictability or frequency. Many traditional objections to character-oriented views lose their force in this way. To give only one example, suppose that as the Nazis come to power, your longtime fair-weather friend, who has never done you wrong before, cheerfully informs on you. A traditional objection states that virtue ethics is committed to excusing his action as "out of character," but if "in character" does not mean "predictable" or "in keeping with historical trends," then "unpredictable" and "out of keeping with trends" does not always mean "out of character," either.

In defense of the critics of virtue ethics, it can be said that virtue ethicists themselves have rarely if ever questioned the connection between character and predictability or stability—and it is easy to see how

this mistake came to be. As I have previously indicated that deep concerns die hard, it is plausible that the person who is deeply concerned,
say, with his students or with his city, would be disposed, *other things
being equal*, to act for the sake of his students or his city more than most.
If one assumes that other things are usually equal, one can conclude that
concern for a certain morally relevant thing does imply considerable
predictability. If one adds some version of the view that concern for some
morally relevant things always goes together with concern for other
morally relevant things, one has to conclude that depth of moral concern implies even more predictability.

Unfortunately for traditional virtue ethicists, both of these assumptions are dubious. This has been shown by various psychological experiments (see Doris 1998; Doris forthcoming; Harman 1999), but it can also
be deduced from more intuitive evidence. The falsity of the second assumption can be seen from the fact that a corrupt lawyer may be more
likely to return your book on time than an activist whose life is devoted to
global justice, or that soldiers who are brave in battle are not any less
likely to fear expressing unpopular opinions in public. It may seem
harder, at first glance, to show the falsity of the first assumption—that
there is a noticeable correlation between the extent to which one cares
about *x* and the frequency of one's acting for the sake of *x*, but this too
can be shown. Imagine that one works in an academic department in
which the workload is typically very high. If one passes through the corridor, greeting each and every member of the department as one walks,
some members are more likely than others to greet one back and to engage one in conversation. One may be tempted to think of those who do
not do so as less friendly or less talkative. This, however, is likely to be a
mistake—an instance of the *internal attribution error* (Harman 1999).
The people least likely to greet one in the corridor are those whose
schedules are the busiest, the grouchiest-looking ones are nearing their
sixth year as assistant professors, and so on; conversely, the people who
are most likely to engage one in conversation are those in the more comfortable stages of their careers. Having realized this, one may still be
tempted to believe that at least the few individuals whose pattern of behavior deviates from this correlation are showing their true colors in
terms of their deep concern, or deep lack thereof. The man who stops to
engage in conversation despite nearing his tenure decision is surely one
who deeply desires to engage in conversation, and the woman who tends

to pass you in the corridor with almost no greeting despite being a full professor on leave is truly unconcerned with making conversation. But this, of course, need not be true. It might be that the man, though misanthropic, has a tendency to react to extreme stress with a compulsion to talk, and the woman, though deeply desirous of her colleague's company, fears making a fool of herself or has been habituated by some sexist norm not to say too much. In a world in which people are rarely allowed to act on all their hearts' desires, it is little wonder that one's actions do not always reflect one's concerns very well.

While these tales show serious problems for the traditional notion of a character trait, they do not show that there is no fact of the matter about moral concern. The person who loves more is not always the person who says "I love you" more often, but some people do love more than others. The person who is more devoted to her students is not always the person who comes to class more often, but some people are devoted to their students more than others. And the connection between depth of concern and moral worth is an important truth aimed at by talk of character.

No Such Thing as a Good Nazi?

This account of moral worth is bound to be incomplete. In fact, it is such almost by definition, for if moral worth has to do with responding to the right-making features of one's action, the full theory of moral worth depends on a full theory of the right, which would tell us what these right-making features are. Are they utility-maximizing features, person-respecting features, or eudaimonia-conducive features? Or are they something else? It is worth noting, though, that intuitions about moral worth also enlighten us about the right. One reason most people believe that ethical egoism is wrong is the fact that we do not tend to hold praiseworthy people who do good for the sake of doing well. If egoism were true, such people would be acting for morally relevant reasons and thus should be perceived as praiseworthy for their actions. Unfortunately, this sort of insight (or any other kind) is not likely to end the debates about right and good actions anytime in the near future, and so there is inevitably going to be some incompleteness in a theory of moral worth.

But while this account is not meant to be complete, two nagging questions need to be addressed. A relatively simple question, concerning the role of moral knowledge, shall be addressed at the end of this chapter. This section will deal with the more complex question of the *misguided conscience*. The world is full of people who are devoted to morally wrongheaded causes. Some of these causes are terribly wrongheaded, like Göbbles'. Others are less wrongheaded but still wrong: perhaps one is devoted to promoting chastity, convinced that chastity is an important moral cause. The chastity promoter, while she is harmless compared to the Nazi, still causes moral harm in the world. She may, for example, choose to donate her money to the Chastity Society instead of the Cancer Society, and she may make a variety of morally wrong choices due to being blind to the virtues of some unchaste individuals or the vices of some chaste ones (e.g., she may vote for the morally inferior candidate or send her child to a private school inculcating false moral views). Whatever the degree of one's wrongheadedness, one must ask, Is there any merit in the devotion of a person to a wrong cause? If a person *does* conquer his desire to help a slave escape, does it always speak only badly of him? Is there ever anything to say in favor of the idealistic Nazi soldier who *does* conquer his inverse akratic urges in service of what he takes, ever so mistakenly, to be a good cause?

Some would suggest that there may be something good about having self-control or the ability to "stick to one's guns" — an ability on which many loyal Nazis prided themselves and which Huckleberry Finn accuses himself of lacking. Note, however, that the loyal Nazi does not necessarily have great self-control — his hatred of Jews and love of power may simply be stronger than any "temptation" for him, a state that does not speak well of him. Similarly, Huckleberry Finn need not be particularly lacking in self-control — it may simply be the case that his reluctance to treat a human being like escaped livestock is stronger than any inhibitions he may have, which does speak well of him. But to the extent that there is a property called "self-control" that is independent of the content of the desires to be controlled, it is hard to see it as anything but morally neutral, a tool that we want the moral agent to have and we hope the immoral agent lacks. Let me explain.

Recall the difference between Aristotle's brave person and Aristotle's self-controlled (enkratic) person. Aristotle's brave person performs as he does on the battlefield *not* because he has great self-control, but because his concern for honor exceeds his fear of death — thus showing not self-control, but virtue. Many cases in which we tend to think that a person has self-control are in fact cases analogous to Aristotelian bravery—cases in which a person is simply more concerned with one thing than another. For example, if I am acting kindly toward Russell even though I am very angry at him, it may show that I have great self-control—that is, an ability to suppress whatever emotions I wish—or it may be the case that I have no self-control at all, but I am so concerned with Russell's well-being that even my anger cannot override my concern. In the latter case, the fact that I act kindly despite my anger shows something good about me. In the former, all it shows is that I have a sort of mental discipline—a morally neutral skill that, like a soldier's training, can be used for bad ends just as easily as for good ones. We want the moral person to have self-control, but only for the same reason we want the moral person to have money—namely, because self-control helps the moral person attain her goals (just as it helps the immoral person attain hers). To come back to Huckleberry Finn, the fact that he is motivated to help Jim despite his convictions may similarly show one of two things: it *may* show that he has less than an ordinary person's self-control, or it may show that his concern for Jim's humanity is so strong that it defeats his convictions and inhibitions. I was assuming that the latter is the case, which would make Huckleberry paradoxically similar to Aristotle's brave person. The brave person's desire to avoid disgrace is stronger than his fear of death. Huckleberry Finn's well-motivated desire to help Jim overrides his attachment to his misguided convictions. The brave person's desire to defend his city is strong enough that it does not need the aid of self-control to win his inner struggle; similarly, Huckleberry Finn's desire to help Jim is strong enough that it does not need the aid of an unusual lapse of self-control or lapse of consciousness (produced by alcohol, stress, etc.) to win in his own inner struggle. In the cases of both Huckleberry and the brave person, it is a virtuous concern that wins the struggle, and that is all that matters to the moral worth of their actions.

Much more will be said about self-control in chapter 4 (where I shall also discuss crimes of passion and Freudian slips). But what has been said so far suffices at least to show one important point: if self-control is morally neutral, it is hard to see how any morally positive value can ever be attached to morally misguided loyalties, for how can anything positive come from a neutral power being exercised for a bad end? To say that there is never any value to a misguided conscience, however, is to do injustice to the complexity of many misguided conscience cases. To see how a misguided conscience can say *something* good about its owner, though, we must first take a closer look at the reasons it usually shows one to be bad.

Why Racists, Sexists, and Megalomaniacs Are (Usually) Bad, Not Just Mistaken

There is a lively argument between historians as to whether Hitler was "sincere"—that is, whether Hitler in fact believed his professed views. The question of Hitler's sincerity is perceived as morally disturbing in a special way. What if it turned out that Hitler sincerely believed that Jews amounted to horribly harmful creatures who are out to destroy humanity, and that therefore he was attempting to do the world a lot of good by helping to get rid of them? Would we have to admit that Hitler was not evil, after all? But if Hitler was not evil, who is?

We may know too little about Adolf Hitler's private life to make a study of his moral psychology, but the little that we know is quite consistent with the possibility that whatever the sincerity of his beliefs about Jews, Hitler despised *morality* and only used its language to capture the heart of the masses. If Hitler in fact despised morality and wished to promote something he knew to be evil, there would be no problem in explaining why he was evil; it is easy to show that he acted for sinister reasons. We can also imagine a Hitler who thinks he has a "new morality"—perhaps a master morality as opposed to a slave morality, or an Aryan morality as opposed to a Jewish morality—according to which killing innocent human beings is often just fine. It would not be a problem to explain why such a Hitler would be bad either: like the extremist, above, he is a person who mistakenly believes that he is acting for moral reasons, but who in fact acts for sinister reasons or out of indifference to (what in fact is) morality, no matter how he happens to name it. But the person whose badness the historians fear they would have trouble accommodating is the person whose anti-Jewish actions were based not on false moral beliefs but on false *factual* beliefs: he mistakenly, or as a result of a damaged brain, believed it to be a fact that Jews were trying to take over the world and subjugate gentiles. Given this false belief, what else could a decent fellow do?

Fortunately for the uncomfortable historians, Hitler does not fit this description very well, but the same question could be raised of many other bad people and evildoers of the more ordinary sort. We can well imagine a more run-of-the-mill anti-Semite justifying her ill treatment of Jews by citing her belief that Jews are subhumans who are trying to conquer the world and that treating them badly may improve the state of the world by letting them know that they are not likely to conquer it in the near future. This person, too, is blameworthy, and, if her racism is rabid enough, she is obviously evil. Yet it seems as if all this person gets wrong is *the facts*: she does not have false beliefs about morality but simply false beliefs about Jews. If she acts badly toward Jews, it seems as if her false beliefs about them—sometimes referred to as her "ignorance"—should excuse her action. Why, then, is she blameworthy?

Racists, sexists, and their ilk are not the only sort of people who are regarded as bad or vicious despite the fact that their behaviors seem attributable to a false belief. Imagine a person who snubs his coworkers because he believes, falsely, that he is much superior to all of them in intelligence, virtue, skill, and practically everything else. Or consider a parent who beats his children quite severely because he believes that beating builds character (one may imagine Klaus Mann's Professor Unrat believing similarly that his cruelty helps his students). These people also seem to have false factual beliefs: the belief that one's coworkers are annoying idiots (assuming that the believer has reasonable definitions of his adjectives) is a factual belief—we can easily imagine what it would be like for it to be true. The belief that children benefit from "good beatings" is similarly a factual belief about child psychology, though a false one. Yet we often take people like the megalomaniac and the child-beater to be blameworthy.

Usually, a false factual belief does seem to be a good excuse, and often it provides an exemption from moral blameworthiness. A paradigmatic case would be the following: Boko Fittleworth (a character in a P. G. Wodehouse novel) overpowers and traps a man whom he spots hiding in his would-be father-in-law's garden shed at midnight, because he believes this man to be a burglar. In fact, the man is not a burglar but a business tycoon whose presence in the shed is part of a secret, unlikely, and harmless plot in which the future in-law is a willing participant.

Though Boko, of course, gets himself in serious trouble with his future father-in-law, and though he owes the businessman an apology, he is still not blameworthy for his action. It is wrong to treat a fellow human being violently, but Boko has a perfect excuse—"But I thought you were a burglar." We need to understand why the anti-Semite and her friends do not have a similar excuse—something like "But I thought you were a member of a worldwide conspiracy."

The beginning of the answer has to do with the epistemic rationality of Boko's belief, when contrasted with the epistemic irrationality of anyone's belief, in this day and age, that all Jews are all monstrously greedy people engaged in a conspiracy to control the world. It is eminently epistemically rational to believe that an unknown man hiding in a known garden shed at midnight and refusing to identify himself is probably up to no good. Thus, Boko's belief is what I would call a false, epistemically rational belief—what we would usually call an *honest mistake*. On the other hand, unless one has just arrived from another planet, armed with a seriously flawed travel guide to Earth, it is difficult for one to reach the belief that all Jews are greedy people engaged in a conspiracy to control the world by way of an honest mistake. Many people who have held such beliefs about Jews met enough Jewish people, and knew enough of history, to be able to see the unlikely nature of that sort of conspiracy. Their beliefs are not honest mistakes, nor the result of mental retardation, but the result of motivated irrationality, sometimes expressed in words such as "I was ready to believe anything about Jews, as long as it was bad."

We do not take people to be bad if they hold bigoted beliefs out of pure ignorance, or mostly out of ignorance. This is hard to show, of course, because such cases of pure ignorance are extremely rare, but I would imagine that if an alien arrived on Earth with a used copy of a generally reliable Guide to the Solar System telling her that all black Earthlings are foolish and all pale Earthlings clever, she would be misled, not irrational, and she would not be bad simply for having made this mistake, even if she acted on it. For a more mundane tale, consider the case of Solomon, a boy who lives in a small, isolated farming community in a poor country. Solomon believes that women are not half as competent as men when it comes to abstract thinking, or at least are not inclined toward such thinking. Solomon's evidence for his belief is the fact that all the women in his community, despite his attempts to engage them in learned conversation, seem to discuss nothing but gossip, family, and manual work, that the few people in his community who are interested in abstract thinking are all men, that no one he knows of has ever doubted that women are worse abstract thinkers, and that the community's small, outdated library contains abstract work written by men only. Solomon's belief is false, but it is not *particularly* or *markedly* irrational. It is not particularly irrational because Solomon is not exposed to striking counterevidence to it, and he is exposed to a consensus and "expert" opinion in its favor (just think how many of our own everyday beliefs are grounded simply on expert opinion and lack of clear counterexamples). True, if Solomon were to think more carefully, he might find reasons to change his mind, but in his case "thinking more carefully" would involve having the intelligence of John Stuart Mill without the advantage of having known at least one woman who is inclined toward abstract thinking. While no person is perfectly rational, it is unfair to accuse a person of being exceptionally irrational just for not being exceptionally intelligent.[13] The boy Solomon is more ignorant than irrational, and he is also, intuitively, more ignorant than morally vicious—he seems much less deserving of the title "sexist pig" than a contemporary American who holds the same view.

Imagine, on the other hand, that Solomon gains a scholarship and finds himself a student in an excellent academic institution, where he proceeds to study his favorite abstract topic. In college, Solomon sits shoulder to shoulder with brilliant female students and is taught by brilliant female professors. At the end of his first year as a college student, if Solomon were rational, he would have changed his mind about the aptitude of women for abstract thinking. If at the school year's end Solomon still believed that all women are bad abstract thinkers, his belief would now be not only false but also irrational. He would no longer be simply mistaken, but *prejudiced*. At the point when we regard him as irrational, we also regard him as suffering from a serious moral flaw.

So an honest mistake is an excuse and often exempts one from blame; prejudice, which is an irrational belief, does not. But why, exactly? There is nothing morally vicious about irrationality per se. After all, there seems to be nothing morally vicious in believing—as irrationally as can be—that Elvis Presley is still alive or that a lottery ticket is less likely to win if it carries the same number as the ticket that won last month.[14] Yet even if there is *nothing* morally vicious in epistemic irrationality per se, there still seems to be something vicious about the anti-Semite, the educated yet sexist Solomon, the megalomaniac, and the child-beater, a vice that does not exist in the person who commits the Gambler's Fallacy.

Consider the sentence "I hate him because he is disgusting." Often, this sentence evokes smiles. It does not seem to provide a true explanation of why "I hate him," because unless there are obvious reasons to think of the object of hate as disgusting in some way or another, the hearer is likely to infer that the speaker puts the cart before the horse: the truth would be more likely expressed in the words "I see him as disgusting because I hate him." Suppose for a moment that all of this is true of Joshua and me. I mistreat Joshua, and I tell you that I do it "because he is disgusting." You, a rational observer, see that no one would see Joshua as disgusting unless her belief formation were colored by hate or some other emotion or desire. You call my bluff: "No," you say, "you treat Joshua like that because you hate his guts. The fact that, with all he has done for you, you still believe that he's disgusting only shows how much you hate him. You really are unfair."

This is a story in which my attribution of an action (mistreating Joshua) to a believed state of affairs (he is disgusting) is not to be taken at face value. Perhaps my mistreatment of Joshua is motivated simply by hatred, the belief "he is disgusting" being a mere epiphenomenon of the hatred. Perhaps my mistreatment of Joshua is simply the result of my wanting to hurt someone and his being a readily available victim, and my belief that "he is disgusting" is an excuse that I develop to rationalize my action, however inadequately. Perhaps I believe that Joshua is disgusting because for some reason or other it is comfortable for me to believe that he is, and my action is my perverse way of confirming and strengthening my belief. In all these cases, the motive for my action seems to be quite unsavory, and all these cases are different from the case in which I mistreat Joshua because I heard from a very reliable (but, in this case, inaccurate) source that Joshua is a serial killer and my actions toward him are understandable or even justified given that assumption. Only the latter case would be analogous to the case of Boko Fittleworth.

I would like to suggest that the anti-Semite and her friends are also generally presumed to act out of unsavory motives, and their claim that they do X because they believe that Y is as suspicious as my "because he is disgusting." Thus, my point is *not* that, à la Robert Adams (1985), the anti-Semite's *belief* is itself blameworthy, but that the anti-Semite's belief plays a rather superficial role in a drama in which a person is motivated by sinister desires. When looking at the blameworthiness of my actions when I hurt Joshua, what matters is the fact that I hurt him because I hated him, and my "because he's disgusting" does not matter much. The anti-Semite hates the Jew "because he's disgusting" or rather believes that he's disgusting because she hates him, or even worse, because she wants to hate *someone*. Sartre has already said that if the Jew did not exist, the anti-Semite would have invented him. Presumably, Sartre meant that if the Jew did not exist, the anti-Semite would have found someone else to scapegoat, and if the anti-Semite did not come across the world-conspiracy idea, she would have found a well-poisoning or a Tzar-killing story to believe instead. The anti-Semite mistreats the Jew because she wants to mistreat someone and is therefore ready to believe anything about the Jews, as long as it is bad. Thus the anti-Semite is not doing what she does because of an honest mistake, but because of a sinister motive; and the more far-fetched her beliefs about the Jews, the more the evidence shows that her sinister motivation is strong. If unjustified hatred is a vice, a hatred so strong that it produces near delusions is an even stronger vice. That is why, if Hitler's strange beliefs about the Jews were the result of hatred's distortion of his perception of the world, it would justify seeing him as *both* evil *and* crazy—the way we see him most of the time.

It is interesting to compare the behavior of those whose motivation resembles the anti-Semite's to the behavior of those who are honestly mistaken—or those who are honestly correct. One characteristic difference between them is that the motivatedly irrational person tends to make more of her belief than the honest believer ever does. The Bus Drivers' Union in England believed that women are weaker than men—and in the 1970s used this belief as a premise in arguing that women should be barred from driving buses. Compare this approach with that of Plato, who also believed that women are weaker then men but pointed out that as this is true only in general terms, any woman who demonstrates that she is strong enough to be a guard should be recruited as a guard. Plato's approach is more characteristic of the person who "simply" believes that women are weaker than men. The bus drivers' demand is so unwarranted by the belief that they claim as its reason that one suspects that the "weakness" argument is a mere rationalization of a desire to keep women "in their place," and if the excuse of "weakness" did not exist, they would have had to invent another one.

Another common difference between the innocent and the motivatedly irrational person is that the latter is likely to show signs of bad faith. The learned officers of the Holy Inquisition based their actions on the belief that they were not punishing their victims, but rather were rewarding and curing them by saving their souls from Hell. Yet, it seems, the inquisitors often treated their personal enemies to their "cure," even if they believed them to be relatively without "sin," and never offered it to their friends, presumably even if they believed them, privately, to have a lot of sins weighing on their souls. Their behavior is significantly different from the behavior of those who, after a good experience with a certain method of therapy, even quite a dreadful one, begin to urge everyone to try it. Thus it seems likely not only that some inquisitors winked inwardly when they repeated their claim that they were not administering punishment, but also that even some of those who never did were motivated in their actions not by the desire to save souls, but by the desire to hurt people they disliked or to exercise indecent amounts of power. The belief that they were saving souls was just a particularly comfortable, sinister rationalization.

Let us take an even closer look at why the anti-Semite and her friends are blameworthy. There are some cases in which the answer is easy: they are acting from morally bad motives. The anti-Semite may be the sort who desires to mistreat others, and so whatever she says about conspiracies, her actual motive is the simple desire to mistreat others. The man who mistreats his children may have a similarly sinister motive, whatever his tales of character. The person who takes herself to be superior to all her coworkers may simply want to have unfair power over people and humiliate them, her real or imaginary superiority being a convenient inner excuse for action. But in other cases, one's motive for acting (and even one's motive for believing) is not by itself evil. For example, perhaps the man who beats his children was beaten himself, and his need to love his own parents, and rationalize to himself the fact that he has allowed them to mistreat him, attracts him to the belief that there is nothing wrong with the way his parents treated him, as they were only trying to build his character; in order to prevent cognitive dissonance, he beats his own children himself. The person who mistreats her coworkers may be deeply insecure and evade this insecurity by telling herself that she is such a genius that her peers' criticisms mean nothing to her. The anti-Semite may be anti-Semitic because all her friends are also anti-Semitic, and she deeply wishes to fit in. Solomon, if he keeps his youthful belief about the intellectual inferiority of women despite the counterevidence offered by his new circumstances, may simply be tired of the onerous job of constantly changing and adjusting his attitude to a new, perplexingly sophisticated world and be clinging nostalgically to the epistemic comforts of home.

All of these motivational stories look quite innocent. Wishing to love one's parents, to avoid insecurity, to fit in with one's friends, or to have a simple view of the world are all perennial motives that influence our actions and beliefs, rationally or otherwise, often enough, whether we are morally bad or good or average. What is wrong, then, with the child-beater whose motives are nothing but the desire to love his parents and improve his children's characters or the anti-Semite who only wants to fit in with her friends? Blameworthiness involves either the presence of a sinister motive for action or the marked absence of concern for morally relevant factors. If no sinister motive is present, the guilt of these agents must have to do with the *absence of moral concern*. Perhaps the child-beater is only trying to love his parents, perhaps the anti-Semite is only trying to fit in with her friends, perhaps the megalomaniac is only trying to evade insecurity—but they are trying to do this *at the expense of others*, at the expense of morality. There is nothing wrong with wanting money, but a person who kills for money is blameworthy because he fails to respond to pertinent moral reasons. The same is true for the person who beats his children in order to better love his parents. He, too, is criminally selfish.

This point needs refinement, because the analogy between the cases seems forced. Consider the following three cases:

(1) A person beats his children quite severely because he wishes to please his parents, who reward him for delivering such beatings.

(2) A person beats his children quite severely because he wishes to please his parents, as above. He is, however, self-deceived about his motives. To make himself feel better, he rationalizes that he beats his children because "it builds character."

(3) A person beats his children quite severely because he believes that beating one's children builds character. His belief is
the result of his strong wish to believe that his parents, abusers
themselves, are decent people; this wish, in turn, is the result of
his wish to love them.

(1) is the typical case of the person who, for love or money, defies morality. (2) is similar to (1), except that a rationalization is added. The person's belief in "character" is, in a sense, irrelevant to his blameworthiness—only one fact matters, namely the fact that he values the approval
of his family more than his children's well-being. Things are quite different in (3). In (3), the child-beater's belief that beating builds character, however irrationally formed, plays a real role in his behavior. His desire to love his parents led him to form the belief. Now, however, he
beats his children not, as in (1) or (2), out of a desire to love his parents
simpliciter, but rather because he believes that his beatings will improve
their characters. Why, then, is he still blameworthy for his action? The
answer is that if he cared appropriately about morality or about the welfare of his children, he would not have formed the belief that severe
beatings build character, or he would not have been motivated by it to
beat his children.

This is a very delicate point, as it can easily be confused with two
false claims. One is the claim that since the beater's belief that beating
builds character is self-deception, he is blameworthy for this very act of
belief formation. After all, he knew at some level that his belief was false
and that it was going to cause him to behave badly, and if he cared more
about his children he would not have caused himself to have that belief.
This claim rests on an overly Cartesian notion of belief formation or self-
deception, and I have explained in chapter 1 my reasons for rejecting the
idea that self-deception is an intentional, voluntary action. Belief formation, as far as I am concerned, is not intentional, as is shown by the fact
that one cannot be forced to change her beliefs at gunpoint. Another
claim I wish to avoid is the claim that we are responsible for our irrational beliefs in the way that one is responsible for "culpable ignorance"
or criminal negligence—the view that we have a duty to "check" on our
beliefs the way that we have a duty to check the brakes on our cars. This
may be true in some limited contexts, but as we do not even know which
of our beliefs need checking more than others, and as it is in the nature

of some kinds of irrationality that one cannot detect it in oneself, it makes no sense to say that we always have such a duty.

On the other hand, it is true, as I said earlier, that what we care about influences our deliberation, perception, and other cognitive processes. Freud's love of antiquities, mentioned in chapter 1, may have caused him to imagine antiquities shops when they did not exist, but he never failed to notice a real antiquities shop, even those that most people would have passed without noticing. If you care passionately about being at work on time, you are less likely to underestimate the amount of time you need to get to work—which is why you, unlike the rest of your group, are never late. If you are a lover of birds and care very little for buildings, you might well remember the bird that you saw on top of Buckingham Palace and not the building itself. If feminism is your life, you may have trouble reading nineteenth-century novels because you feel sorry for the female characters, and if your loved one is a vegetarian, a movie about Argentina is bound to make you wonder how on earth vegetarians get along there. If truth matters to you a lot, it will take longer for you to accept a piece of gossip than it would take for a person to whom truth does not matter much—not because you would feel like you have a duty to doubt it but because you "naturally" will doubt it more.

Similarly, those who care about treating people fairly are not quick to believe a very unlikely, morally incriminating story about a third party, even if this third party is someone of whom they would love to think badly. If a woman is told by an unreliable source that the husband who left her is in fact a criminal, she will probably be disposed to believe the story—except if she cares very much about treating people fairly, in which case she is likely to come to no firm conclusion; the high stakes involved in treating a person as a criminal when he is not one would be too salient for her to accept a cock-and-bull story so quickly. If you care about fairness, you will not easily delude yourself, in the face of counterevidence, that your coworkers are stupid, however soothing of insecurity such a belief might be (of course, if you respect your coworkers' personhood, you would not even find the *actual* stupidity of coworkers a reason to mistreat them). If respect for persons is a deep concern for you—deeper than the desire to be popular with your anti-Semitic friends—you will think more than twice before accepting the view that Jews are not persons in the face of powerful evidence to the contrary. If you care deeply about your children, you will not be quick to believe, in the face of glaring counterevidence, any view that implies that it is help-ful to beat them severely. That is why, while some people who were beaten by their parents beat their own children, many do not. In fact, many people who made excuses for their abusive parents for years snap out of their "denial" the moment they have children whose own interests are at stake. Thus, a person who was severely beaten as a child is justified in being angry at his parents, accusing them of selfishly caring more about maintaining their illusions about their parents or whatnot than about the suffering of their child. Thus, even if the anti-Semite, the megalomaniac, or the child-beater is not motivated by sinister motives, she is still guilty of chilling indifference to moral reasons.

Good Motives, Bad Causes

To recapitulate: believing something such as "Jews are germs" is not an excuse for a bad action if only a mind that is maddened with hatred, or that is chillingly indifferent to fairness and compassion, could accept that belief in the first place. Thus, it seems that if a belief in Nazi doc-trine speaks ill of a person, loyal devotion to Nazism would speak even worse of her. It could only speak well of her to the extent that the devo-tion is fueled by morally *good* motives. Above, we said that the sheer de-sire to "stick to one's guns" is neutral—not by itself a good motive. What good motives *could* there be in one's attachment to a bad cause?

There could be none, if it were true that being an advocate of an ide-ology always implied having the beliefs required by the ideology, and if being an advocate of a person, theory, or country always involved being an advocate of what the person, theory, or country really is. However, things are much more complicated than this. To say that Jennifer be-lieves, for example, in the truth of the Bible is not to imply that it is in general possible to take a text from the Bible, put "Jennifer believes" in front of it, and produce a true statement. Jennifer's love of the Bible may be largely due to a strong sense of the rightness of the "do unto others" slogan and the idea that all human beings somehow deserve love. When Jennifer feels the need to defend the Bible, she feels that she is protect-ing these things—and to the extent that these are things that move her, her devotion to the Bible does speak well of her, regardless of what the Bible might say about homosexuals or the sins of the fathers being visited upon the sons. On the other hand, Dana may be attracted to the Bible largely because it provides her with a good excuse to look down at people she dislikes or to hate homosexuals, in which case her devotion speaks ill of her. The two people may be very different morally, and they would be wrong if they assume, as people often do, that they are likely to get along because "they are both Christians." While they may almost always produce identical statements about their beliefs, we feel that there is a sense in which Christianity "means different things to them."

Because any cause — including a bad cause — may "mean" very different things to different people, and thus a bad cause can mean good things to some people, there will be cases in which a person's attraction to a bad cause would speak well of him. It would rarely speak *nothing* but well of him, because it is rare that the reasons which attract a person to an unwholesome cause are all wholesome, or that a bad cause means nothing but good things to someone, but there may still be something good about it. Klaus Mann provides us with the (surely real) character of Hans Miklas, a young, uneducated, and very naive actor who becomes a member of the Nazi Party while it is still a fringe group. Hoefgen, a fellow actor and a socialist, refuses to share the same stage with him out of dramatized disgust. Yet the reader gets the impression that Miklas is not really a bad man. His attraction to the Nazi ideology appears to rely a lot on his desire for social justice and on his disgust with the (real) corruption around him. In his mind, he associates "German honor" not with conquering other countries, but rather with a corruption-free public life. The meshing of "honor" and social justice in his mind is the result of his believing the propaganda according to which many of the rich who are getting unjustly richer are Jewish. After Hitler comes to power, Miklas, despite being promoted and respected due to his long-standing party membership, quickly discovers that not only has social injustice remained ubiquitous, but it has in fact increased, and so has corruption. He is so devastated that he consciously destroys himself by publicly denouncing the regime. This action authenticates the suspicion that, from the start, his attraction to Nazism was a morally mixed bag, containing an element of true attraction to justice. One wonders if he is not in fact better than his colleague Hoefgen, whose socialism does not stop him from choosing to cooperate with the regime when he can easily leave the country instead. The reason one wonders is not that devotion to a cause, regardless of content, is morally better than fickleness, but because, as

his later actions testify, Miklas's devotion was partially a result of responsiveness to truly moral reasons.

Can one really act for a mix of morally good and bad reasons? It
seems Miklas does, because, though some frustration and hatred have
obviously affected his infatuation with the Nazi movement instead of
some other workers' movement and have made him all too willing to believe anti-Semitic propaganda, a true concern for justice surely con-
tributes to his great disappointment with the Nazi regime. (To complicate the character even further, Miklas's Nazism is also the result of his
ignorance and cognitive limitations, which makes it hard, in his case, to
tell innocent false beliefs from irrational, ill-motivated prejudice.) It may
seem, from a Kantian[15] point of view, that one either is motivated by
morally relevant reasons or is not, without the possibility of mixed motives, but this is not the way we think when we judge people's motivations. Granted, in some contexts it may seem as if it is. To borrow an ob-
servation from Korsgaard, if a student tells us that he has decided to study
calculus for the sake of the intellectual challenges involved, but then we
learn that it is also a required class, we tend to take quite a cynical attitude to his claim that he is motivated by the intellectual challenge. But
consider a student who has always wanted to take calculus since her first
contact with high school physics, but has been inhibited about doing so
because she fears that her cognitive abilities are not up to the task. Upon
entering college, she discovers that a certain degree requirement can be
met by one of a few classes, including Introductory Calculus. She decides to take calculus, thankful for the requirement at the same time as
she fears it. While this student would not have taken calculus if it had
not been required, it would be unjust on the part of her math professor to
treat her on par with her peer who is dragged, kicking and screaming,
into the required class, trying to avoid intellectual challenge to the extent that is compatible with earning a good grade. Analogously, issues of
moral worth become complicated when we consider those whose motives are mixed. To fail to kill a person because she is a person is to respond to moral reasons; to fail to kill a person only because she is a fellow
Jew is not to respond to moral reasons; but what does one say of those
who would not kill someone because she is "both a human being and a
fellow Jew"? As with the tale of calculus, the answer depends on the details of the case and on the amount of concern for Jewishness, as opposed
to concern for personhood, involved in the person's (in)action. Sorting

this out is especially difficult because some people use the word "person" to mean "a fellow Jew," and some people would talk about helping a fellow Jew but mean in this something as close to helping a person as it gets.

Thus we may vindicate Kant's view that, as moral worth depends on the complex matter of people's motives, diagnosing moral worth in real life can be very difficult—perhaps even more difficult than Kant himself believed.

Knowledge of the Virtues

In addition to the view that there must be something morally good in self-control, there is a related, even more venerable view, according to which there is something especially good in having knowledge of the virtues, correct moral convictions, and/or the ability to deliberate well on moral matters. If acting for moral reasons is not the same as acting for what we take to be moral reasons, and depth of moral concern is not the same as conscious commitment to moral principles, how can this be true? I have conceded earlier that Huckleberry Finn would be a better person if his conscious moral convictions were not appalling. However, some people may want to argue that in addition to this fact, it is also true that there is something especially regrettable in the fact that Huckleberry Finn's character deficiency is located specifically in his ability for moral *deliberation*, as opposed to somewhere else. I believe that there is something to this claim, but that the goodness of having the ability to deliberate well about morality can be maintained without denying that Huckleberry Finn's action is morally praiseworthy.

Intellectual knowledge of morality and the ability to deliberate well about all matters moral have obvious things to recommend them. To begin with, an agent in Huckleberry Finn's position, who does not know his virtues from his vices, is likely to try to make himself a worse person, whereas the person who knows his virtues from his vices is likely to try to make himself a better person. More important, there are certain types of morally desirable actions that are very hard to perform if one does not have the right moral principles or at least the ability to deliberate well on moral matters. For example, it is very hard to vote for the right political candidate if one cannot deliberate well on moral matters (and, to some extent, on other matters such as economics and human behavior).

While some of those who voted for Hitler were obviously bad people, others strike us as morally average people (or, in the case of Miklas, somewhat better) whose unreflectiveness, simplicity, and incompetence at deliberation made them easy prey for the candidate who promised jobs, more national pride, and order in the streets. Given the complex moral decisions that even the most mundane life has to offer, it seems that we have a moral duty not to allow ourselves or our children to be too stupid, unreflective, or uninformed, especially with regard to morally relevant issues. The fact that a person — even a good person — cannot deliberate very well or is ignorant when it comes to morally relevant matters has a special sadness to it.

Conclusion

It has been my goal in this chapter to sketch a quality-of-will-based theory of moral worth and show that such a view is potentially useful in understanding some facts of moral life. On my view, people are praiseworthy for acts of good will and blameworthy for acts of ill will or the absence of good will, and the amount of praise or blame they deserve varies with the depth of their motivation or the extent of their indifference. But since, I hold, good will is wanting, noninstrumentally, to perform actions that have whatever property it is that makes actions right, a full account of moral worth is impossible until we know what property it is that makes actions right. I shall not try to fill this gap in this book, nor shall I attempt a full account of acting for reasons. Other gaps that remain in my account concern the significance of my view for moral responsibility and autonomy. I shall discuss this topic in the next chapter.

■ ■ ■

FOUR

VARIETIES OF AUTONOMY

Chapter 3 presented a theory of moral worth in keeping with the goals set out in chapter 1: no privileged role was assumed for conscious attitudes, deliberation, or the agent's awareness of the moral significance of what she or he is doing. A number of questions have remained unanswered, however, and perhaps the most pressing of them is this: What has happened to autonomy? Where, in this whole account of praise- and blameworthiness, is the recognition that the central issue here is the agent's autonomy? Has it been somehow buried implicitly within the discussion of chapter 3, or has it been entirely ignored? To answer these questions, it will be necessary to make some progress first on what they might be asking.

An Overworked Term

"When I make a word do a lot of work like that," says Humpty Dumpty, "I always pay it extra." Some words in philosophy have been working overtime, as anyone who, for example, has attempted to explain to a bewildered student the relations between various "externalisms" and "internalisms" will know. It has to be admitted, though, that the multitude of meanings "internalism" has in our field is not a real problem. Real problems begin when a term of art performs so many tasks that it becomes at least as elusive and complex as the natural-language terms it was supposed to help clarify. I suspect that this is the case with the term 'autonomy'. In philosophical discussions of moral responsibility, attention has shifted somewhat from questions of praise and blame, responsibility and lack thereof, to questions about autonomy: what it is, whether it exists, and so forth.

The emphasis on autonomy has not, I think, been a helpful development. There are at least eight distinct things we sometimes call 'autonomy', and they need to be kept apart. In discussion, we sometimes treat them as if they were all the same, or as if intuitions concerning any of them are equally relevant to the agency theorist who is trying to figure out what true autonomy consists in. The discussion in this section is meant to raise questions about the general usefulness of the concept of autonomy to our theorizing about moral responsibility—to make us wonder if moral responsibility theorists would not be better off going back to investigating praiseworthiness and blameworthiness directly, ignoring intuitions regarding autonomy.

Let us look at the various things that 'autonomy' means. One of these things is what I will call, for convenience, *agent-autonomy*. Agent-autonomy is a relationship between an agent and her motivational states that can be roughly characterized as the agent's ability to decide which of them to follow: it is a type self-control or self-government that persons usually have and that nonhuman animals do not have. This, of course, is a very broad construal of agent-autonomy—different philosophers can agree that we, unlike other animals, "govern" ourselves while having very, very different views as to what constitutes this governing and as to which parts of a person, if any, constitute the "governing" self and the "governed" self. A philosopher may think that our autonomy is a matter of our having second-order desires or that it is a matter of our having the ability to reflectively endorse actions, and so on, and my characterization of agent-autonomy is not meant to choose between these competing theories. Some idea of agent-autonomy is at least implicit in any Kantian account of moral psychology and has been at the center of the work of countless action and agency theorists of many stripes, including the early Harry Frankfurt, Gary Watson, David Velleman, Robert Noggle, Michael Bratman, and Keith Lehrer.

Occasionally, authors use 'autonomy' to mean simply 'agency', and 'autonomous action' to mean simply 'action' (or 'full-fledged action').

This is not the way I propose to use the term 'agent-autonomy'. The way I use the term, *not every theory of action is also a theory of agent-autonomy*, nor does every theory of action include a notion of agent-autonomy. Take, for example, Davidson's theory of action, according to which a movement is an action if it is caused, in a specific way, by a combination of a rationalizing desire and belief. If my glancing at my watch is caused by a desire to know the time and a belief that looking at my watch will tell me the time, it is thereby an action. This theory of action stipulates that a person's movement is her action as long as a certain relationship obtains between the movement and her mental states. It does not go further and require that some relationship obtain between *the agent* and the mental events that cause her action. For my movement to be an action, it is enough, for Davidson, that it is controlled in a certain way by mental events that happen in my brain: there is no extra sense in which the relevant *mental events* need to be controlled by or be a privileged part of *me, the agent*. All of the desires that happen in me are my desires and can, with the help of appropriate beliefs, produce actions: none of these desires are "more truly my own" than others. While Davidson does, implicitly, have a notion of self-control—after all, he talks about akratic actions vs. non-akratic actions—there is no direct way in which control over self (as opposed to control of desire and belief over movement) enters his *definition of action*. My akratic actions are irrational, but they are still actions, on Davidson's view, still my own, still performed for a reason. Thus Davidson's theory of action, is, in my terms, not a theory of agent-autonomy but a theory of action *in which agent-autonomy plays no role* (as opposed to theories of action, like Velleman's, in which it does play a role). It is also possible for a philosopher to have a theory of *agent-autonomy* that is not identical to her theory of action—that is, a theory according to which the phrase 'autonomous action' is meaningful but contains no redundancy, as 'unautonomous action' is also action. I shall say more about this possibility later in this chapter.

Next on the list is the quite distinct sense of 'autonomy' which designates the absence of various kinds of dependence on other people—autonomy as *personal efficacy*, or having the ability to get along well in the world without requiring the help of others. In this sense of 'autonomy', a person can make herself more autonomous by learning how to drive, becoming rich, becoming knowledgeable, or gaining physical strength. This sense of the word 'autonomy' should not be confused with agent-autonomy or self-control because, after all, a rich or educated agent is no more agent-autonomous than a poor or uneducated agent: agent-autonomy, like Sartrean freedom, is the kind of thing the slave in chains has just as much as her master.

Often described as lacking autonomy are those people who seem to lack not efficacy, but various kinds of *independence of mind*: servile and submissive people (Thomas Hill's Deferential Wife is a classic example) and people who blindly accept the views of their gurus or their communities. The psychological situations of these people are often undesirable, and in many cases they involve irrationality or vice. However, they are not always situations in which *agent-autonomy* is lacking. In an old Eastern European joke, a man is urged to stop obeying his wife in every matter and to start following his own free will, whereupon he replies that he *always* follows his own judgment, as freely as anyone, and it so happens that his own judgment tells him to ask his wife what to do and follow her advice. This figure of fun may be perfectly autonomous as an agent, perfectly self-controlled, even though his psychotherapist is likely to tell him that, in a different sense, he needs to increase his autonomy. The feminist who argues that women should be made more autonomous and who then cites early Frankfurt's or Bratman's definitions of autonomy, or alternately faults Frankfurt's definition of autonomy for not explaining why deferential wives are unautonmous, is most likely equivocating without noticing.

A further important notion of autonomy is the notion of *normative*, moral autonomy—the one invoked when people ask to be allowed to make their own decisions and to be free from paternalistic intervention. There are well-known Kantian arguments for a connection between moral autonomy and agent-autonomy, and there is much to be said about them (I will return to some of them later), but for the moment it will suffice to point out that the word 'autonomy' in 'respect for autonomy' cannot simply be assumed, by virtue of similar spelling, to involve agent-autonomy. To see this, consider a paradigmatic case of "autonomy violation" in the normative sense. If someone steals from you, that person violates your autonomy in the normative sense, but it is a prima facie plausible claim that you are no less an autonomous agent as a result: you are no less capable of governing your own actions than you were a moment ago. Or imagine that a doctor lies to a patient or withholds information from a patient about his condition, ignoring the fact that the patient is in the process of making an important employment decision to which his condition would be relevant. Many people would say, in this case, that the doctor made it impossible for the patient to make an autonomous decision. This is, however, not obviously the sense of 'autonomy' that autonomous-action theorists are looking for. Decisions made on incomplete or misleading data are everywhere: to hold that such decisions are deficient in autonomy would seem to make autonomy too scarce a commodity to be the basis of moral responsibility.[1]

So far we have autonomy as self-control, autonomy as material independence and as psychological independence, and normative autonomy. David Velleman, in "Identification and Identity" (forthcoming) makes an additional distinction between autonomy, which he takes to be some form of self-control (i.e., agent-autonomy), and authenticity, or being true to oneself. His distinction is driven by a reading of Frankfurt's latest view of love, caring, and volitional necessity. Until about 1987, Frankfurt's key examples of unautonomous agents were examples of people whom we would normally regard as lacking in self-control or experiencing a lack of it—recall the unwilling addict, the man who is subject to attacks of rage, and other such weak-willed people. But as of his 1988 "Rationality and the Unthinkable,"[2] Frankfurt came to insist that some people are autonomous whom we would ordinarily regard as weak-willed. For example, he talks about people who resolve reflectively to press what they believe to be the button that would facilitate the dropping of an atomic bomb but who find that they "just can't do it," and also of a man who decides to spy on his bride-to-be and finds himself forced to stop because the idea of such spying revolts him too much. These people are not paradigmatic cases of self-control, but Frankfurt sees them not as weak-willed but as constrained by their own deepest values, their volitional essences. Whatever these people may have consciously resolved, the values that stop them from dropping the bomb or snooping are truly their own—otherwise they would not have found themselves repulsed by their respective tasks. These agents are prevented from acting by what they care about—which, according to Frankfurt, makes them what they are. Velleman maintains that this is not truly a theory of autonomy but is rather a theory of authenticity, or personal identity, or the "real self."[3] Here is what Velleman says:

Even if I believed that a person had a motivational essence of this kind, I would not infer that his being governed by this essence was what made him autonomous. Being governed by such an essence might amount to authenticity, perhaps, but not autonomy. In order to see the difference, consider the paradigm case of inauthenticity, the person who manifests what D. W. Winnicott called a "False Self." This person laughs at what he thinks he is supposed to find amusing, shows concern for what he thinks he is supposed to care about, and in general conforms himself to the demands and expectations of others. The motives that his behavior is designed to simulate are motives that he doesn't genuinely have. . . . But is this person lacking in self-control, self-governance, or autonomy? To be sure, he has a problem with autonomy, but his problem is one of excess: he is overly self-controlled, overly deliberate; his grip on the reins of his behavior is too tight, not too loose. His failure to be motivated from within his true self makes him inauthentic, but it seems to result from his being all too autonomous. (Velleman forthcoming, 26–27)

Velleman draws a distinction between *authenticity*, which he takes to be the same as *being true to one's values*, and *autonomy*—self-control or self-governance. He reminds us that there are some people who have a strong measure of autonomy and are in fact known for their exemplary self-governance, but whose very self-control allows them to live out of touch with what one would be tempted to call their "real selves." We can imagine a person who, like the young E. T. A. Hoffman, represses his passion for literature due to his conviction that he should become "a respectable citizen." This person may be very autonomous, but it is natural to say that he is out of touch with his real self. On the other hand, Harry Frankfurt's agents, who surrender to "volitional necessity," may be very true to themselves, but they do not *control themselves*; it may be said that, on the contrary, *their selves control them*, as it were. This is not to suggest, by any stretch of the imagination, the romantic thesis that the autonomous and the authentic are always in conflict, but only to point out that sometimes they are and that therefore they are not one and the same.

Our talk of people being "more themselves" or less so is not all of a piece, either. Peter Strawson, in "Freedom and Resentment,"[4] discusses contexts in which we make statements such as "You must excuse her, she is not herself—she has been under stress." This is a statement about what Velleman calls 'authenticity'; the person's action is claimed to be less blameworthy because, presumably, it does not reflect her true will but only the stress she has endured. Quite different is the kind of talk in which a person reports that she experiences her feelings or desires as alien, or feels "possessed" or "violated" by them or passive toward them, like Frankfurt's enraged man[5] who feels as if his anger is an alien intruder and thus not truly his own. It is the latter kind of talk that gave birth to the idea of *external desires*, and while many accounts of external desires have been given in terms of the structure of the agent's will, the pretheoretical experience of "passivity" toward one's desires often serves as the intuition against which these accounts are measured. For example, the fact that some of us do not experience our vices as alien led Frankfurt to refine his account of externality so as to allow some unwanted traits (vices) not to be external,[6] and the fact that some thoughts are experienced as alien has led him to suggest that there are external thoughts as well as external desires—thoughts toward which we feel "passive."[7] Because autonomy is sometimes thought of as the absence of externality, its phenomenological face, the experience of passivity and alienation with respect to desires, is often thought to be relevant to autonomy.

The very idea of external desires can strike a person as rather strange. If a Victorian lady experiences her sexual desires as alien, intrusive, "not truly her own," our natural reaction is to tell her that she is wrong, that these desires are in fact her own, and that only the false, asexual self-image that she acquired with her upbringing makes her experience them as threatening to her integrity as a person. We would think that she *denies her real self*. Similarly, the man Frankfurt (1976) uses as a paradigmatic example of a person possessed by an external passion—namely, the man who feels possessed or violated by his outburst of rage—need not be the same person to whom we would be inclined to give the Strawsonian excuse of "not being himself"—he may in fact be revealing what we would call his true colors in his outbursts, however honestly he experiences his anger as "not himself." It is perfectly possible for a person to wonder what came over him while his friends tell each other that "he is very much himself today." In other words, experiences of "being possessed" are not always an indication that the desire in question is inauthentic. Nor are they always an indication of lack of agent-autonomy or self-control. Some addicts in religious twelve-step programs experience their sobriety as the will of God taking over, and their akratic, ego-dystonic falling off the wagon as a manifestation of their *willfulness*. Or consider a person who experiences herself primarily as weak-willed, spineless, lazy, and passive. When this person, because of her lack of self-control, takes a course of action or inaction she regards as utterly impermissible, she does not feel invaded or possessed at all; instead, she sadly thinks, *Here I go again. I hate myself.*[8] Imagine now that suddenly, in an emergency, our lazy person begins to act with admirable self-control. As her desires obey her reason and her actions follow her decisions for a change, she may feel, paradoxically enough, as if somebody—somebody cool and competent—has taken her over.

So far we have seen autonomy as self-control, as having power in the world, as psychological independence, as having moral rights, and as authenticity. The foregoing discussion of external desires shows that we need to introduce another figure who, until now, has been lurking in the background of our discourse of autonomy: the figure of the autonomous person as the *self-identified* person, the person with a harmonious and coherent self-image who never experiences her desires as an external threat.[9]

Also lurking at this background are concepts of what may be called *heroic autonomy*: ideals such as Spinoza's freedom, stoic *apathia* or *ataraxia*, Aristotle's life of contemplation, Freud's or Jung's ideals of the liberation that their methods were to aim at bringing, Nietzsche's ideal of the free spirit, and other states that are supposed to be desirable and only attainable by the few. Some notions of heroically autonomous persons may be related to some of the autonomies mentioned before—one may have an ideal of a heroic authenticity, a heroic self-efficacy, perfect inner harmony that leaves no room for externality, or an ideal combining all of the above. One may even imagine an Übermensch whose superhuman power consists of a truly incredible degree of agent-autonomy—a person who always follows his inner party line, always does what he reflectively endorses or what his higher-order desires tell him, and so on. However, agent-autonomy, or at least a substantial degree of it, is supposed to be the default condition of the average adult human being, not merely of the Übermensch. It is especially true that those who take agent-autonomy to be a necessary condition for moral responsibility cannot mean by 'agent-autonomy' any condition that is too much of an ideal and too little of a human reality, unless they wish to hold that very few people are morally responsible. Similarly, those who take agent-autonomy to be a necessary condition for action do not wish to imply that we rarely act. Thus, caution must be exercised when mixing intuitions about autonomy as an ideal condition and intuitions about autonomy as a property that a great majority of humans have, to a large extent, most of the time.

I have left for last one more thing that has often been associated with autonomy, and that is the ability to *respond to reasons*—reasons in general and moral reasons in particular. Autonomy has also been associated with acting for *good* reasons—that is, with acting rationally. While it is not often argued, since Kant, that autonomy is the same as rationality or reason-responsiveness,[10] intuitions about autonomy and the lack thereof are often influenced by intuitions about rationality or reason-responsiveness and the lack thereof, "rational autonomy" being a common expression and "irrational autonomy" not being one. "When we act rationally," says Elizabeth Anderson, "we act for reasons that we endorse. We do not follow blindly where our desires suggest. This is the autonomy of practical reason" (Anderson 1997, 92). On such a view, rational action is always agent-autonomous action—is always action in which the agent, whoever she is, exercises control over her desires. Acting for reasons we endorse is also many people's idea of autonomy, and acting in ways that diverge too much from what we endorse is often regarded as unautonomous. Rational and reason-responsive action is thought of as requiring deliberation or endorsement, and autonomous actions are also often regarded as the result of deliberation or endorsement. (Even some very un-Kantian thinkers connect deliberation or endorsement to autonomy. See, for example, Mele [1995], who argues that being an adequate deliberator is a necessary condition for being an autonomous agent.) Things that impair our ability to respond to reasons, such as alcohol and hypnosis, are supposed to impair our autonomy. Animals are often said not to respond to reasons, and they are often said not to be autonomous.

Identifying reason-responsiveness with agent-autonomy may seem reasonable if one thinks of acting for reasons as always being the result of agent-endorsement, or at least as accompanied by it. In the previous chapters of this book, especially in chapter 2, I argued in various ways that acting for reasons, including acting rationally, is not necessarily related to agent-endorsement or to deliberation. If this is right, it seems less obvious that intuitions about self-control and agent-endorsement belong with intuitions about rationality and responsiveness to reasons. Of course, one would still be tempted to put the label 'agent-autonomy' on reason-responsiveness if one holds that whatever moral responsibility depends upon is called 'agent-autonomy' and if one surmises, correctly, that one cannot be morally responsible unless one acts for reasons. But this is not an interesting finding about agent-autonomy itself; it is a stipulation about the term 'agent-autonomy'.

Why not use the word 'autonomy' to mean "that on which moral responsibility depends, whatever it turns out to be"? Why not say that asking if an agent is autonomous is simply the same as asking whether she is morally responsible? So far, we have seen eight meanings that 'autonomy' can have, or at least eight things that the word 'autonomy' connotes in a way that invokes some pretheoretical intuitions. Whenever we ask, "Is so-and-so autonomous?" instead of "Is so-and-so morally responsible?" we expose ourselves to a tendency to equivocate on some or all of these eight meanings of 'autonomy', or at the very least to be unduly influenced by intuitions about irrelevant senses of 'autonomy'. Thus, phrasing questions in terms of the agent's autonomy instead of in terms of her moral responsibility serves not to clarify, but to further obscure, the already difficult question of her moral responsibility. This is why it is so important to distinguish senses of 'autonomy' and to ask how each one might be related to praise- and blameworthiness, if at all.

Consider an example from Mele (1995), which illustrates how reasoning in terms of autonomy can confuse, rather than clarify, important ethical issues:[11]

> Ann is an autonomous agent and an exceptionally industrious philosopher. She puts in 12 solid hours a day, seven days a week; and she enjoys almost every minute of it. Beth, an equally talented colleague, values a great many things above philosophy, for reasons that she has refined and endorsed on the basis of careful critical reflection over many years. She identifies with and enjoys her own way of life—one which, she is confident, has a breadth, depth, and richness that long days in the office would destroy. Their dean, who shall remain nameless, wants Beth to be like Ann. Normal modes of persuasion having failed, he decides to circumvent Beth's agency. Without the knowledge of either philosopher, he hires a team of psychologists to determine what makes Ann tick and a team of new-wave brainwashers to make Beth like Ann. The psychologists decide that Ann's peculiar hierarchy of values accounts for her productivity and the brainwashers instill the same hierarchy in Beth while eradicating all competing values—via new-wave brainwashing, of course. Beth is now, in the relevant respect, a "psychological twin" of Ann. She is an industrious

philosopher. . . . When she carefully reflects on her preferences and values, Beth finds that they fully support a life dedicated to philosophical work, and she wholeheartedly embraces such a life and the collection of values that supports it. (1995, 145)

It is taken for granted that someone like Beth is not an autonomous agent—after all, Beth has been brainwashed by the Dean Who Shall Not Be Named. The reaction that we have to Beth's story, along the lines of "Surely she cannot be autonomous if her state of mind has been compelled," often serves as an intuition against which to check theories. It is used as such by proponents of historical views of autonomy such as Fischer and Ravizza, and Mele himself is eventually moved by it to include in his own theory of autonomy the condition that the agent have no "compelled" or coerced mental states which the agent did not arrange to have produced in her (187). But consider the following puzzle. There are cases of profound conversions in a person's values that are just as inexplicable to their possessors, just as uninvited, and just as irrational as Beth's conversion. For instance, many people have undergone shifts from being self-endorsed party animals to being self-endorsed industrious workers because of mysterious factors they regard as "age" or the "drying up of hormones." Other people begin to value parenthood—value, not just like—the moment their (formerly unwanted) children are born. Other people have converted from atheism to religion (or vice versa) as the result of an experience of extreme loneliness and pain, and many people's convictions, however well rationalized, are the result of irrational or a-rational factors so unconscious that the agent had about as much opportunity to subject them to reflective criticism as Beth had to scrutinize her brainwashing process. These people are not obviously as lacking in autonomy as Beth and are unlikely to be used as paradigmatic examples of lack of autonomy. And yet the only thing that distinguishes them from Beth is that their irrational conversions *are not the result of a deliberate and wrongful action by another human being*, while her conversion is the result of such an action. A person who converted from atheism to religion as an irrational reaction to pain and extreme loneliness does not strike us as particularly unautonomous, but a person who was deliberately placed in a state of pain and loneliness by a brainwasher to obtain the same result sounds considerably less autonomous. Why is that?

I cannot but suspect that this has to do with the fact that brainwashed Beth, and not the ordinary irrational convert, lacks autonomy in two very specific senses. First, she is quite obviously lacking autonomy in the sense of lacking independence of mind — in the same sense that a person who received all of her convictions from her mother is lacking in autonomy, only worse: after all, there exists another person, the dean, who has given her a substantial part of her value system. Second, it is obvious also that in the moral, normative sense, her autonomy has been violated, because she did not give her permission for the brainwashing operation. The dean violated her autonomy in the same sense that he would have violated her autonomy if he were to switch her long-distance telephone service behind her back. In these two senses, it is obvious that Beth is lacking autonomy. In other senses, it is not obvious at all that she lacks autonomy or that she lacks it more than the other converts mentioned.

Is present-day Beth autonomous in the sense of agent-autonomy or self-control? We would have to say she is — Mele himself states that she is the same as Ann in this way. She does things that she reflectively endorses and cannot be regarded as "wanton," compulsive, and so on. Similarly, present-day Beth is not lacking autonomy in the sense of being particularly irrational or particularly unresponsive to reasons. It is true that the shift in her basic worldview *was* in fact irrational, or unresponsive to reasons, but again, even very rational people have had such shifts, and that does not make their current actions less rational or less responsive to reasons. In her current actions, including staying in the office for long days, Beth may be as responsive to reasons as Ann is. One might wish to introduce a new sense of autonomy — a sense in which a person is only autonomous if all of her convictions are the result of reason-responsive processes or at the very least intentionally induced by her in a self-controlled act of self-indoctrination. But this would be a heroic notion of autonomy, of little use to the moral responsibility theorist. If one wishes to maintain that *only autonomous agents are morally responsible*, one cannot say that the relevant sense of 'autonomy' requires a history that does not include irrational and uninvited changes of outlook due to growing up, growing old, falling in love, loneliness, parenthood, hormones, Prozac, or fatigue, because this would mean that very, very few people would be morally responsible at all.

At the end of the day, the only ways in which Beth may be said to be unautonomous involve the fact that her convictions are secondhand, the fact that the dean is in the habit of violating her rights, and the fact that she is not some sort of super-rational creature who never undergoes irrational or uninvited psychological changes. Yet neither independence of mind, nor having one's rights respected, nor heroic autonomy seemed, prima facie, when considered by themselves, particularly relevant to the question of moral responsibility or lack thereof. Anyone who wishes to argue that Beth is not morally responsible for her actions would need to explain why having been irrationally influenced by an evil human being exempts from responsibility in a way that having been influenced in a similar way by some unlucky chance of a force of nature does not.

Is Beth responsible for her actions? I turn to this question later. For now, let me just point out that this is a real question (as Mele acknowledges), and intuitions run both ways, at times disturbed by personal identity concerns. One need only remember that Patty Hearst, after changing her values as a result of brainwashing, was still convicted for her crimes, to realize that the issue is complex. My point is that the word 'autonomy' obscures the complexity of the issue. It is not clear whether Beth is morally responsible. It seems obvious that in at least two senses, she is not autonomous. By substituting the question "Is Beth autonomous?" for the question "Is Beth morally responsible?," treating the questions as if they were identical, an author may prejudice the reader toward a negative answer to the question of Beth's responsibility, turning a complex question into something trivial.

In discussing moral agents, from Oliver Single to Huckleberry Finn to Hans Miklas, I have focused my attention on the question of their praiseworthiness or blameworthiness. I assumed, as most of us do, that moral praiseworthiness and blameworthiness are essentially related to moral responsibility in the minimal sense that any agent who is morally praiseworthy or blameworthy for her action is, by definition, at least somewhat morally responsible for that action. Thus, any theory that implies, for example, that Oliver Single is not morally responsible is unacceptable, for a nonresponsible agent cannot be praiseworthy, and we should be able to praise Oliver Single. I did not concern myself, however, with the question of whether any of these agents are "autonomous," and my analysis of praiseworthiness or blameworthiness did not include a concept of autonomy. I would now like to raise the question of whether there is anything that we have good reasons to call 'autonomy' which is important to moral responsibility. To be even more specific, I shall be asking if, for an action to be blameworthy or praiseworthy, it is important that it be autonomous in any of these eight senses just listed. I take it that, unless autonomy is a precondition of praiseworthiness and blameworthiness, or unless it affects praiseworthiness or blameworthiness when all else is equal, it is not important for moral responsibility in the way that it has been taken to be.

The Various Autonomies and Moral Worth

Of the eight things sometimes called "autonomy," we have already seen that for an agent to be morally praiseworthy or blameworthy for her action, she does not need to possess heroic autonomy, or there would be very few morally responsible people in the world. It is equally obvious that an agent need not be independent in the sense of having the ability to get along in the world without help from others in order to be legitimately open to praise or blame, nor need she have an "independent mind," nor need it be true that she is fortunate enough not to have her normative autonomy violated (disabled, obedient, and oppressed people have all been held praiseworthy for some actions, blameworthy for others, and rightly so). That rules out four of the things sometimes called 'autonomy' and leaves four others: self-control, reason-responsiveness, authenticity, and identification with one's actions.

Start with identification. I have argued that a sense of alienation—experiencing oneself as passive with regard to a desire—does not correlate in any essential way with lack of self-control or autonomy, but the question now is about the connection between alienation and moral responsibility, or lack thereof. It seems to me that feeling alienated from one's desire or the action it leads to need not correlate with lack of moral responsibility or with variations in praise- or blameworthiness. It is not uncommon for people who commit dramatic crimes to describe themselves as having been "outside themselves," as if "someone else were doing it," during the crime (even Raskolnikov feels as if it was not his own strength with which he was wielding the ax). Oliver Single, too, experiences himself as if he is not using the phone through which he alerts the customs officer: his hand lifts the phone for him, as if on its own. Oliver Single is obviously morally responsible for his actions, and no murderer has ever pleaded insanity simply on the ground that he experienced the deed as if his arm did it rather than he himself. As a rule, people seem to be able to feel alienated from many things—that is, to experience these things as at once belonging to them and alien. For example, a woman who used to be thinner in her youth may stand in front of the mirror and experience her fat thighs as "not really her own," as if someone has latched them onto her. This does not make the fat thighs any less her own. It only means that the fatness of her thighs conflicts with her visceral image of herself. Similarly, I see no particular reason to believe that a desire from which one feels alienated is in any sense "less one's own"—all we know is that the desire conflicts with the person's visceral self-image, which may be accurate or, as in the case of the woman, misguided.[12] At any rate, it seems natural that anyone who performs an action that strikes him as unusual or alarming or inexplicable would be likely to experience it as not his own: this should not by itself be seen to exempt him from moral responsibility or to change praise- or blameworthiness.

In chapter 3, I argued that moral blameworthiness and praiseworthiness depend on responsiveness to moral reasons, which were defined both in terms of the extent to which the morally relevant features of the situation motivate the agent and in terms of the extent to which the agent cares about the morally relevant considerations. It follows from this that both reason-responsiveness and authenticity, if depth of concern is a substantial part of authenticity, are relevant to moral praiseworthiness and blameworthiness, and hence to moral responsibility. Responsiveness to reasons is obviously important for moral responsibility, as praiseworthiness and blameworthiness depend on one's reasons for actions, and creatures not acting for reasons at all cannot be either morally praiseworthy or morally blameworthy (and if, for example, a person with Tourette's syndrome does not act for reasons when he says "Fuck!" he is also not blameworthy for any hurt caused by saying it). One is only morally blameworthy for actions, not for mere bodily movements. Responsiveness to moral reasons is particularly important. One cannot blame or praise a creature who cannot be expected to perceive the morally relevant features of situations any more than an elephant can be expected to perceive legal factors, aesthetic factors, or contexts in which a baseball player should not bunt. The parent, mentioned in chapter 3, who cannot understand the concept of paternalism is not in the same league as the elephant: after all, she can still be expected to understand such things as "harm," "doing to someone what he doesn't want done," and "my room." On the other hand, a severely autistic person who so much lacks the ability to perceive pleasure, pain, and desire in others that he cannot perceive such things as harm and will may be exempt from moral responsibility to that extent.

As for authenticity in Velleman's sense, it comes into play in that, other things being equal, an agent's praiseworthiness varies with the depth of his moral concern, or his blameworthiness with the depth of his sinister motivation, or with the magnitude of his indifference to moral factors. In this sense, it matters not only which reasons the agent is acting for, but also how much his action, for those reasons, reflects him, reflects who he is. The same action for the same motive can be, other things being equal, less blameworthy if it is an action that does not reflect the agent's level of moral concern ("He was just under duress"). This may be the case because the concern was not as great (or weak) as it seemed to be given the action, or because it essentially conflicts with other deep attitudes the agent has without being supported by any, or both.

This brings us, finally, to the question of whether agent-autonomy, or self-control, is relevant to moral responsibility. In the remaining part of this chapter I will argue that *agent-autonomy* is not as important to moral responsibility as is generally assumed. More specifically, I will argue against the claim that we are directly morally responsible only for agent-autonomous actions. I will not argue against the very idea of agent-autonomy, or the claim that it exists or that it is an interesting phenomenon, nor do I wish to claim that it has nothing to do with moral responsibility. I will argue, however, against the claim that only agent-autonomous action is blameworthy or praiseworthy. In the course of this discussion, I shall attempt to point out how this particular claim may be confused with other, similar claims with which I have no quarrel.

Agent-Autonomous Action, Human Action Par Excellence, and Action *Simpliciter*

The first question that must be faced is whether action is possible in the absence of agent-autonomy. As I made clear above, theories of action *need* not have any particular connection to theories of agent-autonomy.

However, there are those who have suggested that the best theory of action is one according to which all actions are the product of self-control or self-governance — of agent-autonomy, in other words. If this were correct, then agent-autonomy would be a necessary condition for any action, and so, *a fortiori*, a necessary condition for any action that is praise- or blameworthy. But what, exactly, would move someone to say that without agent-autonomy one does not really act?

Recall Velleman's tale, quoted in chapter 1. Talking to a friend, I find myself, to my surprise and dismay, raising my voice in anger despite attempts to control myself and be polite. As my friend leaves, it becomes clear to me that my shouting has been motivated by an unconscious resolution to sever the friendship. In this story, I shout at my friend, we may say, "in spite of myself." I violate my own "party line" with regard to what I should do. It is not the case merely that I feel alienated from my shouting; it is also reasonable to assume that there is a sense in which I have failed in self-control. After the outburst, I may reproach myself for my behavior like a leader reproaching inner underlings. Even if I come to see my having parted from my friend as a course of action that had much to recommend it, I may still feel that it would have been better if my decision to part from my friend had gone "through channels" — if my "self-government" had made the decision to withdraw from the friendship, as opposed to being forced into the decision by some inner outlaw organization. It would surely have enabled me to be more polite to my friend and conduct my affairs with him more honorably. If autonomy is self-control or self-rule, it is reasonable to say that in my shouting, I was not acting autonomously.

Is it, however, reasonable to claim that I was not *acting* at all or that *I* was not acting at all? Finding the answer to this question, so critical to moral responsibility, is complicated by a rather confusing fact about common language: the fact that expressions such as "X isn't Y" and "X isn't really Y" are often used figuratively, for good dramatic effect, as in the claims "Budweiser is not beer," "Calgary is not a city," and "Philosophy is not a real job." These are all meaningful statements, but they are quite different from "Orange juice is not beer," "Mount Everest isn't a city," and "Being a smartass is not a real job." If we feel inclined to say that my shouting was not an action or that it was my resentment acting, not me, it is important to pin down whether we are inclined to say it literally or figuratively (and if the latter, what exactly we mean by saying it).

The difficulties that the aforementioned flexibility of language poses to the moral psychologist are pointed out by Velleman in his critique of Frankfurt. In "Identification and Identity" (forthcoming), Velleman cites the following paragraph from Frankfurt:

> Thus Agamemnon at Aulis is destroyed by an inescapable conflict between two equally defining elements of his own nature: his love for his daughter and his being devoted to the welfare of his men. When he is forced to sacrifice one of these, he is thereby able to betray himself. Rarely, if ever, do tragedies of this sort have sequels. Since the volitional unity of the tragic hero has been irreparably ruptured, there is a sense in which the person he had been no longer exists. Hence, there can be no continuation of his story. (Frankfurt 1999, 139)

Velleman thinks Frankfurt is ill-served by such dramatic expressions as "destroyed" and "no longer exists." He reminds us of the fact that Agamemnon's tragedy of Aulis *does* have a sequel—or several sequels. Recall the legend of Agamemnon. After the sacrifice of his daughter, which enables him and his men to sail to Troy, Agamemnon continues to lead the Greeks in the Trojan war. The war is notoriously long and eventful, and Agamemnon's actions and personality provide much of the drama in the *Iliad*. Having obtained victory, he returns home, where he is killed by his wife in revenge for sacrificing their daughter. This legend, Velleman aptly remarks, would lose a lot of its narrative force if we assumed that the man who made the painful decision to sacrifice his daughter did not continue to exist so as to bear the consequences of his decision. Life, history, and fiction provide no shortage of examples of persons who continue to exist after betraying their loves or themselves. To maintain otherwise would be overly romantic and philosophically costly.

In defense of Frankfurt, one could point out that Frankfurt only says that there is *a sense* in which the tragic hero ceases to exist after his tragic choice, allowing for other senses in which he keeps existing. Even allowing for that, however, I think Velleman has a legitimate complaint. Does Frankfurt merely want to tell us that death (and subsequent replacement by a different person) is often a good *metaphor* for the state of having betrayed the object of a true love, as such an act changes the traitor deeply? This would be a fairly convincing claim. But if Frankfurt wishes to defend a literal claim about personal identity according to which different loves make you a different person, he is making a claim that needs more support and defense, as it runs against such basic intuitions as "It is reasonable to punish Agamemnon for killing his daughter," "Agamemnon has genuine memories of the days before he killed his daughter," and so on. Frankfurt sounds sometimes as though he is making the metaphorical claim and sometimes as though he is making the literal claim, and the ambiguity causes the former claim to seem more dramatic and the latter claim more believable. At the very least, Velleman has pointed out a certain lapse of clarity on Frankfurt's part.

A similar failure of clarity, however, threatens any philosopher who relies on relatively complex and loose parts of natural language in her hunt for intuitive justification. A theorist of authenticity like Frankfurt must decide how seriously and how literally to take such expressions as "The conflict has destroyed her" or "The person I was in the sixties no longer exists." Quite similarly, a theorist of autonomy, such as Velleman himself, must decide how seriously and how literally to take such expressions as "it is my resentment speaking, not I." We all understand what Velleman means when he says that I, the agent, did not truly participate in my resentful shouting at my friend, just as we all understand what Le Carré means when he says of Oliver that his arm reaches for the phone, unbidden. Both Velleman's and Le Carré's expressions are meaningful, and the fact that we sometimes use such expressions seems to have significance. But Le Carré, we feel, could easily have written "his arm reached for the phone *as if* unbidden" without loss of content. When Velleman (or early Frankfurt, Watson, etc.) tells us that my incontinent, consciously unplanned yelling at my friend was *not an action*, or not *my* action, that it was a behavior in which *I did not participate*, how serious is he? After all, just as Frankfurt must face the literal-minded critic who reminds him that Agamemnon had an eventful life after being "destroyed" in Aulis, Velleman must face the literal-minded critic who asks, "If she didn't yell at her friend, who did?"

Natural language seems to be ambiguous on the matter. While "It was my resentment, not I" is a natural expression, it would also be natural for my friend, faced with my increasingly irritable behavior, to look into my eyes and say "*You* have already decided, haven't you? Maybe you don't know it, but you have already decided to break off our friendship all the same." We can imagine a case in which my resentment against my friend is justified—brought about, in a manner suggestive of chapter 2, by an accumulation of evidence of my friend's badness that is reason enough to leave him—and I walk away from the meeting thinking "*I should have done it ages ago.*" The plausibility of such talk hints that expressions like "It was my resentment, not I" are mere metaphor. Nonetheless, it is not to be denied that natural language does recognize a difference between the case of my incontinent, ego-dystonic yelling at my friend and the case in which Bertrand Wooster, as part of an elaborate scheme, deliberately plans to hurl insults at Lord Worplesdon in order to make him angry. The question is whether this genuine difference amounts to my yelling *not being my action.*

Alfred Mele (forthcoming) answers that it does not. According to Mele, my incontinent and consciously unplanned yelling at my friend is definitely an action, and I certainly participate in it. What, then, of those who say that it is not an action or that I do not participate in it? These, according to Mele, are akin to people from New York or Paris who say that Calgary is not a city: they have a good point, but they overstate it. Their point is that my yelling at my friend lacks some of the features of the ideal or paradigmatic human action. My raising of my voice at my friend is not, Mele agrees, an instance of human agency par excellence. Mele points out that most nonphilosophers agree that lions, tigers, and bears act: they hunt, they play, they train their young, and these are all actions. What animals cannot do, and humans only do some of the time, is perform human actions par excellence: actions that involve things like deliberation, self-control, and the like. It seems to follow from what Mele says that he sees many accounts of what I have called 'agent-autonomy' or 'self-control' as accounts of human action par excellence, though their authors sometimes mistake them for accounts of action *simpliciter*. The question of what makes something a human action par excellence is deemed interesting and important by Mele, and he develops a view of his own on the subject, but he insists that the question of human agency par excellence is not to be confused with the familiar problem of action theory—the question of what makes something an action.

Velleman, on the other hand, holds the opposite view. My yelling at my friend, which Mele would call an unconscious action, is not my action at all, according to Velleman's "The Possibility of Practical Reason" (2000). True, my yelling at my friend is not analogous to the jerking of an arm during an epileptic fit; as it is intentional, the result "in the right way" of my beliefs, desires, and even unconscious decisions, it deserves to be called a *behavior* and an *activity*. An action, however, it is not. The question of autonomy for Velleman is simply the advanced part of the familiar problem of action theory: once we determine the difference between a man raising an arm and an epileptic fit raising that man's arm, we need to determine the difference between a man raising an arm and a man's anger raising that man's arm, or our definition of action will be incomplete. (Nonhuman animals, it seems, have only activities.)

Velleman's introduction of the term 'activity' raises a very important question. Velleman and Mele agree that there is a real difference between some behaviors, such as my yelling at my friend, and others, such as Bertrand Wooster's planned yelling at Lord Worplesdon. Quite possibly, Velleman and Mele even agree as to which types of behavior to place on which side of the divide—except that for Velleman the divide is between action and activity, while for Mele the divide is between human action par excellence and action *simpliciter*. Why would it matter which of their positions one takes? A philosopher may take those of our doings which we normally call "actions" and divide them into "actions" and "activities," or she may divide them into "ordinary actions" and "human actions par excellence," or, if she wishes, she may divide our doings into "nonautonomous actions" and "autonomous actions." She may say that animals only perform "activities," or she may say that animals can perform actions, but only humans perform *autonomous* actions. What is at stake, really?

The philosophical stakes are in fact quite high, and they have to do with the view, shared by Mele and Velleman, as well as many others, that we are only (directly) morally responsible for our actions. Some discussions of what I call agent-autonomy or self-control are ambiguous in a way that neither Velleman's nor Mele's are—ambiguous as to whether they mean "autonomous action" to be, strictly speaking, the only kind of action there is, or if they mean "autonomous action" to be a special species of action which they attempt to distinguish from other kinds of action, a sort of human action par excellence. In other words, they are ambiguous as to whether we are only responsible for what we do autonomously.

My own inclination is in the direction of Mele's position. We may distinguish between actions in general and human actions par excellence, but this distinction does not correspond to a distinction between movements in general and the subset of movements for which we are directly praise- or blameworthy. We are directly praise- or blameworthy for *all* our actions, whether they exemplify our distinctive powers of agent-autonomy—of self-control, self-government—or not. In defending this position, I would like to be clear that I do not argue against all autonomy theorists, but only against those who believe *that people are only directly morally responsible for autonomous actions*. I shall not argue with those who merely accept the weaker claim that only persons are morally responsible and autonomy is an important part of being a person.[13] And clearly, I have no intention of criticizing the theorist who, by calling my yelling at a friend "unautonomous," only means to say that my yelling or Oliver's defection are not instances of human agency par excellence and cites as evidence the fact that both of them are ego-dystonic or involve unconsciousness. The intelligibility of expressions such as "it was my resentment speaking" makes *this* an easy proposition to accept. Moreover, I agree that if this theorist attempts to define what it is that makes those actions different from others, what constitutes things like ego-syntonicity, self-control, and the first-person perspective, she is doing significant and difficult work that is essential to our understanding of the human mind. The only critical conclusion I derive with regard to this theorist would be similar to Mele's: she should make it clear that her project is *not* fundamentally about moral responsibility.

One argument against the standard claim that we are only responsible for autonomous actions has already been made in chapter 3. Whether one defines the controlling element in self-control as one's reflection, one's second-order desires, one's value judgments, one's plans, one's decision never to regard a certain desire as a reason for action, or the like, one can always imagine Huckleberry Finn's helping Jim (or for that matter, Oliver Single's leaving organized crime) slipping from the definition's grasp and ending up lacking in autonomy. In fact, it would probably be a problem for a theory of autonomy if it *did* define Huckleberry Finn's good deed as autonomous; he is simply not one's idea of self-control (nor is Oliver Single). Huckleberry's action, with its accompanying sense of "I just couldn't do it," is not what one would call an instance of self-control, nor is Huckleberry a person who does what he endorses (he does not endorse his action even *after* he commits it). If one is simply trying to define self-control, not to define 'autonomy' in the sense of whatever it is that moral responsibility depends on, and certainly not to define authenticity, stretching one's definition of autonomy to include the very *akratic* Huckleberry Finn would be hazardous to its meaningfulness. Huckleberry, then, appears to lack autonomy and yet be praiseworthy. Prima facie, this suggests that agent-autonomy is not necessary for legitimate direct ascription of praiseworthiness.

As was also previously pointed out (also in chapter 3), one could hold that what Huckleberry Finn is praiseworthy for is something like a character-building exercise performed in the past that resulted in his having wonderful moral intuitions, but this is quite implausible. Huckleberry simply never engages in character-building exercises. While the claim that what Huckleberry Finn is praiseworthy for must be some character-building action in the past looks clearly implausible, its implausibility only highlights the implausibility of the symmetrical yet much more plausible-sounding claim that is often made causally about blame. The question of one's blameworthiness for one's nonautonomous actions has not yet been addressed by this work. Let us see what to make of it.

Blame and Autonomy

Anyone who takes autonomy to be a necessary condition for moral responsibility needs to—and generally attempts to—account for the fact that prima facie, we blame a lot of people for many, many unautonomous actions. For example, people who have extramarital affairs sometimes do so under circumstances rendering their acts unautonomous on most accounts. They couldn't help it; they acted on a desire that they would not take as a reason for action, a desire that conflicts with their plans and projects, a desire that they believe upon reflection they should never follow; the Devil made them do it, and so on. Yet, as autonomy theorists would agree, this does not exculpate any cheater. Similarly, actions resulting from severe, akratic, ego-dystonic procrastination, the sort that makes the actor feel desperately helpless, are usually still actions for which the agent is held responsible; actions resulting from severely akratic rage (or even from an unconscious desire to sever a relationship with a friend) are also often blameworthy, and advocates of agent-autonomy-based theorists of responsibility do not deny that they are.

Which is why, to account for the blameworthiness of these individuals, they hold that while one is only *directly* responsible for autonomous actions, many unautonomous actions are the result of a failure to exercise self-control, for which the agent is directly blameworthy. While the akratic, ego-dystonic adulterer, procrastinator, or rage-driven person may act in a way that is not autonomous, she can still be held blameworthy for her lack of self-control in the matter. She is, after all, an autonomous agent and thus can be expected to control her sexual desires, laziness, or anger better than she does. Thus, for example, Watson (1977) argues that people who give in to strong but basically normal human desires are to blame for their failure to develop proper self-control. He suggests that this is the reason we do not find fault with people who are motivated by severe chemical addiction or extreme mental distortions—"proper" self-control would not have been enough to prevent them from acting the way they did or could not be expected from them. Velleman makes a similar claim about my indirect moral responsibility for my outburst of anger at my friend.

It is not altogether clear how to interpret this view. What is it the agent is directly blameworthy for? It could be said that the agent is guilty of permitting the unautonomous action to happen. Yet in what sense has the agent permitted the unautonomous action to happen? It cannot be that the agent has somehow *granted* the relevant desire permission to lead her to action because we need to maintain a difference between autonomous and unautonomous actions (or "activities"), and the whole idea of an unautonomous action is, presumably, that it happens despite the absence of such permission (generally, a surrender to a temptation to play instead of working is an autonomous action if preceded by the inner words "Oh, what the hell, you only live once"). What, then, is the agent directly to blame for? It seems that she must be to blame for an autonomous, self-controlled course of action that preceded the unautonomous deed and made the agent susceptible, in the critical moment, to the temptation or rage trigger, while a different course of action would have enabled her to resist it (or even be unmoved by it). Past autonomous action(s) or inaction(s) must be what the agent is blameworthy for, and not simply the fact that the agent is weak-willed. After all, if only autonomous actions are blameworthy, the very fact that somebody is weak-willed is not something she can be blamed for any more than she can be blamed directly for the fact that she has ego-dystonic sexual desires or is given to excessive rage. If agents are only to blame for autonomous actions, they cannot be blamed directly for character flaws, "weak will-power" included. They can, however, be blamed for autonomously doing something that created or enhanced the flaws.

So if we wish to argue that moral responsibility depends upon autonomy, we must hold that the unautonomous offender who is blameworthy must be blameworthy for some past autonomous course of action. But what course of action would it be? To be sure, there are many occasions on which we do hold people blameworthy for failing, as it were, to check their mental brakes. Thus, the person whose wrong action is the result of procrastination may be blameworthy for deciding not to delete the games folder from her workplace computer, for choosing not to buy a day planner, or for taking on too many responsibilities. Perhaps the akratic adulterer should have refused that invitation for dinner while her husband was out of town, and perhaps the angry person, before his outburst of rage, should have taken a deep breath and counted to ten. But this is not all that we blame such agents for. After all, it is sometimes the case that no such "count to ten" measures were available to the agent. It is also sometimes the case that the agent could not be expected to know of such measures in time to use them (perhaps powerful aggressive urges have never appeared in you before, and when such an urge appears it takes you so much by surprise that you do not notice it until you have already done some damage). There are also many cases in which the agent has already taken such measures and in general tried as hard as she could not to follow her "outlaw" desires, but her attempts and measures fail. In many such cases, we still blame the unautonomous adulterer, procrastinator, or angry aggressor. A defender of the moral importance of agent-autonomy might suggest here that the autonomous course of action for which the agent is blameworthy must be some sort of failure that resulted in her current state of weakness of will—resulted in the fact that "as hard as she can" is not very hard. Thus, the agent must be blameworthy for having failed to perform some character-building action or having performed some character-eroding actions.

The main problem I see with this view (ignoring for a moment Huckleberry Finn and the case of praise) has to do with the fact that it necessitates a picture of human life in which we have an incredible amount of control over our characters—an amount of control that most parents only wish they could have over the development of their children's characters. How often do we knowingly and autonomously perform character-building or character-ruining actions? To be sure, occasionally we do. Mr. Tucker, a character in Christopher Buckley's satire *The White House Mess*, knows that entering the White House is likely to turn him into what he calls "a jerk." Yet he chooses to enter the White House, and his moral character is in fact harmed in the ways in which he predicted it would be. From Balzac's Restiniaque to Trudeau's Michael Doonesbury, in fact, fictional characters can be found who make clear-eyed decisions in favor of courses of action that will gain them money or power but will harm their integrity or compassion. I do not doubt such decisions occur in real life. But instances of such decisions are rare—considerably rarer than the autonomy-oriented moral psychologist needs. Successful, intentional, character-building or character-ruining actions performed by a person upon himself are even more rare than successful New Year's resolutions. It is the exception, rather than the rule, that a person's character is substantially self-made, which is why a self-made good character is so impressive in the first place.[14] In most cases in which people lack self-control with respect to some of their desires (or when they simply do not have strong enough "good" desires to combat the "bad" ones), this weakness is primarily the result of early upbringing and all sorts of unintentional psychological reinforcement. To the extent that agents contribute to the creation of their weaknesses by means of their autonomous actions, it is usually not in the straightforward way Tucker influenced his own character. Tucker knew about the way his White House job was likely to affect his character. Quite often, however, an agent chooses her character-shaping actions without any knowledge of the way in which they are likely to shape her character, and does so in circumstances in which she could hardly be expected to know better (any parent trying to shape the character of a child knows how hard it is to make such predictions). One is not usually in a position to predict whether her choice of a job, school, marriage partner, friends, or area of domicile will affect her moral character in some fashion, not to mention the many choices that initially appear too insignificant to fuss about. Thus, it is quite unlikely that what unautonomous blameworthy agents are to blame for is *always and only* some autonomous failure of character-building.

Furthermore, there is a type of case in which there are independent reasons to believe that we are blameworthy by virtue of *having* a certain desire or motivational factor to the extent that we act on it at all, not by virtue of failing to control it. These are cases in which we act on sinister motives, where our reasons for action are in essential, rather than accidental, conflict with morality. If we assume that run-of-the-mill sexual desire is a morally neutral motivation, having no essential conflict with morality, and that there exist a few extreme circumstances under which most people would be moved strongly by sexual desire regardless of their motivational makeup, cases where we cannot say "if you *cared more about your marriage* you would not have done it," we may want to say that under these circumstances, an akratic adulterer's blame has to do not with his adultery itself but only with having led himself into the tempting situation in the first place or his otherwise failing to take steps to circumvent his sexual desire. This could be the case because there is nothing morally bad about simply having sexual desires, and because *ex hypothesi* even a person who cares about morality (or her spouse) very much would be tempted to commit adultery under said circumstances. Things are different, however, if our unautonomous sinner acts not from a neutral desire but out of a malevolent motive, such as sadism or racial hatred. In those cases, one is blameworthy for being at all motivated by such desires, and one can be condemned for having racist or sadistic desires in the first place. As Hursthouse (1997) hints, the confession "I am utterly disgusted by Asian people but I am doing my best to control it" is a far cry better than a wholehearted hatred of Asians, but it is also a far cry from the confession of a morally perfect agent; the ego-dystonic racist who thinks that there is a lot to improve in her moral character, that she could be a better person, is after all correct in her assessment: she *could* be a better person than she is. I take it that similar things are true for the person who says that there are few things he relishes more than the suffering of his fellow human beings, but, realizing that this is wrong, he is trying to control the desire. If an agent acts on that desire, even if it can be shown that he has done everything in his power to curb it, he is still blameworthy for his sadistic deeds.

One may object to this view by pointing out that heaping blame upon people such as the visceral racist or the visceral sadist makes the world a worse place, in that obsession with the blameworthiness of one's visceral feelings and desires tends to backfire.[15] As long as a person knows that her visceral or unconscious desires are bad, the argument may proceed, tormenting her and sanctioning her for desires that she does not endorse may only lead to counterproductive results—no one, after all, can cope with being blamed or blaming herself all the time, and encouraging people to dwell too much on the badness of their visceral desires is likely to result in the activation of psychological defenses that are likely to interfere with them mending their ways. I mention this objection because I am at least partially in agreement with those who fear that attacking an involuntary sinner who already is trying to mend her ways is often a counterproductive—and therefore the wrong—thing to do. It may even be cruel, or at least unforgiving in a context where the virtuous agent would be forgiving. I would like to point out, however, that my view to the effect that the inadvertent sinner is blameworthy does not imply that punishing her—even verbally—is a good thing for society to do or that obsessing over her sins is the right thing for her to do. As I argued in chapter 3, to say that one is blame*worthy* is not to say that one *should be blamed*. Blame may be warranted without an expression of blame being morally desirable.

The Huckleberry Finn objection, the fact that it does not stand to reason that we make or are obligated to make many intentional character-building actions, and the day-to-day practice of holding people blameworthy for having essentially bad attitudes all militate against the view that blame for unautonomous action is really blame for past autonomous action. If this view cannot be held, then it is implausible that agents are morally responsible for agent-autonomous actions only.

Moral Worth, Autonomy, and Brute Beasts

If it is not true that agents are morally responsible only for agent-autonomous actions, is there any other sense in which it could be true that agent-autonomy is required for moral responsibility? For such a sense to exist, it would have to be true that the blameworthiness or praiseworthiness of an unautonomous action is somehow intimately related not to some autonomous action the agent performed or failed to perform, but to the fact that the creature who performed the action is *potentially* autonomous.

In a trivial sense, such a connection does exist. Of all the creatures known to us, we only attribute moral responsibility to humans. Agent-autonomy seems to require a measure of reflective ability that only humans seem to have, and thus, as emphasized by autonomy theorists since Kant, it is the identifying characteristic that distinguishes us from other animals. The set of all moral agents and the set of all potentially agent-autonomous creatures appears to be identical. One is a moral agent if and only if one is an agent-autonomous creature—though it is worth mentioning that at this point, we only know it is true in extension, the way we know that one is a creature with kidneys if and only if one is also a creature with a heart. Admittedly, the extensional equivalence does not look like a pure coincidence. It may appear that if we deny that some notion of agent-autonomy is needed to ground moral responsibility, we imply that nonhuman animals can be morally praiseworthy or blameworthy. This would be a counterintuitive conclusion, even if one is ready to grant that animals have moral rights.

Due to the popularity of agency theory and the flourishing of Kantian ethics, it is often assumed that if one asks what the moral difference is between us and other animals, only one answer is possible: the autonomy of practical reason. It is interesting to see what answers appeared to those who had not yet heard of the autonomy of practical reason. In *Leviathan*, Hobbes succinctly gives the following view:

> To make covenants with brute beasts is impossible, because not understanding our speech, they understand not, nor accept of any translation of right, nor can translate any right to another: and without mutual acceptation, there is no covenant.

Hobbes is only speaking here of contracts.[16] But if we wish to explain why animals are not moral subjects, it may be an interesting exercise to see how far such commonsense facts as animals not understanding our speech can take us before we have reached anything quite as complicated as agent-autonomy. The exasperating fact that your cat cannot understand your request that she be careful in handling your computer keyboard from now on counts for a lot when you remind yourself that she is exempt from moral responsibility for knocking it off the table again. Now let us expand the Hobbesian notion of "not understanding our speech" and speak simply about things that animals, given their intellectual capacities, do not understand. Let us again consider a situation in which we are tempted to blame a nonhuman animal but think better of it. April, a child, discovers that the family dog destroyed her dinosaur-shaped toy. She becomes angry; "But it's *my favorite dinosaur!*" she screams. We may well imagine a parent explaining to her, "He's only a dog, darling. He does not understand that it's your favorite dinosaur." The dog does not understand *mine*, *favorite*, or *dinosaur*, not even in the murky, visceral way a small child does. Similarly, the dog's mind presumably cannot grasp—nor can it track, the way even unsophisticated people can—such things as increasing utility, respecting persons, or even friendship. As Hobbes hints, even if some protoversions of these notions exist in the animal's mind, these are not concepts that it can sophisticatedly apply to humans. Thus, even if this animal can act for reasons, to some extent, it cannot respond to *moral reasons*, even though it may occasionally come close. In the previous chapter, I maintained the view that moral praiseworthiness and blameworthiness are judgments of responsiveness to moral reasons, and to judge a dog vicious for not responding to moral reasons would be similar to judging a dog a philistine for not being able to appreciate Mahler. Dwelling on this banal list of things that dogs cannot understand shows us that finding an explanation as to why animals are not moral subjects does not require any appeal to autonomy.

One may argue, of course, that the dog's lack of autonomy is somehow part of the cause for the dog's lack of understanding of concepts such as property and its inability to track moral reasons. This, however, is unnecessary speculation. After all, dogs are also incapable of high aesthetic appreciation, and they cannot appreciate the wisdom of a quarterback's decisions when they watch football, either. We do not feel any particular need to say that a dog's failure to appreciate Beethoven or to judge Michigan's offensive line has to do with its lack of autonomy; and our tendency not to fault dogs for not responding to moral reasons is quite analogous to our tendency not to judge them critically as aesthetic philistines or as bad judges of football games. What I do not wish to deny is that the inability of dogs to respond to some of these features of reality has to do not only with brain capacity *simpliciter* but also with their inability to think abstractly or reflect. While I insisted, in chapter 2, that rapidly acting athletes, such as a football player executing a brilliant last-minute pass, are acting for reasons and are doing so without deliberation, I never denied that their nondeliberative inferences are based on some beliefs about the games they play and their rules, things that can only be learned with some aid from specifically human higher faculties—not the least of them, as Hobbes would remark, the ability to take verbal instruction, which presumes the ability to think in words—to reflect and deliberate.

Despite the many differences between Huckleberry Finn and the fast-acting athlete, something similar seems to apply to him: his nondeliberative inferences are made against a background of beliefs that can only be formed in specifically human ways. While no one taught him that black people are persons worthy of respect, and no deliberation is involved in his coming to respect them, his coming to respect them is only possible *against the background of other beliefs*, such as the belief that friends should be helped, the belief that property should be respected, and so on—beliefs that can only be formed with some help from one's own or other people's reflection. Moral education is more complicated than learning to play football, but it seems clear that some ability to deliberate and some ability for abstract thinking are necessary for it. If this is true, then I have to admit that the connection between moral accountability and autonomy is stronger than simply the fact that only creatures with high-capacity brains can have either—it is also true that both are unique to reflective creatures. Thus, while autonomy is *not* a constitutive feature of moral responsibility, having some kinds of *higher faculties* or reflective abilities may be a psychological precondition for being responsive to moral reasons, and since by most accounts agent-autonomy is about using reflective abilities to decide how to act, it is very likely that having such higher faculties and reflective abilities is also a psychological precondition for autonomy. Even having ego-dystonic and ego-syntonic states of mind—having an "ego" in the first place—seems to require reflection. That said, the fact that moral responsiveness and moral responsibility share a psychological precondition with agent-autonomy—that they are both part of the "package" of being a reflective and very intelligent creature—does not by itself reopen the case for treating autonomy as grounding moral responsibility, and certainly not for treating autonomous actions as the only actions for which we are responsible.

I do not claim to have a full account of what it is that makes humans separate from other animals and makes them capable of having moral norms and notions, any more than we know the answer to related questions, such as what it would take to make an intelligent computer. It may be, however, that the fascinating investigation into that which makes us separate could gain from the thought that there could be various different factors involved, as opposed to one property called "autonomy."

FIVE

BLAME, AUTONOMY, AND PROBLEM CASES

With chapter 4, the significance of questions about autonomy has become much clearer, and a general argument has been given that one central sense of 'autonomy'—that of agent-autonomy—is not a necessary condition for direct moral praise- and blameworthiness. But this general argument is likely to meet with a chorus of objections deriving from particular examples. Accordingly, in this chapter I deal with a number of particular examples which appear to show that agent-autonomy is a necessary condition for moral praise- or blameworthiness. In each case, I attempt to understand the details of the example and to show that commonsensical conclusions about praise and blame can be held, and accounted for, if one follows the theory of moral worth developed in chapter 3.

Moral Worth, Autonomy, and Deviant Mental Conditions

Consider cases of people whom we ordinarily regard as having reduced agent-autonomy. These include people whose mental states are medicalized by today's American culture, with widely varying degrees of plausibility, such as addicts, compulsives, depressed and deluded people, as well as sufferers from identified neurological disorders (dementia,

Tourette's syndrome). What can a theory that has no use for agent-autonomy say about these cases? Consider also cases in which we exempt people from moral responsibility because they seem too crazy, or because they are very drunk or otherwise drugged. On an account of moral worth that does not ground moral responsibility in agent-autonomy, why would these conditions be exempting or excusing?

There are far too many sorts of mental deviance, and far too many empirical theories of the nature of each form of deviance, for me to cover every case. A few will be touched on, however, and the pattern of the responses will be clear. In general, the excusing quality of various forms of insanity and strange mental conditions has to do not with the way they affect agent-autonomy, but rather more generally with the way they affect *responsiveness to moral reasons,* or *good and ill will.* In attributing moral worth we normally rely on certain assumptions as to what a person's behavior shows about her responsiveness to moral reasons—what it implies about the agent's good or ill will. We assume, for example, that the person who stands in front of us in broad daylight realizes that there is a person in front of her (and therefore if she suddenly steps on our feet, her action shows ill will or indifference). Or we assume that some good actions are so easy to perform that anyone who fails to do them displays great moral indifference. People with strange mental conditions defy such assumptions: they may, for example, be incapable of seeing that there is a person in front of them, and actions that would be easy for normal people may be hard for them. As a result of this, we are forced to revise our standard assumptions as to the amount of good or ill will implied by their actions, and so to revise our assessment of their moral worth.

To give an easy example: Dr. P., Oliver Sacks's primary case in *The Man Who Mistook His Wife for a Hat,* commits the incredible blunder for which he became famous because of a very rare neurological condition that impairs the way his brain processes visual data (it is in the nature of the disorder that the victim is not aware of his affliction). Needless to say, his irrationality is *un*motivated—it is not the case that he sees his wife as an object out of disdain for her or as a convenient rationalization for pushing her around. Suppose that, as a result of mistaking his wife for a hat, Dr. P. grasps his wife in a way that obviously pains her. We normally assume that a person who handles another person so as to cause her physical pain shows, at the very least, a lack of responsiveness to moral reasons—he should care more about his wife's well-being, we think. But because of his strange brain condition, Dr. P.'s action speaks no ill of him; it betrays neither ill will nor the absence of good will on his part, but simply the fact that he wanted to grab his hat.

In other actions performed by people with strange minds, we may only partially adjust our view of the agent's will. For example, if we discover that someone is severely depressed we reasonably assume that her neglect of minor duties does not demonstrate as much ill will or absence of good will as it would usually demonstrate, and her performance of certain other duties demonstrates more good will than usual. I say that for some neglectful actions, depressives would be *less* blameworthy, because if one is depressed, one need not be unusually indifferent to moral reasons in order to neglect one's moral duties; but one may still be blameworthy for neglecting duties, with the share of one's blame increasing the worse one's behavior is. For example, we assume that even for a depressed person, neglecting a duty to feed a child requires unusual indifference to moral reasons. Many other strange mental conditions are like that: we tend to see them as a sort of weight that makes certain actions require less ill will and some actions require more good will than is required under normal circumstances.

In addition, there are weird mental states that do not constitute any sort of excuse or exemption. The sort of person popularly referred to as a "homicidal maniac" is often regarded as both crazy (we may want to study his brain or his childhood or both) and evil. The same goes for the "morally insane" Svidrigialov in *Crime and Punishment*: the oddness of this man's mind simply *is* the total absence of moral responsiveness.

In these cases no reference needs to be made to agent-autonomy. However, one may object there are other cases in which it is hard not to mention autonomy. Take the cases of ADHD (attention deficit/hyperactivity disorder) and Tourette's syndrome. In *Adult ADD*[1] we are told of John, an ADHD sufferer, who saw a house from the window of his car, admired it, and, within a few minutes, bought it. John and his wife were not, at the time, looking for a house or thinking of moving: the house was purchased impulsively, like candy next to the grocery store cash register. It seems to be the case that with some people who are diagnosed with the disorder, ADHD simply *is* a lack of agent-autonomy. John, by and large, has ordinary beliefs and ordinary desires; the difference between him and other people seems to be that he does, to an astonishing degree, go wherever impulses take him. Someone else, upon seeing the house, might also like it and feel a craving to live in it, but someone else would subject his craving to deliberation and would simply pass by; for John, the craving immediately triggered action, even though he had been told many times to think before he acts. Admittedly, the normal person's response to the craving for the house would often result not from deliberation *simpliciter*, but from an emotional response that "checks" the craving and leads, if the craving is strong enough, to doubt and deliberation. Still, John is missing something that can reasonably be called a form of self-control or agent-autonomy—the ability to stop before acting, think, and implement his practical conclusion—and this seems to be exactly why his wife did not take him to be very blameworthy for buying the house, though she insisted that he see a psychiatrist. Similarly, some contemporary research suggests that sufferers of Tourette's syndrome often act on urges that many people have, except that most people easily, almost unthinkingly, stifle these urges, while something in the Touretter's brain makes this stifling impossible or even counterproductive. Thus, many people have the urge to straighten asymmetrical objects or to utter obscenities in oppressively respectable situations, but for most of us there are mechanisms that keep these urges in check—usually before the thought even crosses our conscious minds. The Touretter seems to have damage to these mechanisms. Again, the Touretter who says "Fuckers!" in the middle of a family gathering is excused, or almost excused, from blame, and the excusing nature of Tourette's—unlike the more complex and debated excusing nature of addiction—seems to have to do strictly with a lack of self-control or autonomy.

How does my view treat these cases? While the absence of autonomy matters to the way we view these cases, it only matters *indirectly*. What matters directly is that John's buying of the house and the Touretter's obscenities do not indicate ill will or moral indifference on their parts. The fact that they are lacking ordinary human self-control or autonomy is simply a factor in their psychologies which explains *why* their bad actions do not indicate ill will on their parts. Consider Dr. P. again. The fact that Dr. P. is disposed to mistake his wife for a hat—*honestly* mistake her for one—explains why his carelessly grasping his wife does not show ill will on his part. Similarly, the fact that John has no self-control matters because, given his organic deficiency of self-control, his buying of the house does not entail indifference to his duties to the family budget, and the fact that someone has Tourette's syndrome entails that his public cursing implies no more disrespect than most of us display while sitting still. The cases of John and the Tourettic person do not show that moral accountability has something *special* to do with agent-autonomy any more than the case of Dr. P. shows that moral accountability has something special to do with the processing of optic signals. A defect in self-control, a defect in the visual processing centers, and the fact that one is extremely poor all act as excusing conditions, to the extent that they do, in exactly the same way—through the way they alter our assumptions that a person who did something bad did it out of a marked lack of moral concern.

A Story of Three Kleptomaniacs

Similar things are true for those staple examples of agent-autonomy theory, the unwilling drug addict and the unwilling kleptomaniac. Whatever our opinion of what drug addiction and kleptomania are like—and of course, we do not yet know much about these conditions—the fact that we do not blame the stereotypical kleptomaniac or the stereotypical drug addict for the immoral acts they might commit which follow from the kleptomania or addiction can be explained by the fact that their actions do not carry the usual implications regarding their moral concern. Better still, such considerations help us explain the situations in which we are *not sure* how much blame is attributable to a certain compulsive person, because some facts about her mind or brain are not clear to us. Such considerations also explain why cases in which different people show the same symptoms for different reasons raise different intuitions about their degrees of blameworthiness. At times, the moral concern approach accounts for differences in intuition that exclusive focus on agent-autonomy tends to blur. For this purpose, let us look at three cases of kleptomania—two imagined and one drawn from life.

Here are the two imagined cases of kleptomania:

> *Lana*, who is generally a morally virtuous person and has a responsible approach to life, experiences a recurrent strong urge to steal and occasionally succumbs to it. The urge appears suddenly whenever she is in a shopping mall, and concerns items that she regards as cheap and that

she neither wanted before seeing nor wants after having stolen. Once she is out of the mall, the urge to steal is gone, and if she has stolen an item, she feels guilty and secretly returns it. She does not understand the urge. She feels most comfortable when she is far away from shopping malls, but her life is such that it is hard to avoid them completely. Desperate and embarrassed, she regards the urge as a problem and consults a therapist.

Greg also has an urge to steal, to which he sometimes, but not always, yields. He also feels that when he steals, he does so "in spite of himself." Like Lana, his crimes are petty and are not motivated by need. Greg does not doubt for a moment that stealing is wrong. He is embarrassed by his crimes and resolves many times never to commit them again, which works for short periods. In addition, he fears the consequences of getting caught. "I shouldn't keep doing this," he tells himself honestly. "This is wrong." He tries to change. But he when he recalls the last time he successfully managed to steal a fashion item from a prestigious store he can't help smiling a little, the way a parent may secretly smile at a child's mischief even as he punishes it. He smiles when he remembers how foolish the respectable-looking customers looked to him as he operated behind their backs—he has always somewhat resented respectable people and is fairly uncomfortable with having become one himself. Also, he has always been attracted, in spite of himself, to adventures, risks, dares, and forbidden actions, for their own sakes. He has a history of risky business deals. His friends, who don't know about his thefts, complain that he is irresponsible and urge him to stop treating life as a mere game. He agrees but finds it hard to resist temptation, including the temptation to steal. Shoplifting, for some reason, gives him a thrill that no legitimate game can provide. "What's wrong with me," he sometimes wonders, "that I get such a kick from something so wrong?"

Both of these cases would qualify as kleptomania under *DSM IV*[2] psychiatric criteria. However, Lana strikes us as a good person with an errant urge to steal, who, if blameworthy, is much less blameworthy than the ordinary thief, while Greg, when we look at the details of his case, appears to us as a culpably callous person who has occasional pangs of conscience and is lucky enough to have a psychiatric definition to use as an excuse. Lana's urge to steal, while rather resilient, is not simply akratic but exists in open, essential conflict with the rest of her relevant attitudes, cerebral and visceral, and this explains why she always returns the goods, why she feels very distressed, and why she seeks therapy.

In her case, the assumption that her action implies moral indifference is tempered simply by the fact that the rest of her behavior and emotional life does not seem like that of a morally indifferent person. The fact that such an isolated desire nevertheless manages to motivate Lana, despite so much apparent moral concern on Lana's part, leads us to suspect that, like the Tourettic individual, she may have some sort of brain condition which does *not* consist in a strong desire to steal, but rather in a mechanism that translates weak desires into strong urges, an "impulse control disorder." If this is true, she is exempt or almost exempt from blame. If it turned out that there is no such disorder and her urge does emerge from a resilient, ill-integrated, unconscious desire to steal for some reason or another, she will be blameworthy, but considerably less so than the average akratic adulterer who claims that the Devil got into him, as the depth of Lana's errant desire is offset by the depth of her essentially conflicting attitudes, such as her commitment to morality and sense of decency.

Things are different with Greg. Greg, in many ways, is a lot like the average akratic adulterer who claims that the Devil got into him: he has a moral concern that opposes his misdeed, but not enough such concern. Lana could throw up her hands and say, "Look, how much more concern for morality do you expect me to have?" With Greg, in contrast, it seems to be plainly true that if he cared more for morality, he would not steal, or he would steal less often. He is quite lucky to have psychiatric labels such as "kleptomania" as an excuse.[3]

Now consider a third case of kleptomania, a real case reported in Kaplan and Sadock (1991, 487). The psychiatric-textbook kleptomaniac, it seems, is a tad more complicated than the philosophy-textbook kleptomaniac:

> *Lisa*, a 20-year-old unmarried billing clerk, was referred for psychiatric evaluation by the criminal court judge. Lisa, who had previously been placed on probation by the juvenile court, was now being tried as an adult for yet another charge of theft. She had deposited cash payments made to the physician for whom she worked into her own account. Lisa was accompanied to the psychiatric interview by her mother, a well-dressed, upper-middle-class matron who provided additional (and often contradictory) information to that given by Lisa.
>
> Lisa had been charged and convicted of theft twice previously, but those offenses reflected only the times she had been caught and

her mother had not been able to successfully intervene. In fact, Lisa had been repeatedly apprehended for shoplifting and had, on several occasions, "borrowed" the credit cards of her friends and her mother, charging thousands of dollars for clothing, jewelry, food, and cosmetics. As a child and young adolescent, Lisa had frequently stolen money from her father's wallet and her mother's purse. Teachers at school had learned that if anything was missing, Lisa's desk or locker was the first place to look. When Lisa was apprehended, her mother would make plausible excuses for Lisa and then pay for whatever loss she had caused. Everyone, including Lisa, agreed that she had no need to steal. Her mother was indulgent and provided her with essentially anything she wanted.

Lisa continued, however, to steal and lie repeatedly. Lisa lied about everything: how much money her father earned, how many boyfriends were pursuing her, and how well she was doing at school. When caught stealing, she inevitably had a facile, reasonable excuse for why she had something that did not belong to her. To further complicate her story, Lisa also secretly engaged in bulimia and would, once or twice a week, binge and induce vomiting.

From a psychiatrist's viewpoint, the information about Lisa's family was very revealing. Her father was described as a successful surgeon whose compulsive gambling had led to repeated financial crises that had been kept secret from the children. He was also described by the mother as a "pathological liar" who skillfully covered his absences (to see his bookie) from the hospital and office with plausible excuses. His father (Lisa's paternal grandfather) was an alcoholic, as was Lisa's maternal grandfather.

The overriding dynamic in Lisa's family was the attention provided to her older brother, a professional baseball player. Almost all family activities throughout her childhood had centered around this brother and his athletic accomplishments. Her father may not have been able to take time from his busy medical practice to attend Lisa's piano recitals, but he never missed a Little League or high school baseball game. Lisa's mother doted on the handsome young man, indulged him, and rescued him from his minor misdemeanors.

Lisa was referred for psychological testing that revealed mild dyslexia, in addition to the underlying depression and mixed impulse control disorder (kleptomania, bulimia, and compulsive lying) diagnosed by the psychiatrist. Once again, with the behind-the-scenes interventions of her mother, the judge ordered a brief period of probation and mandated psychiatric treatment. Lisa canceled the first appointment that was scheduled after the end of her probation and never returned for further treatment.

Lisa is a befuddling case, because the facts are ambiguous in many ways. Does Lisa have a nonpsychological "impulse control disorder," which "runs in the family"? But then what to make of the story of her family's withholding of love, which suggests that she is motivated by something simpler—a desire to draw attention and support from her mother? In the latter case, she would seem at least somewhat blameworthy, as many people have such a strong desire but do not resort to doing immoral things to satisfy it, indicating that lack of normal moral concern is a relevant factor in her motivation ("We haven't had the love that every child ought to get" sounds like a feeble excuse in the mouths of the juvenile delinquents in *West Side Story*). But does her deep depression, as diagnosed by the psychiatrist, not reduce the amount of blame she deserves? Does she have an impulse control disorder *and* a desire for attention? What part does each of them play? Does the fact that she discontinued psychiatric treatment show a lack of moral concern on her part? Or does it show that treatment failed to work?

"Brief parole with psychiatric treatment" seems to more or less cover the confused intuitions we have about this case. It seems clear that Lisa, like Greg, is too blameworthy *not* to be considered legally responsible. Her case brings to mind once again Kant's remark that the courts should not be concerned with the subtleties of human motivation. On the other hand, not taking account of her depression, her youth, and her family environment, as well as the possibility of an impulse control disorder, seems a bit heartless. She is not Robert Harris, the apparent psychopath described by Gary Watson (1987), whose parents and youth prison experience seem to have turned him into an evil, vicious, wholeheartedly murderous adult. Watson maintains, and I agree, that however much we may regret that bad experiences turned a sweet child into a murderous adult, Harris the adult is a bad person and is as blameworthy as can be for his cold-blooded murders, which he wholeheartedly endorsed and desired. But Lisa is not like that. Her motives need not be sinister and there is no evidence that her lack of moral concern is bad enough to amount to utter heartlessness. One wants to give her the opportunity to see a therapist on the chance that her moral concern may motivate her to change, given better support than that available from her parents. I do not have anything less ambiguous to say about Lisa, but then any theory of moral worth or of moral responsibility that would imply that Lisa's case is easily decided, given the scant facts we know about her and the scant knowledge we have about the human brain, has a problem; it implies, falsely, that life is simpler than it is. Any theory that divides our bad actions too neatly into the clearly blameworthy and the clearly nonblameworthy (whether or not it conceives this dichotomy in terms of autonomy) risks becoming such an oversimplifying theory.[4]

Whatever one's theory of moral responsibility or moral worth, bringing it face to face with real accounts of deviant mental and neural conditions is a worthwhile task. Let me give one last example of the effects of such confrontation. Heroin withdrawal has been described by one sufferer in the following words:

> I felt a cold burn over the whole surface of my body as though the skin was one solid hive. It seemed like ants were crawling around under the skin.

> It is possible to detach yourself from most pain . . . so that the pain is experienced as neutral excitation. From junk [heroin] sickness there seems to be no escape.

> I was too weak to get out of bed. I could not lie still. In junk sickness, any conceivable line of action or inaction seems intolerable. A man might die simply because he could not stand to stay in his body. (Burroughs 1977, 97)

"Unwilling" heroin addiction is usually an excusing condition. Unwilling tobacco addiction is not. Why is it so? It is surprising that compatibilist attempts to explain why the heroin addict has such a good excuse focus on all kinds of things about the structure of his will but rarely consider the agony of heroin withdrawal. People are generally excused if they have performed an immoral action under the threat of real physical torture: one does not need to be particularly indifferent to morality in order to succumb to torture. The heroin addict, even if he really wants to stop, is confronted by what amounts to torture; and the power of the desire to avoid torment is sufficient to explain why it is so hard for him to stop.[5] The cigarette addict, on the other hand, faces rather less severe withdrawal symptoms. Thus many cigarette addicts stop smoking, and thus they do not have such a compelling excusing condition—even if it turned out that, in the technical sense of creating an impulse to consume it again, tobacco were just as addictive as heroin. It is exactly the relevance of such facts that is often obscured by focus on the 'autonomy' of the addict.

Freudian Slips and Lapses of Reason: Is Unconsciousness Ever an Excuse?

In the above discussion of deviant mental conditions, an account of moral worth that is based on quality of will rather than agent-autonomy is defended. Much of what I have said about deviant mental conditions holds true for relatively ordinary people who act in a deviant way in a particular set of circumstances: good will, ill will, and moral indifference add up to moral worth, and to the extent that an action is attributable to nonrational factors that have no bearing on the agent's level of good will, ill will, or moral indifference, the blame or praise warranted is less. Serious mental conditions involve such factors, but with more ordinary people, things like stress, fatigue, the affects of mild drugs, or the fact that one has just caught his wife in bed with a lover all serve to reduce the amount of praise and blame earned.

More complicated, or so it may seem, are the roles of unconsciousness and inattention as reducers of praise and blame. To Velleman (2000) we owe thanks for putting into philosophical circulation Freud's remarkable story of the broken inkstand. Freud testifies that he is not a clumsy man and that his spatial skills are generally quite good, and then he tells us the following tale:

> My inkstand is made out of a flat piece of Untersberg marble which is hollowed out to receive the glass inkpot; and the inkpot has a cover with a knob made of the same stone. Behind this inkstand there is a ring of bronze statuettes and terra cotta figures. I sat down at the desk to write, and then moved the hand that was holding the pen-holder forward in a remarkably clumsy way, sweeping on to the floor the inkpot cover which was lying on the desk at the time.
>
> The explanation was not hard to find. Some hours before, my sister had been in the room to inspect some new acquisitions. She admired them very much, and then remarked: "Your writing table looks really attractive now; only the inkstand doesn't match. You must get a nicer one." I went out with my sister and did not return for some hours.

But when I did I carried out, so it seems, the execution of the condemned inkstand. Did I perhaps conclude from my sister's remark that
she intended to make me a present of a nicer inkstand on the next fes-
tive occasion, and did I smash the unlovely old one so as to force her to
carry out the intention she had hinted at? If that is so, my sweeping
movement was only apparently clumsy; in reality it was exceedingly
adroit and well-directed, and understood how to avoid damaging any
of the more precious objects that stood around. (Freud 1965, 217–218)

Velleman thinks Freud's destruction of the inkstand is not an action.
On my account, it is an action, an action performed for a reason, albeit
unconsciously. Is Freud blameworthy for knocking down his inkstand?
Obviously, he is not *very* blameworthy.[6] First of all, all he does is destroy
a small piece of his own property. His misdeed is a minor misdeed—the
sort of thing that some charming mischief-maker in a novel could do and
invoke nothing but an indulgent shake of the head from the reader.
Freud's sister could afford the inkstand and probably intended to buy her
brother a present of a similar value at some point in any case. The motive
for the misdeed, too, does not involve grand vice: just the petty selfishness of someone—who, we know, was not always financially comfortable—who wants a nicer inkstand and does not want to get one himself.
There is no doubt, however, that Freud would have been more blameworthy had he destroyed the inkstand consciously, knowing full well that
his purpose was to manipulate his sister. Why is that?

When a person pays attention to what she does, she makes it more
likely (though does not guarantee) that more of her beliefs and desires
that are relevant to the matter—conscious and otherwise—will come
into play and motivate her (see the last section of chapter 2). Imagine
that John walks to a coffee shop, but he is absorbed with thinking about
the Dow Jones average and so he really does not pay attention to his
walking or where he is going. John has a lot of beliefs and desires that are
relevant to his walk, and some of them obviously motivate him even
though he pays no attention to them: for example, when he jaywalks
across a major road, he does it for a reason. Still, if he only paid more attention to what he was doing, his deep desire to stay alive and his long-
standing belief that the road over which he jaywalks is absurdly dangerous would have motivated him much more powerfully, and he would
have waited a few more minutes before crossing instead of performing a
reckless feat of jaywalking. Now imagine that John picks up your pen

and puts it in his pocket, and he does so because he wants a pen. He does not, however, notice that he is doing it, as he is absorbed in his heated conversation with you about the Dow Jones average. It may be that John has just as much concern as anyone for other people's property rights, that he has the belief that the pen is your property, and that if he only paid attention to what he was doing with his hands, this belief and this concern would have motivated him and he would not have taken your pen. If all of this is true of John, then he is less blameworthy for taking your pen than he would be otherwise, because the fact that his moral concern did not prevent him from stealing your pen is partially attributable to his being distracted—not to moral indifference. If, on the other hand, it were true of John that even if he were not distracted, he would have stolen your pen, then the fact that in this particular instance he stole it unconsciously does not provide him with an excuse (such would have been the case if John was a pickpocket whose hands sometimes "thought more quickly" than he did).

To go back to our original question: why would a conscious ink-stand-execution be more blameworthy than an unconscious one? If Freud were to hatch a conscious plot to knock down his inkstand in order to manipulate his sister, his relevant moral concerns would have gotten ample chance to nip the plot in the bud. A Freud who manages to consciously knock down his inkstand is a Freud proving himself lacking in moral concern more than a Freud who pays no attention at all to his action or the motives that led to it.

The sort of action we call a "Freudian slip" often deserves very little praise[7] or blame. The excuse in such cases generally attributes one's deed to one's unconscious in either of two senses: first, as above, in the sense that it would not have happened with conscious attention, and second, in the sense that we feel that the best of us, if we were distracted, could have done something similar, because we all harbor, to the same harmless extent, the sort of petty motives involved in your average slip: jealousy, inappropriate sexual desires, futile wishes, and so on. Naturally, some unconscious actions are much more serious affairs, in the sense that it takes marked ill will or marked lack of good will to perform them, even unconsciously. The story Freud cites of a skilled circus performer who "accidentally" kills her jealous husband by bungling, with a precision reminiscent of Freud's execution of his inkstand, a key action in their performance, is a case in point (Freud 1965, 245). Her action cannot be written off to her being distracted, because she is perfectly capable of performing her trick under distracting conditions and only marked lack of good will makes her susceptible to distraction. She is very blameworthy, though she would have been more so if she had been able to perform the same deed consciously. Then again, there are unconscious actions that are the result of motivational constellations that would have produced them even if the agent had been conscious of his intentions, and in these cases, unconsciousness is no excuse, and the word "slip" is not easily applied to the action.

An account of moral worth that is not autonomy-based need not deny, then, that consciousness has a role in the assignment of praise and blame, and that there are many cases where, other things being equal, a conscious act speaks well or ill of the agent more than an unconscious act. It can do so without denying that unconscious acts can be very praiseworthy or blameworthy indeed.

Hypnotists, Brainwashing Experts, and Brain Surgeons

Having dealt with questions regarding animals and people with deviant minds, let me look at one more celebrated type of case which is often mentioned in connection with autonomy and moral responsibility—the case of the person operating under the influence of a nefarious neurosurgeon or hypnotist, who instills in him a bad desire. In response to early Frankfurtian theories, for example, it is often said that a hypnotist or nefarious neurosurgeon may take over a person's higher-order attitudes just as easily as her lower-order attitudes, and so a person may be Frankfurt-autonomous and still be a slave to the hypnotist. This objection relies on the intuitive appeal of the hypnotized person as a paradigmatic case of deficient autonomy—and as a paradigmatic case of a person who is not morally responsible for her action. Faced with my line of argument, one is likely to ask the following question: what, except the lack of autonomy, explains the fact that a person who acts on an artificially induced desire is not morally responsible? Unlike the Tourettic individual, the hypnotized agent in whom a bad desire has been instilled is, by definition, acting on ill will, and so only his lack of autonomy appears to explain the moral slack he is given. In response to this question I would like first to argue that it is fairly problematic to regard a person as lacking *agent*-autonomy for the sole reason that she has been hypnotized or surgically modified, and second I would like to offer a preliminary view of the praise- and blameworthiness of these agents without appealing to *agent-autonomy*.

Before I proceed with my arguments, it is worth mentioning that real-life hypnosis, as far as it is understood at all, does not seem to be the straightforward method of *desire-induction* that philosophers imagine it to be. Sometimes it seems to be more similar to one of its more popular images—a method for causing the hypnotic subject to find herself performing certain actions despite not having desires to do them, because the hypnotist has found a way to command the person's body while bypassing the usual channels of desire. At other times it resembles yet another popular image: the hypnotist inducing an association in the mind of the subject—say, between pizza and worms—that results, unsurprisingly, in the agent forming a desire (say, to avoid pizza). Another thing hypnosis, like sleepiness, may do is loosen a person's inhibitions or weaken her ability to reason, thus making it easier to encourage her to perform certain actions given desires she already has. This sort of situation, unlike the monstrous desire-induction of philosophical science fiction, is not very different from other deviant mental conditions that are not human-made, conditions in which standard assumptions about the kind and depth of motivation needed to motivate an action no longer apply. The excuses we make for the hypnotized subject may very well be based, like the excuses given to other deviant people, on the feeling that he is not, after all, acting on a bad desire or at least that he is not acting on a strong bad desire. In subsequent paragraphs, therefore, I shall discuss, not real-life hypnosis, nor any other technique of causing people to act strangely by means other than desire-induction. I will discuss only science-fictional desire-induction—the sort of case, for instance, in which an evil neuroscientist, Dr. Nefarious, installs in Hapless Patient's brain a desire to kill the Canadian Minister of Sports and Recreation, either alone or with desires and beliefs to match, and as a result HP, who until yesterday had never heard of such a minister, commits the crime. In some versions of the story, he commits it akratically, and in others he endorses it and takes it for his very own.

People like Dr. Nefarious's Hapless Patient have been touted as paradigmatic unautonomous agents. HP is, however, a strange choice for that role, and perhaps a dangerous one for the agent-autonomy project. I do not mean to say that he is not a proper test case for the purpose of evaluating compatibilist and incompatibilist approaches to moral responsibility, where he has already done some important jobs. He is not, however, an unproblematic test case for theories of agent-autonomy, because however unfree he may seem in other ways, he need not lack agent-autonomy. His Appetite need not be opposed to his Reason, his first-order desires need not oppose his second-order desires or whatnot, because we can always imagine that Dr. Nefarious has tampered with the agent's "higher" or "privileged" attitudes—the governing bodies in his self-rule. To suggest that agent-autonomy theory needs to exclude the hypnotist is to risk turning the agent-autonomy project on its head. Why, then, is it commonly assumed that HP is a paradigmatic unautonomous agent? Much of the intuitive appeal of the idea that there is no one less autonomous than the victim of the magic hypnotist or neurosurgeon derives not from the appeal of the concept of agent-autonomy—self-control, as opposed to being passively dragged along by one's desires—but rather from the appeal of the concept of autonomy as *psychological independence from others* (or as a general term for "freedom").

As free thinkers, we tend to recoil at the thought of one individual being too much, and too exclusively, under the influence of another person. We feel scorn or compassion for the wife who always does what her husband tells her, the subservient disciple of the guru, and so on. We tend to attribute to these people a lack of autonomy, but as I pointed out earlier in this chapter, what they lack is autonomy in the sense of independence from others, not agent-autonomy. Like the man in the Russian joke, they may very well follow their own will, which tells them to follow others. The frightening thing about Dr. Nefarious and her ilk is that they deprive their Hapless Patients of their psychological independence to an extreme degree. Hapless Patient is at the mercy of Dr. Nefarious and so is, in a sense, a paradigmatic slave—which does not by itself make someone a paradigm of absent *agent*-autonomy. If we ignore the fact that HP lacks independence-autonomy, what additional reasons might we have to think of him as lacking *agent-autonomy*? Only the fact that his artificially induced desire, or belief-desire complex, is formed irrationally and not in response to reasons. But we have been down this road before. If we were to hold that agents who act on irrationally formed desires or decisions lack autonomy, we would have to pay a high price. It would mean, for instance, that a person's decision to vote Republican is not autonomous if it is a result of a fallacy or if it is unconsciously driven by wishful thinking or habit, or that a writer's decision to write a sad story is not autonomous if a gray day or a migraine or a lack of iron in his diet forced his hand. If we allow our own physical and brute-psychological nature to be an enemy of our autonomy, we reach a view that only a Kantian metaphysics postulating a mysterious coexistence of a noumenal and phenomenal self can accommodate. The price of calling HP 'unautonomous'—the price of holding that anyone who has gained or lost beliefs and desires acts irrationally or a-rationally is unautonomous—is practically to admit that being human excludes being autonomous. It also involves all of the trouble incurred in extending the meaning of 'autonomy' to include rationality.

What, then, of the moral worth of HP's actions? I think there are three kinds of scenarios which need discussion. In one sort of scenario, the "Patty Hearst scenario," Dr. Nefarious creates a bad person out of HP, and HP is like a born-again Robert Harris, a "born-again" case of bad constitutive moral luck. In this sort of scenario, HP is fully blameworthy for bad deeds done after Dr. Nefarious's intervention. In other scenarios, Dr. Nefarious creates in HP something similar to a compulsion, or a very unwilling addiction, and HP deserves little or no blame. In yet a third kind of scenario, puzzles about personal identity make it very hard to figure out the assignment of blame.

How does Dr. Nefarious make HP commit the murder? The standard story is that she instills an irresistible desire in him. But desires are only irresistible or resistible given the motivational structure of the specific agent involved. For most people under most circumstances, the desire to avoid death is quite close to irresistible, and still this desire is resistible to a devoted soldier, a suicide bomber, a person extremely attracted to danger, or a very sad person. For many people, the desire to chat on the Internet is relatively easy to resist, but to a person who is extremely lonely, chatting on the Internet can become so irresistible that it can become something very similar to frightening physical addiction, and just as destructive. Heroin addiction is very powerful, but people have succeeded in quitting, and there are even a few rare reports of people who managed be "moderate heroin users."[8] A universally irresistible desire would be a desire that is irresistible within any human motivational structure under all circumstances. Presumably, the desire to avoid some extreme forms of torture is such a desire, but I suspect few others are. Usually, when we talk about irresistible desires, the irresistibility is of some more qualified kind.

So Dr. Nefarious, in order to make HP commit the murder, not only has to instill a desire in HP to kill the Canadian Minister of Sports and Recreation, but she also has to make the desire irresistible to him. Many of the methods available to her involve *turning HP into a murderer* (albeit a strange one). For example, Dr. Nefarious may instill in HP an intrinsic desire to kill the Canadian minister that is much stronger then all his other desires, and in that way irresistible to him. This would be turning HP into the equivalent of a person who hates another so much that he can't stand the thought of his existing, and would—akratically or otherwise—forfeit the satisfaction of all of his other desires in order to kill him (a sort of fanatic with a particularly strange cause). Or she may give him a desire to kill the minister that is fairly strong but change the rest of his personality in such a way that the desire would be completely unopposed. In both cases, HP currently has the psychology of a bad or blameworthy person, except that he acquired that psychology in a strange way.

If this view sounds strange, consider the case of Patty Hearst—perhaps as close as reality gets to the story of Dr. Nefarious. Brainwashed by her captors, Hearst joined their terrorist organization and was eventually convicted for her crimes despite the fact of her nonrational change in motivations. Note that it matters very little to our judgment if she has indeed been brainwashed deliberately or if she just converted, irrationally, due to the duress she was under (the "Stockholm Syndrome"). In either case, a drastic change in her belief-desire set happened irrationally and rather quickly, and in either case the person who stood before the court seems to have been a wholehearted terrorist who was blameworthy for her actions, not an innocent woman acting under great duress. Stress may cause people to act out of character, but it may also truly *change their characters*, and this is what seems to have happened in the case of Hearst.

Now, just as in the discussion of HP's *agent-autonomy*, one is distracted by the fact that he is dependent on Dr. Nefarious, so in discussing HP's moral responsibility one faces the following distracting factor—that *Dr. Nefarious* obviously *is* blameworthy for turning HP murderous, and thus in an indirect way for causing the murder. Similarly, if Hearst's captors intentionally made a terrorist out of her, they are also blameworthy for making her so. Dr. Nefarious and the terrorists are analogous in this way to Robert Harris's parents, as discussed in the previous section. One can also be distracted by the fact that HP's desire to kill the Canadian minister and Hearst's political convictions were acquired very nonrationally; but then the desire to have sex is also acquired nonrationally, and people who act on it, if they do something wrong, are still blameworthy. I have argued above that if we treat nonrational personality changes as excluding subsequent autonomy, too few people are autonomous. Similarly, if we exempt from blame any murderer or terrorist whose convictions or character were acquired irrationally, we would exempt too many murderers and terrorists.

But turning HP into a murderer is only one way to give him an irresistible desire to kill the Canadian minister. Dr. Nefarious might, instead, turn him into a person with a (very) deviant mental condition. She might induce false beliefs in him that would make the murder a reasonable thing to perform—for example, a coherent delusion that the minister is about to take over Canada and become a dictator. She can craft a nonpsychological, neurological condition in which the thought of not killing the minister will induce very severe physical pain in poor HP—a caricature of drug addiction. In these cases, HP will surely be much less blameworthy, if at all. Or she may turn him into a caricature of impulse control disorder. Imagine that you wake one morning with a desire to murder the Canadian Minister of Sports and Recreation, and nothing else has changed in your brain. If you are anything like me, you will find yourself with a desire radically lacking in integration. That is, your desire will be so essentially opposed to the rest of your attitudes, including your deepest ideas and concerns, that it would make the offending desires of the most unwilling heroin addict or kleptomaniac look positively wholehearted. This is the state we often imagine postoperation HP to be in. But how can a desire so ridiculously opposed by any other part of the patient's mind motivate him to murder? Either Dr. Nefarious has made the desire ridiculously deep, in which case she has turned him into a murderer, after all, or she gave him a neurological impulse control disorder that ruins the ordinary relations between the depth of desire and motivational power, making him an extreme caricature of Tourette's or kleptomania or ADHD, a person in whom a desire of ordinary depth results, due to some brain mishap, in a ridiculously strong urge that cannot be subdued even by the fact that the rest of HP's psyche, including his deepest concerns, opposes it. In such a scenario, HP merits very little blame, simply because his action manifests very little ill will or lack of good will.

I have looked at two kinds of scenarios—HP is changed into a murderer, or a more sophisticated trick is played upon him.[9] But perhaps much of our tendency to look at HP as exempt from blame comes from our response to a third kind of scenario: HP is changed into a murderer, *and then changed back.* Imagine that HP, an ordinary person, is changed into a murderer by Dr. Nefarious. After he kills the Canadian minister, Dr. Nefarious has no use for him, and she allows him to revert to his previous, morally average personality. Later, his lawyer cites Dr. Nefarious's medical operation as his defense. Am I going to argue that no such defense is available to him? No. I only wish to argue that the defense genuinely available to HP is a very extreme, very decisive variant of the defense available to a good person who committed a crime fifty years ago, long before he found Jesus and underwent tremendous positive changes in personality: "My client is a completely different man now." Part of the eerie nature of the Dr. Nefarious story is that it involves creating, in a manner of minutes, deep changes in a person that normally take decades to form. In the case of the person who committed a crime fifty years ago and who makes a very convincing argument for being a very different person now, we often are grabbed by the intuition that it would be futile to disturb the life of a nice person because of a distant previous self for which he has presumably already punished himself with deep remorse. The case of Dr. Nefarious is admittedly more complicated. As we imagine Dr. Nefarious to have unlimited powers to change HP's brain to fit her plans, the case of the changed and rechanged HP raises hard questions of *personal identity* that seldom, if ever, arise in real life. Should we punish Dr. Jekyll for the actions of Mr. Hyde? The question of whether we should blame HP for the actions of the modified HP is the same question, perhaps posed even more sharply, because some of the more romantic interpretations of Stevenson's story are ruled out (that is, HP Hyde did *not* spring out of HP Jekyll's own suppressed desires but was arbitrarily created by Dr. Nefarious). Whether we should blame HP Jekyll for HP Hyde's action is a hard question, and the air surrounding it is not exactly thick with reliable intuitions. I take it that a case involving puzzles about personal identity should not be used as a test case for theories about moral responsibility.

Concern, Autonomy, and
Constitutive Moral Luck

The preceding sections have argued that, in spite of appearances to the contrary, it is possible to deal with familiar problem cases without theoretical assistance from the notion of autonomy. A quality-of-will-based theory, such as the one presented in this work, can make all the fine moral discriminations that need to be made without giving special moral significance to self-control. Yet I have no doubt that philosophers accustomed to thinking about these problem cases in terms of autonomy will have, at the least, lingering doubts. Can autonomy, in the sense of agent-autonomy, of self-control, really be ignored in a theory of moral worth? This section will consider one possible source of these lingering doubts and do its best to dispel them.

My suspicion is that autonomy-based views of moral praise- and blameworthiness may be particularly attractive to those who wish to deny or minimize the role of *constitutive moral luck*[10] in moral life. The idea of constitutive moral luck is the idea that luck, in the form of incidental historical facts about your upbringing, genetic makeup, and incidental life events, can make a person morally worse or morally better, and that a person can be blameworthy or praiseworthy for actions performed out of a motive to whose existence luck has contributed. For example, a person who akratically shouts at his friend may later curse his early upbringing for having given him a bad temper and wish he had better luck with his parentage.

The sense that it is unfair to blame a person for something that is the result of luck can lead a philosopher to develop an incompatibilist approach to moral responsibility, according to which either an action is not causally determined or it is not truly morally blameworthy: however bad your luck, you "had the choice," in some libertarian sense, to yell or not. A philosopher who is committed to the view that actions are causally determined but still wishes to deny or minimize constitutive moral luck may find attractive the view that we are only responsible for agent-autonomous actions, where "autonomous" is interpreted in compatibilist rather than libertarian terms. Thus, without resorting to libertarianism, the autonomist may hold that you are not blameworthy for your outburst of "bad temper," but only for not having exercised control over your bad temper. This produces a sense in which "you had a choice" whether to yell or not that is not contra-causal. This is not to say that autonomy-based views of moral responsibility attempt, successfully or unsuccessfully, to deny the existence of constitutive moral luck, but only to suggest that the sense that there is something wrong with constitutive moral luck is one reason one can find an autonomy-based account of blameworthiness attractive and a concern- or quality-of-will-based account of moral blameworthiness unattractive. Those who find the possibility of constitutive moral luck a worry find that this is a worry that quality-of-will-based accounts of praise- and blameworthiness raise, much more than autonomy-based accounts do. Let me discuss the extent to which my account entails the existence of constitutive moral luck.

When Gary Watson (1987) argues that Strawson's view of praise and blame should lead us to hold that Robert Harris is blameworthy, he provides an argument according to which a quality-of-will-based account of blameworthiness should commit itself to the existence of some constitutive moral luck. Robert Harris, a real-life criminal described by Watson, is the quintessential cold-blooded murderer, who seems to actively, wholeheartedly rejoice in the suffering of his fellow human beings. This human monster, regarded as such even by his fellow death-row inmates, seems to be a product of a grotesquely horrible childhood: his parents were relentless in their physical violence and emotional hostility toward him from the day of his birth, he was subjected to further cruelty at a correctional school, and almost no one, it seems, showed him the affection he needed in his formative years. As a result, a person developed with no concern whatsoever, conscious or otherwise, for his fellow human beings or their moral codes.

Harris is all ill will and no good will, he acts for sinister reasons, and he is utterly unresponsive to moral reasons. Thus, for reasons described by Watson in detail, an ill-will-based account of blameworthiness must hold that he is blameworthy. We can feel sorry for the child who was tormented by his parents, and we can feel sorry for him, among other reasons, because his parents *turned him into a bad person*.[11] The adult, however, already *is* a bad person—a thoroughly bad one. Naturally, he is not to blame for creating his bad character (in a way that Mr. Tucker may be partially to blame for creating his bad character by choosing to run for office). Harris's *parents* (and the penal system) are blameworthy for creating his bad character, but that need not reduce from the blame he deserves for the murders he committed; there is enough blame to go around, one could say. A virtuous person may rightly thank her parents for "instilling a sense of duty" in her, but she is still praiseworthy for her dutiful actions, even as her parents are praiseworthy for instilling a sense of duty in her. Similarly, Harris's parents are blameworthy for creating a monster, but once created, Harris is a monster and blameworthy for actions that he performed out of monstrous motives.[12]

To admit that Harris is blameworthy is to admit that some constitutive moral luck exists. Watson's (and my) view of Harris has many supporters. It also has many detractors, who find the idea of constitutive moral luck objectionable. Before attending to this issue, however, I would like to point out that my account of blameworthiness and praiseworthiness entails less constitutive moral luck than one might first suspect. This is because the person whose parents gave him something to which he refers as his "bad temper" is not always a person whose parents gave him genuine ill will or absence of good will, and the person who has an "angelic temper" is not always genuinely virtuous. If a person's "bad temper" is the result of a blood-pressure problem, constant arthritis, or depression (which in some sufferers expresses itself in anger rather than sadness), my account holds that it is unfair to blame him as much as someone else who does not have that problem. After all, it takes more moral concern for this person to avoid the sort of behavior associated with "bad temper." If a person's angelic temper is nothing but a sort of timidity or a sort of uncritical social adaptability that happens to fall on the ground of a decent society, my account agrees that there is nothing particularly praiseworthy about her. Of all the things that genes and environment can give a person, only good will and ill will can make her a better or worse person. Other things, like introversion or an "easy-going" nature, cannot do so, even though they can occasionally can make it easier or harder to do some morally required things. They can also, of course, color one's moral reputation a great deal, but they do so unfairly, as a combined result of the immense difficulty one has in understanding other people's motives and the human tendency to label people "nice" or "not nice" on rather scant evidence.

The fact remains, however, that my account allows for "Watsonian" constitutive moral luck: upbringing, history, and perhaps genetic disposition can contribute to making someone a better or a worse person, though the factors involved are complex and cases as clear as Robert Harris's are rare.

There are many respects in which we evaluate people's cognitive and motivational dispositions, their sensitivities and sensibilities and responsiveness to different sorts of reasons. Imagine, for example, an economics professor making the judgment that a certain student is, or would make, "a bad businessperson." He has no appreciation of economic factors and no will to succeed, she explains. This assessment is not changed if I tell her about the family circumstances that practically ensured that no desire to win or appreciation of economic factors could develop in the child that became this student. "Too bad," the instructor would insist, "but now he's a bad businessperson." A similar conversation can be imagined about other judgments, such as this: "She is a complete philistine. She could not care less about art and beauty. Maybe there is a way to change that, but I have not found it." On my view, because we cannot always control our own character, moral judgments such as "She is a jerk" must sometimes be treated in the same way. I realize that some would regard this view as counterintuitive, and others would hold that if it is true, this is an unfortunate state of affairs, disturbing beyond the sort of unfairness involved in the fact that some of us will never be prudent, assertive, musical, or graceful. Why is this?

Naturally, one could say that if life is unfair with regard to morality, this is especially sad news because morality is more important than prudence, art, and so on. But I suspect that the difference between one who finds constitutive moral luck to be disturbing and one who finds it as trivial as "constitutive business luck" also has to do with a disagreement as to the nature of blame.[13] Some people take blame to be analogous to punishment or derivative from it in some way, and they treat holding someone blameworthy as analogous to holding the view that a person should be punished or should be given something that is similar to punishment—perhaps punished in our minds, if not in our courts. I take blame to be not an inner version of a social sanction or a "practice," but a belieflike attitude similar to fear or various kinds of esteem. Blame is not primarily something required or prohibited, like punishment, nor even something that can be appropriate or inappropriate, the way that a brave attitude is appropriate for a soldier. It is first and foremost *warranted* or *unwarranted*, the way that my fear of getting a flu shot is warranted only if flu shots are dangerous to me and my admiration for Primo Levi's writing is only warranted if he is in fact a great writer. To hold someone blameworthy is not, in itself, to hold that any course of action is appropriate in regard to him, but rather to hold that a certain attitude toward him is epistemically rational: there was ill will, there was a wrong act, thus blame is warranted. In this way, on my view, blame is analogous to holding someone to be a bad businessman or a lousy artist. On the other hand, if one thinks that holding a person blameworthy is basically holding a certain prima facie view as to *what should be done to her*, the analogy breaks down. An egalitarian may hold that everyone, smart or stupid, musical or unmusical, graceful or ungraceful, should be treated equally, because luck makes people stupid or unmusical or ungraceful. If "a bad (blameworthy) person" means "a person who should be punished," and punishment is a way of treating a person more badly than one treats others, then "Harris is bad" is not at all like "Harris is stupid." That luck made Harris stupid is just a fact or a falsehood, but if "luck made Harris bad" means that luck made Harris *a person that should be treated more badly than others*, our liberal or egalitarian intuitions are offended.

On my view, "Harris is blameworthy" does not mean or entail "Harris should be punished" any more than "Harris is a bad businessman" means or entails "Harris should be rejected from Harvard Business School." Punishment is but one way, which is often but not always morally justified or required, to deal with blameworthy people. A full account of the complex relationship between blameworthiness and punishment is out of the scope of this work. However, if one keeps in mind the separation between blameworthiness and the appropriateness of punishment, I think one will find that intuition supports the idea that Harris (and others like him) really is blameworthy.

Autonomy as the Basis for Normative Autonomy: A Few Doubts

The discussion of autonomy to this point has been mostly deflationary. The idea has not been that there is no such thing as autonomy, or that particular accounts of autonomy are false, or even that autonomy is utterly unimportant, but rather that most versions of it, especially agent-autonomy, are not as important as often assumed. Now, the spirit of this discussion is likely to invoke in some readers the following thought: perhaps agent-autonomy is not directly important to moral responsibility in the way that action theorists often assume. However, *agent-autonomy* is still a very important thing, because it grounds normative autonomy, also known as *respect for persons* or as *respect for people's autonomy*. It may not be *the same* as normative autonomy, but it is needed to ground it.

Answering this claim is, strictly speaking, off-topic for this book, which is about moral worth, and by extension moral responsibility, but not about normative autonomy. I have no intention, here, of answering all the arguments that have been made for such a connection or of refuting all the theories that imply such a connection. But, as I do accept that some sort of respect for persons is an important part of morality, I wish to insert a skeptical note about the relation of *agent-autonomy* to morality. That is, I would like to make a few arguments, not to the effect that a connection between agent-autonomy and normative autonomy does not exist, but that it does not *obviously* exist and that the impression that there is a simple connection between agent-autonomy and normative autonomy is greatly inflated by the fact that the word 'autonomy' is used for both. If there is a connection, which there may be, the connection is complicated, and the neo-Kantian who wishes to demonstrate it has at least some of the burden of proof.

I argued earlier that normative autonomy and agent-autonomy are not the same thing—if a person has stolen from me, my normative autonomy has been violated, but I am as agent-autonomous, as self-controlled, as before. I shall not repeat this argument. I have also argued that autonomy is not the only thing that sets human beings apart from other animals, though it may be related, via contingent facts about the mind's machinery, to other things that set human beings apart from animals, such as responsiveness to moral and other particularly complex sorts of reasons. A dog's incapacity to respond to such things as morality and its inability to develop artistic tastes or to judge football games, as I argued, are all of a piece. Differences between humans and animals with respect to moral accountability cannot then be assumed to follow from differences in agent-autonomy rather than differences in cognitive capacities or other differences. The same point can be made about rights: from the fact that humans have more rights than dogs (if this is a fact) and the fact that humans but not dogs are agent-autonomous, it hardly follows that dogs' inferior moral status derives from their lack of agent-autonomy.

Perhaps the impression that normative autonomy is based on agent-autonomy develops in response to the fact that individuals and states can do to children, the mentally disabled, and others lacking in agent-autonomy things that they cannot do to others possessing agent-autonomy. In particular, individuals and states are justified in treating these groups with a degree of paternalism that would be wrong if practiced on competent adults. It is beyond the scope of this book to work through the complex questions of when one is allowed to override considerations of normative autonomy in the way one treats an innocent person — questions that have given political philosophy many of its headaches — but it is unlikely that much can be gained in the quest for answers by studying agent-autonomy. Twelve-year-old children, for example, are often quite as agent-autonomous as many adults — though they are not as smart, knowledgeable, competent in achieving their goals, or the like. The fact that they do not have a right to be free of paternalistic intervention may have something to do with their rationality or ignorance, but not, it seems, with their autonomy. If one wishes to find out whether people should be allowed to ride motorcycles without helmets, one is not likely to base one's opinion on whether those who ride without helmets are self-controlled or not — it is the same question whether the riders fail to wear helmets akratically or by deliberate choice. Nor do questions of agent-autonomy come up if one wonders whether to hide an upsetting event from a friend who is about to face an important interview. The temptation to allow paternalistic behavior seems to arise in cases in which people are likely to make unwise, irrational, or incompetent choices in matters where the stakes are high, and the temptation seems to be tempered by the fact that establishing stupidity and irrationality is not very easy, and it seems to be the strongest when one has more than the usual amount of knowledge about the psyche of the person at whom the paternalism is directed ("I *know* she'll thank me for this in the morning"). While some irrational decisions and irrational people are unautonomous, lacking in self-control, it is far from true that all of them are.[14]

Another context in which one could be tempted to see agent-autonomy as deeply related to normative autonomy is the context in which one is called upon to respect a person's decision even though it seems to be inauthentic: to respect what a person thinks she wants, wants to want, or decides to do even when it conflicts with what she, as it were, *really wants*. An infamous scene in Ayn Rand's *The Fountainhead* depicts the hero, Howard Roark, violently raping a woman. The woman, Dominique, struggles with him, but we are told that in her heart—at this stage, quite unconsciously—she wants him, and it is hinted that Howard, being a genius, already knows this. Despite Rand's suggestion to the contrary, however, it is morally wrong to force a person to have sex even if one happens to have good reasons to believe that she unconsciously wants to have sex. If her Reason says no, it does not matter that her Appetite might be the more authentic, or even rational, part. In situations such as these, it is tempting to think that respecting a person's autonomy is analogous to respecting a person's "party line": if Dominique's party line is that she should not have sex with Howard, the authority of her "self-government" is to be respected. It seems as if, in this case at least, a person's deliberated-upon best judgment is in some way worth more than the rest of her beliefs and desires. But upon a second look, one discovers that respect for people's *decisions* is not always respect for their *agent-autonomy*. Imagine that Dominique plans to have sex with Howard, although he will be her first sexual partner and she is very nervous about what sex will be like. She honestly (and accurately) tells him that she wants to have sex with him and then akratically insists "No!" when he attempts to touch her. If Howard is to respect her normative autonomy, he should respect her ego-dystonic, non-agent-autonomous refusal just as much he should respect a party line refusal. Just as morality seems to ask us to respect some people's choices even when they are quite irrational, it also tells us to respect many choices that fail to express agent-autonomy.

One could object that perhaps there is something special about sex in this way, as it is intuitively a matter on which a person's right to change her mind is greater than usual (there is something morally dubious, for example, about a contract in which A solemnly promises to have sex with B). What, then, about examples of a more mundane nature?

Emma, a student who usually goes to bed at five in the morning and wakes up at noon, has an important meeting at nine in the morning. She makes her husband, Philip, promise to wake her up at seven in the morning, no matter how much she protests. Philip wakes her up, and she rebukes him with "Go away." In this case, Philip's moral duty is obviously to respect her autonomous decision from last night and not her desire that he go away.

But what matters here need not be the lack of agent-autonomy in Emma's rebuke (if it is in fact lacking in agent-autonomy). The issue may be not autonomy of decision but quality of decision.[15] The just-awakened Emma is cognitively impaired. She makes a low-quality choice; she is acting stupidly (a weakening of self-control may have partially contributed to the fact that she is acting stupidly, or it may not have been an issue). A stupid choice in the face of high stakes, where both the low quality of the decision and the nature of the stakes are as obvious as, in real life, they can be—these are the standard circumstances in which paternalistic intervention is morally tempting, especially a paternalistic intervention whose goal is to make it likely that the person makes a high-quality decision. One does not need to think that rationality always entails deliberation to think that a conscious person is more likely to make such a decision than a half-conscious one, and so it seems proper to make Emma conscious and let her decide again whether to go to the meeting. Note the important role played by the height of the stakes here. On lazy *weekend* mornings, many spouses in Philip's position have respected a low-quality decision of their partners to stay in bed, even if an autonomous request for a wake-up service was filed the night before. To complicate the case further, there is also the fact that Emma made Philip *promise* to wake her up. When to break a promise to keep someone tied to the mast until the siren's song is over is a complicated issue all by itself, and I am not at all sure that such promise-breaking is only warranted if the person seemed self-controlled when soliciting the promise or uncontrolled when informing you that he wishes to visit the sirens. The impression that respecting people's normative autonomy is respecting their party line is partially created by the fact that, quite often, respecting people's normative autonomy is respecting their *word* and respecting *promises made to them*. In practice, respecting people's autonomy often involves taking their word as to what they want, and what people say aloud often (though not always) reflects their inner party lines—especially when they perform acts such as promising or signing contracts.[16]

These, of course, are not meant to be anything like conclusive arguments against the claim that agent-autonomy grounds normative autonomy. This section was only meant to raise doubts as to whether the connection between agent-autonomy and normative autonomy is as perfectly obvious as it sometimes seems.

Conclusion

If I am right, autonomy in the sense of self-control is less important to moral responsibility, praiseworthiness, and blameworthiness than is generally assumed. I suspect, however, that autonomy, in some form or another, has always been and will always be fascinating to us, for reasons that have to do not so much with moral responsibility but with perennial riddles involving the amount of control that human beings can, or cannot, have over their lives.

Consider, this time, a poem:

> Out of the night that covers me,
> Black as the pit from pole to pole.
> I thank whatever gods may be
> For my unconquerable soul.
>
> In the fell clutch of circumstance
> I have not winced nor cried aloud.
> Under the bludgeonings of chance
> My head is bloody, but unbowed.
>
> Beyond this place of wrath and tears,
> Looms but the horror of the shade,
> And yet the menace of the years
> Finds, and shall find me, unafraid.
>
> It matters not how strait the gate,
> How charged with punishments the scroll,
> I am the master of my fate;
> I am the captain of my soul.
> — "Invictus," by William Earnest Henley

Henley's poem can be moving, or infuriating, or both, depending on one's mood, one's interpretation, and the way one has recently been treated by fate.[17] As remarked by Bernard Williams many times, the search for some modicum of control over one's fate, the search for something within us that is immune to the vagaries of luck, is a constant human concern. In a simple, crude sense it seems quite obvious that we do not have such control, as our lives are at the mercy of circumstances: "Man plans and God laughs," says a Yiddish proverb. If we cannot have such control over our circumstances, can we not at least control the inner citadel—and be captains of our souls?

The tendency to believe that we are captains of our souls has a rival tendency in the human heart—the tendency to believe that we are, as it were, slaves of our souls, that we have fates and identities and inner voices that we cannot escape with our laughable reasoning capacities any more than Jonah could escape his mission. Reason is a shallow fraud, as is any idea of control over our lives, and salvation lies in surrender to these voices, say thinkers from William Blake to Carl Jung.

But we are not captains of our souls, nor are we servants of our souls. Quite simply, we *are* our souls. And this is not always such a bad thing.

NOTES

Chapter 1

1. Compare this to a less dramatic situation familiar to novelists—the one in which a character takes a special care with his clothes before meeting another character, and so the reader, but not the character, knows that sexual intentions are present.

2. Assuming that what is often claimed is in fact true, and 90 percent of American drivers think of themselves as above average.

3. Lazar claims that on the rare occasions when we do intentionally try to induce a false belief in ourselves (her example is a man who tries, for self-interested reasons, to induce religiosity in himself by going through the motions of religious ceremony), what we have is not really hot irrationality, but an attempt, which may be practically rational, to induce cold irrationality. In the absence of a pill that makes you believe irrationally that you are likely to ace an interview, you may try the less reliable but equally "cold" method of repeating the words "I am great" under your breath.

4. This quotation and many others like it are found in Szasz's (1977, 180–207) tragicomic survey of the history of "masturbatory insanity."

5. It is worth mentioning that Frankfurt's later work does not share this concept of externality—a concept that attributes importance to the ego-syntonic or ego-dystonic quality of desires. The trend started by Frankfurt's 1971 article, however, is still continued by many authors. I will say more about it in chapter 4.

6. White (1988).

7. Nisbett and Wilson (1997).

8. I have cast this in familiar Korsgaardian terms, though it does not in fact appear in *Sources of Normativity*.

9. The novel in which the reader is invited to watch, with a precarious sense of superiority, how a character with an excessive sense of self-control is driven to his or her doom by his or her demons is almost a genre by itself. See, for example, the main character in Richard Yates's novel, *Revolutionary Road* (Boston: Little, Brown, 1961).

10. See Smith (1994, 137) for his version of the disclaimer.

11. See Darwall (1986).

12. If, for instance, Tamara is an incurable romantic who has both far-fetched hopes and far-fetched fears concerning Todd that say more about her fantasy image of him than the likely advantages or disadvantages of the marriage.

13. A notable exception to this is in Harry Frankfurt (1988), where people act rationally and against their deliberative conclusions. I say more about such cases in subsequent chapters.

14. Launched by Strawson (1962), Frankfurt (1969), and Frankfurt (1971), and perspicuously described by Watson (1987). See also the way Smith (1983; 1991) develops this idea.

Chapter 2

1. In writing about the rationality of an agent's action, I am referring to the *rationality displayed by the agent* in performing that action. A rational course of action, as I understand it here, is a course of action that the agent is actually rational in taking as opposed to a course of action the agent would take if she were rational. For more on this distinction, see Darwall (1986).

2. An analogous conflict of perspectives appears in ethics: if an ethical theory is seen as a moral agent's manual, it is a failure for it not to provide easy, practicable instructions for getting out of certain dilemmas, while if an ethical theory is aimed solely at providing an account of the moral, it may be a blow to the theory's credibility if it entails that one can easily find one's way out of certain dilemmas—after all, a true account of moral life should not imply that the moral life is epistemically easy. For an ethics-related discussion of the relation between accounts and manuals, see Railton (1984). The idea that it is not always an advantage for a moral theory to provide easy solutions to practical dilemmas is often expressed by proponents of virtue ethics. See, for example, Hursthouse (1991).

3. See Williams (1981, 24).

4. Davidson first pointed out that *akrasia* is not an ethical problem, as it occurs in cases such as the tooth-brushing case. He also defends the view that *akrasia* is the result of irrationality in reasoning, as opposed to the result of volitional

failure (I take it that an agent taking a course of action because of a volitional failure would not be any more rational than an agent acting out of a failure of reasoning). He does not, however, address the possibility that akratic action can sometimes be neither the result of failure of reasoning, nor the result of volitional failure, nor the result of any sort of normative failure whatsoever, but rather a rational action.

5. The literature based on this assumption is enormous and includes authors who are very different from Davidson. See, for example, Pears (1984) and Mele (1987).

6. Different theories describe the schism in different ways — for example, as the schism between absolute and relativized judgment. This is immaterial to my argument. I am willing to agree that there exists inconsistency or incoherence in the akratic person's mind, but I insist that sometimes far greater irrationality is manifested if the agent follows her best judgment than if she acts against it.

7. Frankfurt puts it to us that if a person decided, upon deliberation, that he should destroy the Earth in order to avoid a minor injury to his finger but cannot bring himself to perform the destruction, he would be somewhat irrational, but if, on the other hand, he were to make such a decision to destroy the Earth *and* have no inner barriers to following through with this decision, then he would have completely taken leave of his senses. Many best judgments, Frankfurt indicates, take a somewhat crazy person to form, but a much crazier person to actually follow, and shouldn't our intuitions about sanity and insanity be relevant to the way we view rationality and irrationality? I agree with Frankfurt that intuitions about sanity similar to those invoked by his Earth-destruction story should not be ignored by anyone giving an account of rationality, and later I use them to help support my conclusion. However, in relying exclusively on intuitions about sanity and insisting that the Earth-destroyer as described would be irrational whatever else is true of his desires, Frankfurt is vulnerable to the accusation that his conclusion depends on the assumption that there are external reasons for actions. My own argument depends on no such assumption.

8. While I agree with McIntyre's criticism of the *akrasia* literature, I find that her positive arguments are aimed more at the irrationality of being obstinate and the benefits of the ability to be the kind of person who is sometimes weak-willed than at the actual rationality of some akratic actions.

9. Hill, while not actually arguing for the rationality of some akratic actions, gestures toward this conclusion in pointing out that cases of acting against one's best judgment are very different from one another and do not, upon sensitive examination, point to the existence of a unified phenomenon that one may label "weakness of will" and regard universally as a vice.

10. This is not to say that acting rationally always involves acting out of self-interest, as some of one's desires may be altruistic.

11. Smith later points out that it would be more precise to say that the person who believes that she should φ in C is committed to believing that if she were fully rational, she would desire that, were she her actual, imperfectly rational self, she would φ in C. Smith makes this correction, for example, in his reply to Swanton (1996) in order to answer objections based on the idea that sometimes one's hypothetical, fully rational self is so different from the actual self that it makes little sense for the two selves to desire the same things. I take his response to be generally effective, and in any case the difference between the versions of Smith's claim does not matter to my subsequent discussion.

12. It is especially not my point to ascribe to Smith any particular theory about the genesis of akratic action.

13. If we thought of Sam not as developing or failing to develop a desire to become a hermit, but as developing or failing to develop the absolute judgment "I must become a hermit" from his all-relativized judgment that he should become a hermit, the big picture would not change: it would still make Sam's psyche more coherent not to develop that absolute judgment, which would accommodate one belief but contradict many more.

14. A similar position to the coherence view of rationality is the view that judgments of practical rationality, like judgments of probability, are always judgments of rationality given a certain set of beliefs or conditions. Smith may be alluding to this position in arguing that Sam would be irrational in not becoming a hermit given that he believes that he should become a hermit. I would, however, argue that given the whole story about Sam's beliefs and desires, he would be less rational in becoming a hermit than in not becoming one, and that since the latter involves more that is relevant to what Sam has a reason to do, it is a better basis for determining whether, all things considered, Sam acted rationally or not.

15. A judgment recalling the remarks of Frankfurt in "Rationality and the Unthinkable" (1988).

16. My point regarding Paul's case and Sam's case does not depend on the claim that emotions have cognitive content. Even if they do not, it is still true that Sam is not irrational simply because he felt anxiety while he was deliberating, but because anxiety, or something else, caused him to make a poor inference. In the case of Paul, even if one does not assume that his anxiety was by itself somehow reasonable, it is obvious that it did not prevent him from reaching a practical conclusion in a reasonable manner.

17. In some contexts, the view that *akrasia* is a form of irrationality is contrasted with the view that it is the result of failure of self-control or volition. I find it hard to see how failure of self-control or volition can be a rational process—if it is not irrational, it is nonrational.

18. Again, this is evident in nearly all of the extensive literature about weakness of will. From "How Is Weakness of the Will Possible?" (Davidson 1980) to

"Where Does the Akratic Break Take Place?" (Rorty 1980) and many more, the question always appears to be taken to mean "What kind of unfortunate mental glitch causes one to act against one's best judgment?"

19. Thus, he is not acting for what Davidson calls "renegade reasons"—he is not acting for reasons that he already considered and dismissed but for reasons that he overlooked.

20. Once again, it does not matter whether we take Sam's failure to abide by his decision to be a failure to develop a desire or failure to develop a Davidsonian "absolute" judgment from a Davidsonian "relativized" judgment. In either case, he fails to form the desire or absolute judgment because of good evidence to the effect that the desire or absolute judgment is inappropriate or false, and his only irrationality is in failing to revise the (relativized) judgment he reached by deliberation.

21. Or perhaps, despite wondering what made her stay in the program for so long, she never bothers to examine her reasons for quitting or is unable to cite them due to her lack of introspective skill. Whether Emily or Sam comes to a reflective understanding of the irrationality of her or his former best judgment, or whether they eventually appreciate the reasons for their failures to follow them, does not affect my argument for the rationality of this failure.

22. Similar results are discussed by Churchland (1995).

23. One account of rationality that would seem to fit would be the one offered by Scanlon in his 1998 book or in his forthcoming article, "Reasons and Passions." I do not wish to defend this specific account of desire and reason, though I agree with his arguments in "Reasons and Passions" against the idea that there exists a Faculty of Reason.

24. I clarify the specific relation of moral knowledge to reflection and deliberation in chapter 4.

25. As you grow experienced, I am told, educated "instinct" and "intuition" will play a larger and larger role.

Chapter 3

1. I elaborate on this point in "Hamlet and the Utilitarians" (Arpaly 2000a); a similar point, with a fascinating discussion of the various ways in which emotions can be appropriate or inappropriate, is found in D'Arms (2000).

2. For an alternative, sophisticated treatment of Huckleberry Finn, see Hill (1998). Driver (1996) also takes for granted that Huckleberry Finn's action is meant to be understood as praiseworthy, but her account of this praiseworthiness is completely independent of Huckleberry's motives and reasons. An interesting discussion of one kind of inverse *akrasia* is in Frankfurt's "Rationality and the Unthinkable" (1988).

3. There is nothing very unusual about perceiving fairly sophisticated truths without perceiving that one is perceiving them—as people discover retrospectively when they realize that they can find their way around a city they had thought was still foreign to them, or when the confession of a cheating spouse is surprisingly unsurprising, as was argued in chapter 2.

4. Hursthouse (1999, 195) addresses a previous version of my argument.

5. For a Huck-friendly view of moral reasons, see Scanlon (forthcoming). Railton (unpublished) also defends a Huck-friendly account of moral reasons.

6. The person who cares about morality, but not very much, is implicitly discussed in Susan Wolf's "Moral Saints" (1982) and more recently, and explicitly, in work by Sigrun Svavarsdottir (1999).

7. One can, if one is so inclined, apply Michael Smith's (1994) discussion of the distinction between concern for morality *de re* and *de dicto* here.

8. A *fortiori*, I shall not try to develop a fully fledged positive view of what it means to be concerned about something in the first place. I am not committed here to Frankfurt's view of caring, but I am not sure that I say anything in this paper with which it is incompatible—at least given the assumption that wanting to have a desire does not imply thinking that one *should* have it.

9. For a sense of the diversity of prevailing views, see, e.g., Dretske (1988), Stalnaker (1984), Strawson (1994).

10. By "essentially conflicting attitudes" I mean attitudes that conflict because of their content and not merely because of some accidental factor making it hard or unrealistic to act in accordance with both of them. For example, love of sports and love of philosophy may conflict accidentally if it so happens that one has to choose between a philosophy talk and a basketball game, or between a sports-related career and an academic one. The conflict here is a contingent one—it has to do not with the nature of sports or philosophy but rather with the fact that one cannot be in two places at the same time, or with having merely "one life to live." On the other hand, there is an essential conflict between one's love of philosophy and a craving to live the life of a "simple soul," between (certain forms of) Christianity and lust, etc.

11. My discussion of the philanthropists owes a lot to Hursthouse (1997) and Foot (1978).

12. The connection between virtue and depth of concern is evident, though never quite explicit, in Foot's *Virtues and Vices* (1978).

13. Some authors, such as Moody-Adams (1994, 291–309), would argue that since Solomon's beliefs were influenced by cultural bias, he is still irrational. I agree that some cultural bias is present in everyone's early education. However, since we all have to form beliefs under conditions of ignorance, Solomon's belief is only about as irrational as most of our everyday beliefs, and thus it can be compared favorably to the belief of a twentieth-century American

sexist, which is formed in circumstances where many more human beings would "know better." To use Russell Hardin's expression, Solomon is more "epistemically crippled" than anyone the reader is likely to know (Hardin, forthcoming).

14. For a discussion of authors who believe that there is something morally bad in irrationality itself, see, for example, Richard Feldman (2000) or Guy Axtell (1997).

15. See Herman (1993).

Chapter 4

1. After all, a person who has made a decision on the basis of nonculpable ignorance is still praiseworthy if he does what seems morally imperative, or blameworthy if she neglects an apparent moral imperative.

2. In Frankfurt (1988).

3. See Wolf (1993).

4. Strawson (1962).

5. Described in Frankfurt (1976).

6. Frankfurt (1976).

7. Frankfurt (1976).

8. It may be that it is common in North American culture to viscerally expect self-control from oneself and experience any failure of self-control as disturbing, baffling, and surprising. On the other hand, Russian novels are full of people who perceive themselves and humans in general as weak and passive, and are pleasantly surprised, and grateful to God, for any exception to this (for example, Lebedeyev in Dostoevsky's *The Idiot*).

9. Timothy Schroeder and I presented an extended version of these arguments in "Alienation and Externality" (1999).

10. David Copp (forthcoming), however, argues for autonomy being identical to rationality.

11. Though I pick on Mele, similar examples could have been drawn from John Martin Fischer and Mark Ravizza (1998).

12. For a further discussion of visceral self-images, see Schroeder and Arpaly (1999).

13. Michael Bratman may be such an author. When claiming that planning is essential to autonomy, Bratman does not attempt to show that we are not responsible for unplanned actions but rather that creatures who never plan are never morally responsible and are not full-fledged persons. See Bratman (1999).

14. The claim that we have little control over the development of our character is made and defended by Sher (2001).

15. Thanks to David Velleman for bringing this objection to my attention.

16. Though the ability to make contracts and being a moral subject are very similar things for him.

Chapter 5

1. Tom Whiteman et al. (1995).

2. The standard diagnostic tool of North American psychiatry.

3. Note, however, that even if Greg is blameworthy it still may be true that therapy could do him good.

4. Agent-autonomy is not characteristically thought of as coming in degrees, as metaphors of self-government invoke such notions as "outlaw desires"—and things are, after all, either legal or not. However, I do not wish to imply, and there is no need to assume, that any theory that uses the concept of *agent-autonomy* is guilty of this kind of false dichotomy. It would be interesting to see more autonomy-based treatments of cases in which accountability comes in degrees.

5. Textbook treatments of addiction appear, with some qualifications, to support such a view. See, for example, Doweiko (1996), chapter 11, esp. 142–143. Similar treatments are given in Carson and Butcher (1992), and Rosenhan and Seligman (1995).

6. Interestingly enough, Freud did seem to agree that we are at least sometimes blameworthy for unconscious actions, though he doubted whether the courts should take any interest in them (Freud 1957–1974).

7. For an example of a praiseworthy Freudian slip, see Freud (1965), 219.

8. Ann Marlowe, in her memoir *How to Stop Time* (1999), describes years of her life in which she used heroin regularly but kept her consumption at a low enough level and her addiction at a mild enough stage that her white-collar job was not affected and her "heroin budget" did not increase, though the addiction was powerful enough for her life to "revolve around the drug" in her spare time. It is not surprising that she seems to have been, before and while taking the drug, happier and richer than a stereotypical heroin user.

9. Another scenario is the one in which HP has always been the murderous type, and all Dr. Nefarious had to do was to add to his mix a specific desire to kill the Canadian minister. For HP's pretreatment personality to be such that his newly instilled desire would not be fiercely opposed by the rest of him, he needs to be very callous in his attitude toward human life. In this case, his desire to kill the minister would be like any number of murderous desires he would develop in response to irrational factors such as anger, stress, or the color of the sky. True, it is a stranger desire than most of these, but this *is* a science-fiction example.

10. A concept introduced by Nagel (1982) in "Moral Luck."

11. For that matter, we can feel sorry for the adult as well, for being a bad person and not knowing the joys that concern for one's fellow human beings brings. The ability to feel sorry for someone is not always a sign that we do not hold him to be bad.

12. Here my views conflict directly with the view expressed by Wolf in "Asymmetrical Freedom" (1980). I hold that there is, in essence, perfect symmetry between the case of Harris and the case of a wonderful person who was raised by wonderful parents. Harris aside, when it comes to ordinary people, I suspect that the fact that we tend to be more forgiving of bad traits created by bad parents than dismissive of good traits created by good parents has to do with the Tolstoyesque fact that it takes very little for a person's moral upbringing to go wrong and a lot for it to go right.

13. I thank Tim Scanlon for this point.

14. Countless authors would disagree with me about the irrelevance of autonomy to such cases of "violating a person's autonomy" as manipulation. For example, Dworkin (1988), Berofsky (1995), and Owen (1995).

15. My idea of "quality of decision" is similar to Alan Wertheimer's (forthcoming) idea of "quality of consent." Wertheimer directed my attention to the fact that in some legal contexts, a low-quality consent (such as the consent of a drunk or tired person) is consent enough, while in other contexts (generally contexts in which the stakes are high, as with medical decisions), "high-quality consent" is required.

16. Note that taking this view does not, in any way, make us consequentialists.

17. I wrote this section, and chose to quote "Invictus" in it, long before a terrorist named Timothy McVeigh chose to use the poem as his last words. No allusion is intended.

REFERENCES

Adams, R. 1985. "Involuntary Sins." *Philosophical Review* 94, 3–31.

Anderson, E. 1997. "Practical Reason and Incommensurable Goods." In R. Chang (ed.), *Incommensurability, Incomparability and Practical Reason*. Cambridge, Mass.: Harvard University Press. 90–109.

Aristotle. 1985. *Nicomachean Ethics*. T. Irwin (trans.). Indianapolis: Hackett Publishing Company.

Arpaly N. 2000a. "Hamlet and the Utilitarians." *Philosophical Studies* 99, 45–57.

———. 2000b. "On Acting Rationally Against One's Best Judgment." *Ethics* 110, 488–513.

Arpaly, N., and T. Schroeder. 1998. "Praise, Blame, and the Whole Self." *Philosophical Studies* 93, 161–188.

Audi, R. 1990. "Weakness of Will and Rational Action." *Australasian Journal of Philosophy* 68, 271–281.

Axtell, G. 1997. "Recent Work on Virtue Epistemology." *American Philosophical Quarterly* 34, 410–430.

Bennett, J. 1974. "The Conscience of Huckleberry Finn." *Philosophy* 49, 123–134.

Berofsky, B. 1995. *Liberation from Self: A Theory of Personal Autonomy*. Cambridge: Cambridge University Press.

Bratman, M. 1999. *Faces of Intention: Selected Essays on Intention and Agency*. New York: Cambridge University Press.

———. 1996. "Identification, Decision, and Treating as a Reason." *Philosophical Topics* 24, 1–18.

Burroughs, W. 1977. *Junky*. New York: Penguin Books.

Carson, R., and J. Butcher. 1992. *Abnormal Psychology and Modern Life*. 9th ed. New York: HarperCollins.

Churchland, P. S. 1996. "Feeling Reasons." In A. Damasio, H. Damasio, and Y. Christen (eds.), *Neurobiology of Decision-Making*. Berlin: Springer-Verlag. 181–199.

Copp, D. Forthcoming. *Rationality and Autonomy*.

Damasio, A. 1994. *Descartes' Error: Emotion, Reason, and the Human Brain*. New York: Putnam.

D'Arms, J., and D. Jacobson. 2000. "The Moralistic Fallacy." *Philosophy and Phenomenological Research* 61, 65–90.

Darwall, S. 1997. "Self Interest and Self Concern." *Social Philosophy and Policy* 14, 158–178.

———. 1986. "Rational Agents, Rational Acts." *Philosophical Topics* 14, 33–57.

Davidson, D. 1985. "Deception and Division." In E. LePore and B. McLaughlin (eds.), *Actions and Events: Perspectives on the Philosophy of Donald Davidson*. New York: Blackwell. 138–148.

———. 1982. "Paradoxes of Irrationality." In R. Wollheim and J. Hopkins (eds.), *Philosophical Essays on Freud*. Cambridge: Cambridge University Press. 282–305.

———. 1980. "How Is Weakness of the Will Possible?" In D. Davidson, *Essays on Actions and Events*. Oxford: Oxford University Press. 21–42.

Doris, J. Forthcoming. *Lack of Character: Personality and Moral Behavior*. New York: Cambridge University Press.

———. 1998. "Persons, Situations, and Virtue Ethics." *Noûs* 32, 504–530.

Doweiko, H. 1996. *Concepts of Chemical Dependency*. 3rd ed. New York: Brooks/Cole Publishing Co.

Dreier, J. 1996. "The Moral Problem." *Mind* 105, 363–367.

Dretske, F. 1988. *Explaining Behavior: Reasons in a World of Causes*. Cambridge, Mass.: MIT Press.

Driver, J. 1996. "The Virtues and Human Nature." In R. Crisp (ed.), *How Should One Live? Essays on the Virtues*. Oxford: Clarendon Press. 111–130.

Dworkin, G. 1988. *The Theory and Practice of Autonomy*. Cambridge: Cambridge University Press.

Feldman, R. 2000. "The Ethics of Belief." *Philosophy and Phenomenological Research* 60, 667–695.

Fischer, J., and M. Ravizza. 1998. *Responsibility and Control: A Theory of Moral Responsibility*. New York: Cambridge University Press.

Flaubert, G. 1965 [1856]. *Madame Bovary*. P. de Man (trans). New York: W. W. Norton.

Foot, P. 1978. *Virtues and Vices*. Berkeley: University of California Press.

Frankfurt, H. 1999. *Autonomy, Volition and Love.* Cambridge: Cambridge University Press.

———. 1988. "Rationality and the Unthinkable." In H. Frankfurt, *The Importance of What We Care About.* Cambridge: Cambridge University Press. 177–190.

———. 1976. "Identification and Externality." In A. Rorty (ed.), *The Identities of Persons.* Berkeley: University of California Press. 239–251.

———. 1971. "Freedom of the Will and the Concept of a Person." *Journal of Philosophy* 68, 5–20.

———. 1969. "Alternate Possibilities and Moral Responsibility." *Journal of Philosophy* 66, 829–839.

Freud, S. 1957–1974. "Moral Responsibility for the Content of Dreams." In *The Complete Psychological Works of Sigmund Freud*, vol. 19. J. Strachey (trans.). London: Hogarth Press. 131–134.

———. 1965. *The Psychopathology of Everyday Life.* J. Strachey (ed. and trans.). New York: W. W. Norton.

Hardin, R. Forthcoming. *Trust and Trustworthiness.* New York: Russell Sage Foundation.

———. 1988. *Morality within the Limits of Reason.* Chicago: University of Chicago Press.

Harman, G. 1999. "Moral Philosophy Meets Social Psychology: Virtue Ethics and the Fundamental Attribution Error." *Proceedings of the Aristotelian Society, 1998–1999.* 315–331.

Herman, B. 1993. *The Practice of Moral Judgment.* Cambridge, Mass.: Harvard University Press.

Hill, T. 1998. "Four Conceptions of Conscience." *Nomos* 60, 13–52.

———. 1986. "Weakness of Will and Character." *Philosophical Topics* 14, 93–115.

Hobbes, T. 1996. *Leviathan.* Richard Tuck (ed.). New York: Cambridge University Press.

Hursthouse, R. 1999. *On Virtue Ethics.* New York: Oxford University Press.

———. 1997. "Ethics and the Emotions." In D. Statman (ed.), *Virtue Ethics.* Georgetown University Press. 99–118.

———. 1991. "Virtue Theory and Abortion." *Philosophy and Public Affairs* 20, 223–246.

Kant, I. 1964. *Groundwork of the Metaphysics of Morals.* H. Patton (trans.). New York: Harper & Row.

Kaplan, B., and H. Sadock. 1991. *Synopsis of Psychiatry.* 6th ed. Baltimore: Williams and Wilkins.

Korsgaard, C. 1996. *The Sources of Normativity.* Cambridge: Cambridge University Press.

Kramer, P. 1993. *Listening to Prozac.* New York: Viking.

Lazar, A. 1999. "Deceiving Oneself or Self-Deceived? On the Formation of Beliefs 'Under the Influence'." *Mind* 108, 265–290.

Le Carré, J. 1999. *Single and Single*. New York: Scribner.

Lehrer, K. 1990. *Metamind*. New York: Oxford University Press.

Marlowe, A. 1999. *How to Stop Time: Heroin from A to Z*. New York: Basic Books.

McDowell, J. 1979. "Virtue and Reason." *The Monist* 62, 331–350.

McIntyre, A. 1993. "Is Akratic Action Always Irrational?" In O. Flanagan and A. Rorty (eds.), *Identity, Character, and Morality*. Cambridge, Mass.: MIT Press. 379–400.

Mele, A. 2000. *Self-Deception Unmasked*. Princeton, N.J.: Princeton University Press.

———. 1995. *Autonomous Agents*. New York: Oxford University Press.

———. 1987. *Irrationality*. New York: Oxford University Press.

Mill, J. 1979. *Utilitarianism*. G. Sher (ed.). Indianapolis: Hackett Publishing Company.

Moody-Adams, M. 1994. "Culture, Responsibility, and Affected Ignorance." *Ethics* 104, 291–309.

Nagel, T. 1982. "Moral Luck." In G. Watson (ed.), *Free Will*. New York: Oxford University Press. 174–186.

Nisbett, R., and T. Wilson. 1997. "Telling More Than We Can Know: Verbal Reports on Mental Processes." *Psychological Review* 84, 231–259.

Noggle, R. 1995. "Autonomy, Value, and Conditioned Desire." *American Philosophical Quarterly* 32, 57–69.

Owen, D. 1995. "Philosophical Foundations of Fault." In D. Owen (ed.), *Philosophical Foundations of Tort Law*. Oxford: Clarendon Press. 201–228.

Pears, D. 1984. *Motivated Irrationality*. Oxford: Oxford University Press.

Railton, P. 1984. "Alienation, Consequentialism, and the Demands of Morality." *Philosophy and Public Affairs* 13, 134–171.

———. 1997. "Mark Twain's 'Sound Heart and Deformed Conscience': Rational Beings and Being Rational." John Dewey Lecture, University of Vermont. 18 October.

Rorty, A. 1980. "Where Does the Akratic Break Take Place?" *Australasian Journal of Philosophy* 58, 333–346.

Rosenhan, D., and M. Seligman. 1995. *Abnormal Psychology*. 3rd ed. New York: W.W. Norton.

Sayre-McCord, G. 1997. "The Metaethical Problem." *Ethics* 108, 55–83.

Scanlon, T. Forthcoming. "Reasons and Passions." In S. Buss and L. Overton (eds.), *Contours of Agency*. Cambridge, Mass.: MIT Press.

———. 1998. *What We Owe to Each Other*. Cambridge, Mass.: Harvard University Press.

Schroeder, T., and N. Arpaly. 1999. "Alienation and Externality." *Canadian Journal of Philosophy* 29, 371–388.

Sher, G. 2001. "Blame for Traits." *Noûs* 35, 146–161.

Smith, H. 1991. "Varieties of Moral Worth and Moral Credit." *Ethics* 101, 279–303.

———. 1983. "Culpable Ignorance." *Philosophical Review* 92, 543–571.

Smith, M. 1997. "In Defense of *The Moral Problem*: A Reply to Brink, Copp, and Sayre-McCord." *Ethics* 108, 84–119.

———. 1996. "Normative Reasons and Full Rationality: Reply to Swanton." *Analysis* 56, 160–168.

———. 1994. *The Moral Problem*. Oxford: Blackwell.

Stalnaker, R. 1984. *Inquiry*. Cambridge, Mass.: MIT Press.

Strawson, G. 1994. *Mental Reality*. Cambridge, Mass.: MIT Press.

Strawson, P. 1962. "Freedom and Resentment." *Proceedings of the British Academy* 48, 1–25.

Stroud, B. 2000. "Practical Reasoning." In E. Ullmann-Margalit (ed.), *Reasoning Practically*. New York: Oxford University Press. 27–38.

Stump, E. 1988. "Sanctification and Free Will." *Journal of Philosophy* 85, 395–420.

Svavarsdottir, S. 1999. "Moral Cognitivism and Motivation." *Philosophical Review* 108, 161–219.

Swanton, C. 1996. "Is the Moral Problem Solved?" *Analysis* 56, 155–160.

Szasz, T. 1977. *The Manufacture of Madness*. New York: Harper and Row.

Velleman, J. Forthcoming. "Identification and Identity." In S. Buss and L. Overton (eds.), *Contours of Agency*. Cambridge, Mass.: MIT Press.

———. 2000. *The Possibility of Practical Reason*. Oxford: Clarendon Press.

———. 1992. "What Happens When Someone Acts?" *Mind* 101, 461–481.

Whiteman, T., N. Novotni, and R. Peterson. 1995. *Adult ADD*. Colorado Springs, Colo.: Pinon Press.

Watson, G. 1993. "Responsibility and the Limits of Evil." In J. Fischer and M. Ravizza (eds.), *Perspectives on Moral Responsibility*. Ithaca, N.Y.: Cornell University Press. 119–149.

———. 1987. "Free Action and Free Will." *Mind* 96, 145–172.

———. 1977. "Skepticism about Weakness of Will." *Philosophical Review* 86, 316–339.

———. 1975. "Free Agency." *Journal of Philosophy* 72, 205–220.

Wertheimer, A. Forthcoming. "Intoxication and Consent to Sexual Relations."

White, P. 1988. "Knowing More Than We Can Tell: 'Introspective Access' and Causal Report Accuracy 10 Years Later." *British Journal of Psychology* 79, 13–45.

Wilkes, K. 1994. *Real People: Personal Identity without Thought Experiments.* Oxford: Oxford University Press.

Williams, B. 1981. *Moral Luck.* Cambridge: Cambridge University Press.

Wolf, S. 1993. "The Real Self View." In J. Fisher and M. Ravizza (eds.), *Perspectives on Moral Responsibility.* Ithaca, N.Y.: Cornell University Press, 151–170.

———. 1982. "Moral Saints." *Journal of Philosophy* 79, 419–39.

———. 1980. "Asymmetrical Freedom." *Journal of Philosophy* 77, 151–166.

INDEX

judgment. *See* best judgment

Kant, Immanuel, 9, 69–72, 81, 84, 86, 87, 89
kleptomania, 153–158
Korsgaard, Christine, 4–5, 19–20, 22, 23–25, 113
Kramer, Peter, 13

language, 133–136
lapses of reason, 159–161
Lazar, Ariela, 12, 13
Le Carré, John, 3, 57, 135
Lehrer, Keith, 118
Leviathan (Hobbes), 145
Listening to Prozac (Kramer), 13
localized amorality, 82
luck, 169–177

Madame Bovary (Flaubert), 67–68
Mann, Klaus, 112
Man Who Mistook His Wife for a Hat, The (Sacks), 150
McDowell, John, 94
McIntyre, Alison, 37
megalomania, 101–111
Mele, Alfred, 12, 13, 14, 126–127, 136–137
mental deviance, 149–153, 159, 167
mental events, 119
mere inclination, 76
metaphor (and the idea of external desires), 134–135, 136
Mill, J., 70
misguided conscience, 8, 10–11, 99, 100–101
Moore's paradox, 34
moral concern, 84–93, 95–96, 108, 132
moral desirability, 69–70
moral education, 147, 189 n. 12
moral indifference, 91, 159

moral knowledge, 74–75, 114
moral luck, 165, 169–173
Moral Problem, The (Smith), 37, 44
moral psychology, 81
  agency and secret agent, 3–8
  belief formation "under the influence," 11–14
  complexity of, 3–31
  deliberation and reflection, 20–25
  external desires and closet homosexual, 14–16
  first-person perspective, 17–20
  inadvertent virtue and misguided conscience, 8–11
  self-control and unconscious motivation, 17–20
moral reasons, 71–73, 79, 84, 131, 146, 150
moral responsibility, 128–148, 162, 174. *See also* blameworthiness; moral worth
moral worth, 67–115, 159
  and autonomies, 130–132, 144–153
  blame and moral unresponsiveness, 79–83
  and character, 93–98
  definition of, 69
  degrees of moral concern, 84–93, 95–96
  moral responsiveness *de re*, 73–79
  and motivation, 69–70, 73, 83
  racism, sexism, and megalomania, 101–111
  responsiveness to moral reasons, 71–73, 79, 84
  theory of, 7–8, 10, 30, 98
motivation
  deficiency of, 83
  "diehard," 86, 87–88
  good and bad, 111–114
  of Huckleberry Finn, 76